DATE DUE

DEMCO 38-296

THE IRONY OF REFORM

TRANSFORMING AMERICAN POLITICS

Lawrence C. Dodd, Series Editor

Dramatic changes in political institutions and behavior over the past three decades have underscored the dynamic nature of American politics, confronting political scientists with a new and pressing intellectual agenda. The pioneering work of early postwar scholars, while laying a firm empirical foundation for contemporary scholarship, failed to consider how American politics might change or recognize the forces that would make fundamental change inevitable. In reassessing the static interpretations fostered by these classic studies, political scientists are now examining the underlying dynamics that generate transformational change.

Transforming American Politics brings together texts and monographs that address four closely related aspects of change. A first concern is documenting and explaining recent changes in American politics—in institutions, processes, behavior, and policymaking. A second is reinterpreting classic studies and theories to provide a more accurate perspective on postwar politics. The series looks at historical change to identify recurring patterns of political transformation within and across the distinctive eras of American politics. Last and perhaps most important, the series presents new theories and interpretations that explain the dynamic processes at work and thus clarify the direction of contemporary politics. All of the books focus on the central theme of transformation—transformation in both the conduct of American politics and in the way we study and understand its many aspects.

FORTHCOMING TITLES

*Extraordinary Politics: How Protest and Dissent
Are Changing American Democracy,*
Charles C. Euchner

*The Divided Democrats: Ideological Unity,
Party Reform, and Presidential Elections,*
William G. Mayer

Revolving Gridlock,
David Brady and Craig Volden

New Media in American Politics,
Richard Davis and Diana Owen

Seeing Red: How the Cold War Shaped American Politics,
John Kenneth White

Governing Partners: State-Local Relations in the United States,
Russell L. Hanson

The Tragic Presidency,
Robert L. Lineberry

Congress and the Administrative State, Second Edition,
Lawrence C. Dodd and Richard L. Schott

THE IRONY OF REFORM

Roots of American Political Disenchantment

G. Calvin Mackenzie

WestviewPress

A Division of HarperCollinsPublishers

Riverside Community College
MAR '97   Library
4800 Magnolia Avenue
Riverside, California 92506

JK 271 .M13 1996

Mackenzie, G. Calvin.

The irony of reform

Transforming American Politics

"One Million Lawyers," written by Tom Paxton, copyright © 1984 by Pax Music (ASCAP). All rights reserved. Used by permission.

Tables 5.1 and 5.2 and Figures 5.2 and 5.3 reprinted by permission of Congressional Quarterly Books.

Table 6.3 copyright © 1981 by Jethro K. Lieberman. Reprinted by permission of Georges Borchardt, Inc., for the author.

All rights reserved. Printed in the United States of America. No part of this publication may be reproduced or transmitted in any form or by any means, electronic or mechanical, including photocopy, recording, or any information storage and retrieval system, without permission in writing from the publisher.

Copyright © 1996 by Westview Press, Inc., A Division of HarperCollins Publishers, Inc.

Published in 1996 in the United States of America by Westview Press, Inc., 5500 Central Avenue, Boulder, Colorado 80301-2877, and in the United Kingdom by Westview Press, 12 Hid's Copse Road, Cumnor Hill, Oxford OX2 9JJ

A CIP catalog record for this book is available from the Library of Congress.
ISBN 0-8133-2838-1 (hc).—0-8133-2839-X (pbk)

The paper used in this publication meets the requirements of the American National Standard for Permanence of Paper for Printed Library Materials Z39.48-1984.

10   9   8   7   6   5   4   3   2   1

For Sally

Of course, there is no way in this cockeyed world of ruling out the extraordinary-cause-for-the-extraordinary-effect. You come by boat to Mann Gulch by way of the cliffs of the Missouri River where extraordinary ocean beds stood up and fought each other, but it seems as if the more that becomes known about big cock-eyed things, including the actions of men and women as well as cliffs, the more they seem to reduce to one little cockeyed thing fitting closely to another of the same kind, and so on until it all adds up to one big cockeyed thing. It's never confusion, though, because ultimately it all fits—it's just cockeyed and it fits and is fire. And of course that is extraordinary.

Norman Maclean

YOUNG MEN AND FIRE

CONTENTS

TABLES AND FIGURES

TABLES

FIGURES

PREFACE

The unlikely beginning of this book occurred in a hot New England attic in 1988. There, while in the process of moving to a new home, I came across a box full of college notebooks I had not looked at for almost twenty-five years. I pulled one out and opened it—a notebook from a course on Congress I had taken in the mid-1960s. As I turned the pages, I was reminded of a course vividly taught by a young professor who knew his stuff. The notes were well organized and richly detailed; they reminded me how much I had learned in that course and how it had helped inspire me to pursue a career as a teacher of government.

But in turning the pages, I noticed one other thing about those notes. They were all wrong. They were not wrong at the time, of course; but they were all wrong now. Virtually everything that we knew to be true about Congress in the 1960s no longer obtained. Everything was different. As an institution, Congress had been almost completely remade.

In the months that followed, I could not shake that experience. It made me wonder that if by focusing too narrowly on the subjects of my own research and teaching, I was missing something much more profound that was happening in American politics. If you stand too close to the front end of an elephant, it looks like a snake. I wondered if I was looking at elephants and seeing snakes.

I began to collect relevant books and articles, and during a sabbatical leave I burrowed into them. Every day I took a bag full of books to some comfortable place—the meadow behind my home, the ocean shore, a canoe on a Maine lake—and read about life and politics in America in the twentieth century. History, science, sociology, culture, technology: I read it all and struggled to see how it fit together. What emerged was a powerful picture of change, especially change in the way Americans govern themselves. The more I read and thought and talked to other people, the more astonished I was at the sweep of this change and at its impact on our politics and government.

Something powerful and complex and not a little mysterious had happened in America, and the pivot of the century—and, in many ways, of all of American historical development—appeared to be World War II.

The politics of the last decade of the twentieth century barely resembled the politics of the prewar period. If a revolution had occurred in America, the changes would not have been much more dramatic.

And yet for all the change, Americans seemed more dissatisfied with their public life than at any time in this century. How could that be? How could so much change have yielded so little satisfaction? That perplexing question impelled me through all of the months that I read about and thought about and wrote about the politics of postwar America.

What I have tried to write here is a work of synthesis, not of original scholarship. This is a long essay that tries to concentrate on the shape of the forest, not the exact dimensions of any one tree. I have tried to connect the disparate developments in politics and government and to place them in a cultural context. Political reform in the second half of the twentieth century has not simply been the product of some intense negotiations among elites. Reform of our politics has also broadly reflected social, economic, and cultural changes that have rocketed through and transformed our society in the postwar world.

I have tried to view postwar developments broadly, to connect them to one another, and to weave together strands of published thought and analysis that help explain their meaning. In a way, I have written this book for my friends and family. I have failed them often in trying to answer their questions about the strange and apparently illogical things they hear and read about; I owe them better answers than I have given them.

All the answers are not here, but some are. Perhaps, at least, reading this book will help my friends and family—as writing it has helped me— see that big changes are not always the result of sweeping national movements or new ideas or political violence, that sweeping transformations can accumulate as well as explode, that many people pulling each other in different directions can end up in a strange place where none of them intended to go.

G. *Calvin Mackenzie*
Bowdoinham, Maine

ACKNOWLEDGMENTS

This book percolated to completion over a period of several years. During that time I was blessed with the able and ingenious help of several excellent research assistants: Lisa Prenaveau Andrzejewski, Chris Selicious, and Colin Harrington. I much appreciate the hours they spent checking facts, tracking down elusive information, and performing all the other critical tasks of careful scholarship. In addition, I am grateful that this project deepened my opportunities to get to know these fine people.

During my years at Colby I have had daily conversations with two brilliant, practical, and creative political scientists: Sandy Maisel and Tony Corrado. These conversations and the insights I gleaned from them have constantly sharpened my thinking about the topics discussed in this book. They were also great fun.

My dear friend historian Rob Weisbrot was the most acute critic of this work and the greatest source of encouragement to pursue it. A lot of loose ends and false leads fell from earlier drafts after they failed to pass the Weisbrot test. For his great good sense and his genuine interest in my work, I am deeply in Rob Weisbrot's debt.

The team of professionals with whom I worked at Westview—Jennifer Knerr, Brenda Hadenfeldt, Jim Grode, Rachel Hegarty, and Gail Renlund—were wonderful colleagues on this project. Their support, efficiency, and care made the production of this book a real, and unusual, pleasure. Larry Dodd lent his sharp editiorial eye and many good ideas to this project. The book also benefited from a close reading by Robert Spitzer and Donald Robinson.

I wrote this book after more than twenty years as a practicing political scientist. Over those years my thinking about politics and government has been shaped and inspired by the extraordinary work of many of my colleagues in this discipline. This book draws heavily on that body of scholarship. I am pleased to acknowledge how much I have learned, and how much I owe, to those whose work is cited here.

Finally, the most important acknowledgment of all: I am grateful for the opportunity to learn from the smart and fascinating people who sit around the dinner table in my home: Rebecca Knight, Andrew Mackenzie, Peter Mackenzie, and Sally Mackenzie. This book will not answer all their questions, but I hope it will help move our conversations along.

G.C.M.

INTRODUCTION

In October 1946 RKO released a motion picture called *The Best Years of Our Lives.* It was a film about the experiences of three World War II veterans, a film about optimism and disillusionment. It captured almost perfectly the spirit—and the shadows—of the time. In 1947 the film won nine Academy Awards.

One of those Academy Awards went to Harold Russell, a real veteran who had lost both his hands in the war. This was Russell's only Hollywood film; he moved on to become a successful businessman. Looking back on those immediate postwar years, he later said, "The guys who came out of World War II were idealistic. They sincerely believed that this time they were coming home to build a new world."[1]

They, and the generation of baby boomers they produced, did build a new world. In fact, they built a world dramatically different from the one into which they had been born. This is a book about that world, about how it differed from all that had gone before, and especially about the impact it had on the way Americans govern themselves. This is a book about change—profound change.

We take the year 1947 as our starting point. Americans still listened to the radio in 1947, and they still read newspapers. Television was just beginning its journey from science fiction to universal home appliance, and the number of daily newspapers was larger then than now. Racial segregation was still a fact of American life: in schools, in the workplace, in public accommodations, even in the American armed forces. Most American women—nearly 70 percent—did not work outside their homes. The traditional family where Dad worked and Mom stayed home with 2.9 children was a statistical reality. Most families were like that, and their likeness was everywhere: billboards, movies, magazines, textbooks.

Americans lived in the city or in the country; there was little in between. The nation's large urban areas dominated life and politics. If you were not one of the 14 percent of civilians who worked on a farm, the likelihood was that you worked in a city. And if you worked in a city, you had little choice but to live there. The nation's highway and mass transit systems simply could not support a society of commuters.

And if you worked in the city in a blue-collar job, chances were good that you were a labor union member or under pressure to become one. After the struggles for recognition and rights endured by the labor unions in the previous quarter century, they were experiencing their heyday in the late 1940s. So prominent were labor unions in the public mind that a piece of legislation aimed at curbing their influence, the Taft-Hartley Act, became the most visible and contentious issue in the Eightieth Congress that convened in 1947.

Although a presidential election was to occur the following year, there was little presidential campaign activity or media speculation in 1947. No candidates announced their intention to run, and political professionals, virtually all of whom held public office, were making no commitments to any candidate. It was too early: The campaign season fell in election years, not before.

When 1948 arrived, candidates slowly appeared and began the nomination pursuit. There were a few presidential primaries that year, most notably in Nebraska, Pennsylvania, and Oregon, but no candidate ran in all of them, and some ran in none. Governor Thomas E. Dewey of New York, the eventual Republican nominee, finished behind three other Republicans in the combined primary vote, receiving only 11 percent of the votes cast. It mattered little, for the nominations would be decided by the party kingpins at the conventions, not by primary voters.

The candidates for the nomination were experienced and familiar figures, each with a significant political base. They were among the leaders in their parties, and they would seek to obtain the nomination by appealing for the support of other party leaders in much the same way that leadership selection occurs in most advanced democracies.

The parties chose President Harry S Truman and Governor Dewey as their candidates, and the two men competed in the fashion of their time. Traveling on trains, they crisscrossed the country, making hundreds of speeches at local gatherings. Party officials across the country worked their wards to turn out support for their nominee. From time to time, the candidates would make half-hour speeches broadcast nationally by radio. These emphasized themes and issues and rarely mentioned the opponent by name. There was little paid political advertising, except in the final days, when both parties encouraged their supporters to vote.

This was the first presidential election year in which there was any real scientific opinion polling. George Gallup's young organization sampled the national electorate periodically for its candidate preferences. But neither candidate employed a pollster, and the issues and themes Dewey and Truman emphasized were selected by instinct and intuition, not from poll data. Opinion samplings in the final weeks supported the conventional wisdom: Dewey would win. Only the voters, it turned out, thought otherwise.

It is hard to comprehend that many of us were alive in that time, for it seems from the 1990s like ancient history, like a world greatly distanced and radically different from the one in which we Americans now live. And it is. In the nearly five decades since World War II, America has changed. Its population has nearly doubled. Its demographic profile is profoundly different, with fundamental changes in all the core units of society: family, home, work, school, and church.

And in that time, American politics and government have undergone a revolution, but not in the conventional sense in which a dispossessed group challenges the establishment, visions differ and ideologies clash, the outs seize power from the ins and then systematically alter the procedures of politics, the operations of government, and the substance of public policy. No, the recent revolution in American politics was slower to unfold, more subtle and inchoate, less apparent to the naked eye—but far-reaching and enduring nevertheless.

It is the argument of this book that the postwar decades were a period of political change as significant as any in our history. America has gone through such changes before: the Progressive era and the New Deal, for example. But the recent period is different from all the others: It occurred without popular consensus, without direction or consistent leadership, without ideological underpinnings, and without intent.

This absence of intent is especially noteworthy, for it helps explain the discontent and disaffection that so many Americans currently feel about the quality of their public life. In each of our previous periods of significant political change, one group of citizens, bound by a shared understanding of what was wrong with their government, formed a consensual agenda for change, then sought to obtain power through the political process to implement that agenda. The Anti-Federalists who became the Jeffersonian Republicans, the Jacksonian Democrats, the Populists and Progressives, and the New Deal Democrats all started somewhere and aimed somewhere. The response to change in previous periods of transition was not always neat; there were adjustments and alterations along the way. But it is a relatively simple task of historical analysis to trace the problems, the proposed responses, and the political actions undertaken to implement them in each of those cases.

Such is not the case with the postwar transformation of American political life. It fits none of the historical patterns. To illustrate its peculiarity, consider a hypothetical possibility. Suppose, for example, that a group of reformers had come together fifty years ago to plan a massive restructuring of American politics that would result in:

- The creation of more than fifteen thousand special interest groups with Washington lobbyists and more than four thousand political action committees (PACs) spending almost $400 million on national elections.
- A presidential selection process that virtually excludes from influence the country's most experienced and knowledgeable political figures; that is never ending and tedium inducing; that is managed by hired professional technocrats with little commitment to any issue or group of voters; that replaces reasoned debate with fifteen-second sound bites; that gives more weight to the vote in New Hampshire than in California.
- An increasingly bureaucratic and impotent presidency that concentrates as much energy on news management and public relations as on policy and legislation.
- Legislative and executive branches often controlled by different political parties and constantly engaged in efforts to checkmate each other.
- A Congress in which party leaders often cannot lead, incumbents are nearly always reelected, staff members exercise enormous discretion, and budgets are debated four times each year by four different sets of committees in each house.
- A policy process in which judges, who are unelected and hold lifetime tenure, often make the most important decisions on critical substantive issues.

No rational group would have planned such a revolutionary agenda. No one would have supported it had this agenda been proposed. It responds to no widely perceived set of problems, it is not informed by any coherent theory of politics or government, and it does not strengthen the loyalty of any substantial segment of the American people to the government. But this is the agenda we implemented. And the task of this book is to explain how it happened.

Two simultaneous trends weave through twentieth-century American politics. One is the steady growth of federal government authority relative to individual Americans and relative to the other governments in the states and municipalities. Authority has grown and centralized. Government has spread its jurisdiction ever more broadly over the lives of individual citizens, and to a steadily increasing extent it has been the government in Washington—not those closer to home—that most affects individual lives.

For American citizens in the first decade of this century, the federal government was usually a distant irrelevance. It did not impose income taxes, regulate many businesses, control the airwaves, interfere in the financial markets, operate a national pension system, pay for health care, support the poor, fund the schools, operate a large standing army or navy, view itself as a world superpower, or generate reams of publicity about its own work.

The federal budget at the end of the first decade of this century was $694 million. Most of that was raised from customs duties, and nearly 70 percent of it was spent on veterans' compensation and the operation of the War and Navy Departments. With so little to do, the government was absent from the capital (and the public consciousness) for much of each year. But over the decades that followed, all of this changed. Accelerated by war, economic crisis, and the major reform energies of the Progressive period, the New Deal, and the Great Society, the role of the federal government steadily grew. It became the most influential participant in the national economy, it created a welfare state, and it emerged after World War II as the leading player in international relations. Perhaps the single most profound change in twentieth-century American life is the growth of government and of the federal government especially.

While the functions and responsibilities of government were growing, a second and related trend was occurring. The presidency, Congress, and the courts all underwent intense institutional development. The primitive and often part-time institutions that ran the country at the beginning of this century have become large, complex, and bustling enterprises. The presidents through Herbert Hoover managed to lead the country with the assistance in the White House of a few clerks and secretaries. Current presidents are surrounded by a formal executive office structure and hundreds of aides.

Members of Congress before World War II usually had other jobs, which they left only for the few months each year while Congress was in session. In Washington their offices employed an assistant and a secretary or two. A score of committees, each with a very small staff, handled all the legislative business. Now Congress has several hundred committees and subcommittees, more than twenty thousand staff employees, and a virtually year-round session.

And so it was with the federal courts. In the century's first decade, there were barely one hundred federal judges. They had limited authority and handled a total of only thirty thousand cases over the whole country in an average year. Courts were typically in session for only a few months each year. Judges did their own research and wrote their own opinions. Today there are more courts and judges handling more cases than ever before. The judicial branch has grown to include an administrative office and a variety of special purpose courts. And the scope of judicial jurisdiction has steadily expanded.

It is not surprising, of course, that the institutions of the federal government have grown and developed as the federal role has expanded. What is surprising perhaps is that the two trends are not more closely related. None of the reform periods of this century, with the partial exception of the Progressive era, provided any administrative blueprint to support the enlargement of substantive authority each was generating. Americans radically refashioned the role of the federal government without systematically redesigning or seriously contemplating the impact on its administrative structure or political processes.

The shape of public administration and the political process both changed, but these changes were not driven by some central conception or theory tied to the enlargement and changing allocation of governmental authority. Instead, administration and politics changed on their own, usually in piecemeal fashion and often in response to self-interested incentives. As the scope of federal authority grew, institutions developed to better compete to control it. And political interests—or, as we usually call them, special interests—mobilized to obtain for themselves a larger portion of the expanding pie of federal benefits. Structural and procedural changes in government and politics have been little more than riders on the wind of substantive change.

We do not, therefore, have a set of late-twentieth-century institutions managing the redefined business of a late-twentieth-century government. Nor do we have a political system closely adapted to the needs and character of that government or the people it serves. What we have is institutions with roots still deeply planted in a time of small and limited government seeking to operate a government that is no longer small or limited. And we have a political process that seems to bear no significant relationship either to the government it is supposed to staff and inform or to any other apparent purpose, except the service of incumbent officeholders and certain well-financed special interests.

We have a problem. It is a large problem, and it cannot be ascribed to the inadequacies of any individual or set of political leaders. When failure persists and political attachments weaken despite changes in leadership and party configuration, it becomes apparent that the causes are systemic and not just personal or partisan flaws.

The government's ability to forge consensus, resolve complicated problems, achieve closure, and properly manage its finances has diminished, in some cases to the vanishing point. The capacity of the American political system to provide an effective outlet for popular concerns, to steadily infuse public life with alternative visions and creative new leaders, and to impose responsiveness and accountability on public officials has steadily deteriorated. The chorus of disaffection swelling in the American people has no hollow ring. Something is very wrong.

Part of our current distress is a delayed legacy of the American constitution. A few years ago we celebrated the bicentennial of that document and highlighted its longevity and splendid accomplishments. We paid less attention to the fundamental tension that afflicted its Framers and remains unresolved to this day. The Constitution sought to create a government that was at once able to control and be controlled by its people, a government that could be simultaneously competent and democratic.

The Framers were brilliant, imaginative, and politically astute. But they were students of two experiences that taught them competing lessons. As children of the American Revolution, they were deeply skeptical of concentrated authority. As citizens under the Articles of Confederation, they knew the costs of fragmented authority. So they wrote a constitution that tried through a series of delicate compromises and balances to have it both ways: to create necessary power while discouraging undesirable concentrations of power.

They provided no enduring solutions to the conundra with which they wrestled. Indeed, those among them who went on to positions in the government they had created were soon wrestling anew with the same questions. And over the ensuing two centuries, their successors have struggled as well with the imperfect balance the Framers created.

Like the Framers, Americans continue to be schizophrenic about concentrated authority. We have wavered back and forth, experimenting with strong leadership occasionally, especially in war and crisis, but mostly emphasizing representation and seeking to protect the parts against the whole. Today, we have reached a curious and largely ineffective compromise. The federal government has more authority than ever before but little capability to use it for a coherent purpose. Government is simultaneously powerful and incompetent. Like a great brontosaurus, government is large and muscular but afflicted with a tiny brain and a frail central nervous system. So government is perceived to be at the same time too weak and too strong, impotent and oppressive.

The American people expect more from government than ever before, yet resent its intrusions into their lives. They want an increasing array of services and benefits from government but are restive with their costs. So there are a resounding loss of faith in government and a corrosive decline in support for its leaders and employees. The result is the greatest crisis of legitimacy since the Civil War. Americans grow increasingly angry at their government and dubious of its claims on their paychecks and restrictions on their freedom.

We have undergone a half century of sweeping social and political change, and we are now living, in widespread discomfort, with its consequences. In the chapters that follow, we will trace the developments that brought us to this point and explore their implications for the American experiment in self-government on the eve of the millennium.

We begin by examining the cultural context for political change, how American society has evolved over the past half century. Then we explore the profound alterations that have occurred in our political process, the way we choose and inform our leaders, and the way we hold them accountable. This leads us to an analysis of the major institutions of government: Congress, the presidency, and the courts. We conclude with a discussion of the meaning of the reforms that have so altered American politics in the past half century and with some suggestions—more instructive than feasible perhaps—for correcting the three principal failures of contemporary government:

- The inability to concentrate power for collective purpose
- The disjunction between politics and government
- The fragility and transience of coalitions in government

Nowhere in this book is there an argument for a return to some golden age. We have never really had a golden age in the American experience. Democracies are hard to operate, politics is always awkward, and governing is always difficult. We have managed to muddle along through most of our history with a set of eighteenth-century institutions that, through hard work by underappreciated politicians and some good luck, we have managed to adapt to changing circumstances. We could do so because government was not very important to the lives of most Americans. Until World War II, most Americans paid no direct taxes to the federal government and received few or no direct benefits from it. We could abide the inefficiencies—even the occasional stupidities—of government because there were also occasional moments of brilliance and because, when all was said and done, government did not matter all that much.

After World War II, everything changed. Government assumed a steadily growing place in the lives of all of its citizens—in no small part because groups of citizens finding it harder to cope with powerful social and economic forces wanted more government. But when government functions expanded, when the costs of government grew, all of us became more sharply aware of its actions. We became stakeholders. And when we did, we often increased our demands for government services and our expectations for government operations. And when government fell short in meeting our needs or expectations, we grew disenchanted.

Some Americans may long for a return to a golden age of smoothly functioning government and happy citizens. But those notions are romantic. Such an age never existed. Americans have always had a love-hate relationship with their government. They loved the ideals of democracy, freedom, equality, and free enterprise. But they struggled and suffered with the practical application and preservation of those concepts. The task of struggling and suffering was never simple and rarely pretty.

But now the costs and difficulties of democratic self-government are larger than they have ever been. The task of making our old institutions and patched-together processes work in our own time is more vexing than ever. This book does not argue that what we need is to return to some golden age when everything was wonderful. It argues instead that we have always struggled to make our Constitution fit contemporary problems and realities and that the struggle is harder now because those realities have altered so dramatically in the past half century.

THE NEW LANDSCAPE
OF AMERICAN LIFE

In the years that followed World War II, America remade itself. The population nearly doubled. Booming economic growth provided most Americans with unprecedented freedom from want and access to lifestyles that earlier generations had found only in dreams. The invention and mass marketing of new technologies changed the way Americans communicated, conducted their businesses, educated their children, planned their families, managed their homes, and entertained themselves.

America at the end of the twentieth century is a country profoundly altered from the one that emerged from World War II. It is no surprise that American politics has changed so sharply in the last half century; American leaders have a new and different country to govern. They could no more operate in the manner of Woodrow Wilson or Franklin Roosevelt than those leaders could have emulated Thomas Jefferson and Andrew Jackson. A changing society sets a new political stage, and American society has never changed more rapidly or more deeply than in the past half century.

Politics is always shaped and constrained by its setting. Successful governments are rarely transplantable from one cultural context to another or one time to another. Each society and each era create their own opportunities, encouraging certain kinds of politics and discouraging others. That is precisely what has happened in the United States in the second half of the twentieth century. Conditions that once yielded and sustained a politics heavily reliant on two dominant parties, on state and local political machines, on personal interaction between leaders and followers, and on limited government involvement in business and personal lives have diminished, in some cases disappeared entirely. Those conditions have been replaced by others that encourage new forms of politics and new levels of government activity. In this chapter, we look at the most important of these changes in the American political landscape.

AMERICA AT WAR'S END

The sensitive observer would have begun to notice the changes even before the Japanese attack on Pearl Harbor initiated the greatest mobilization of armed forces in American history. There were stirrings of change everywhere. Paved roads were beginning to be laid across the countryside and into and out of the large metropolitan centers. National corporations and national marketing were emergent economic forces. Consumer products that had been luxuries a generation earlier—cars, radios, washing machines, refrigerators—were becoming more commonplace. Public higher education was growing, and college was less and less a privilege reserved for the wealthy.

The Depression had focused attention on the government in Washington in altogether new ways. That government was becoming the center of national activity, growing in size and cost. Federal government spending, still tiny by contemporary standards, had crept up from $3.1 billion in 1929 to $9.1 billion ten years later.[1]

These were the beginnings of change. Yet to most outward appearances, America in the late 1930s did not look very different from America at the end of the nineteenth century. Although the swelling of American cities was well under way, this country was still predominantly rural, its economy heavily engaged in agriculture. In 1936 more than 10 million people, nearly 20 percent of American workers, were employed on farms. Most Americans who did not work on farms wore a blue collar and carried a lunch pail to work. Most of them were men since social roles still required women to stay home and tend to the family. Few young people aspired to or attended college. Family incomes were still meager, averaging $1,231 a year in 1939. And in an age before government welfare programs and safety nets, most Americans were vulnerable to the forces of nature, shocks in the economic cycle, and the twin dreads of illness and old age.

World War II was a jolt to all of that. No other event in American history, not even the revolution for independence, wrought such dramatic change in so short a time. Some of that change had begun before the war, but the war supercharged it and ensured its permanence. The war was, as historian Geoffrey Perrett noted, "the closest thing to a real social revolution the United States has known."[2]

The clearest change was economic. The war put the American economy back on its feet and started it on a long and sturdy path of growth. The gross national product (GNP) increased at an average annual rate of 9.4 percent from 1940 through 1945. Personal incomes, after barely increasing at all in the 1930s, more than doubled in the 1940s. Wages and salaries of all American employees grew from $50 billion in 1940 to $147 billion in 1950.

This enormous infusion of money into the economy affected almost everyone. The distribution of this new wealth was more equitable than any social or economic planner could possibly have envisioned, reaching down deeply into the lower rungs of the economic ladder. Prior to World War II, American society was notable for the absence of a significant middle class. The upper one-third lived quite comfortably; the lower two-thirds struggled constantly at the edge of survival. The war hauled everyone up. Americans who could not previously have hoped to own their own home, send their children to college, take vacations, or feel relief from financial worry found themselves after World War II in a country with much broader horizons.

A grateful nation welcomed home its 15 million veterans with a broad and generous array of programs for their benefit. These included mustering-out pay, weekly stipends until employment was secured (membership in what veterans called the "52–20 club"), and a network of medical facilities to treat the sick and wounded. But two postwar veterans' programs—part of what came to be known as the GI Bill—had much more sweeping consequences.

One of these provided government mortgage loan guarantees for veterans buying a home. In 1940 only 43.6 percent of American homes were owned by their occupants. The simple fact was that most members of the American working class had great difficulty saving enough money for a downpayment and then securing the necessary credit to buy their own home.

Home loan guarantees changed all of that. And in the process, they changed the American landscape. Houses began to spring up everywhere in the greatest home building boom in history. In the decade after World War II, the Veterans Administration alone guaranteed more than $121 billion in home mortgages. Almost 15 million new housing units were constructed in that decade, nearly four times the number built in the previous decade. By 1956 more than 60 percent of American homes were owned by their occupants. With those new houses came new communities and new cultures and a whole new politics.

The other veterans' program with deep and lasting effects was the GI Bill's education benefits. Veterans who went to college or sought advanced technical training had their tuition paid by the federal government and received a monthly stipend for family support. With this encouragement, American veterans flooded into overwhelmed colleges and universities. An average of almost four hundred thousand bachelor's degrees were awarded each year in the decade from 1948 through 1957, nearly four times the annual average of the 2 decades preceding World War II. And the number continued to grow steadily thereafter. This provided the booming postwar economy with the best educated workforce in its history and created opportunities for those who availed themselves

of the GI Bill to earn incomes and establish lifestyles that had been beyond the dreams of their parents and grandparents. Because of the GI
Bill, higher education in America was no longer merely a privilege of the
elite. For a broad range of American families, it became an expectation.

The war also forced Americans to confront racism in a way that most
had been able to avoid since the end of Reconstruction. In fundamental
ways, the war was about racism: about claims of Aryan superiority and
about racial genocide. Even the sturdiest blinders could not permit
Americans to fight a war against racism abroad and overlook the practice
of racism at home. The war stirred the pot of American race relations and
brought it to a boil. Over 1 million black Americans served in uniform
during the war, many of them from communities that systematically denied them the right to vote and to get a decent education. Employment
opportunities in war industries induced hundreds of thousands of blacks
to leave the South and move to where the jobs were in American cities.
From 1940 to 1950, almost 2 million black citizens made this trek north
and west. This was one of the great internal migrations in human history,
and it began to change the national political implications of the race issue.

During and immediately after the war, a small group of dedicated attorneys, headed by Thurgood Marshall and Charles Houston and operating under the imprimatur of the NAACP Legal Defense Fund, had
begun to challenge the legal foundations of racial segregation. In 1944
they won a case opening primary elections in the South to blacks as well
as whites. In 1948 they persuaded the Supreme Court to render unen-
forceable racially restrictive real estate covenants. And in 1950 they forced
the law schools at the Universities of Maryland and Texas and the graduate school at the University of Oklahoma to admit black applicants.

The necessities of war had also created unprecedented opportunities
for women in the workplace. It was not simply that there were jobs for
women because so many men had entered the armed services. Many of
those jobs were in occupations to which women had traditionally been
denied access because of their perceived physical limitations. But during
the war, women took jobs in physically demanding and sometimes dangerous occupations and in so doing demonstrated the unwisdom of traditional ideas of female capabilities.

When the war was over, many women returned to their tasks as homemakers and turned their jobs over to returning veterans. But the number
of women in the workforce stayed substantially above prewar levels,
work and career became far more common female aspirations, and an important point had been made to those employers who doubted that
women could do difficult or dangerous jobs. Sex role stereotypes would
never again be as rigid as they had been before the war.

In all of these ways, World War II opened up American society. Millions of young men left their homes to go to war. They became more cosmopolitan and less parochial in the process. The walls of economic class were crumbling from the force of economic growth and ready access to higher education. A housing explosion was creating new communities and altering older ones. The movement for black liberation was under way. And the seeds had been planted for a new enlightenment by and about American women. "My generation," James Michener was to write, "after suffering years of hardship and deprivation, stormed back and, in a sense, fought just as bravely to build a new America."[3] It was a new America that no longer fit the simple verities or stereotypes of the decades before the war. Nor was it a new America that comfortably fit the structure of prewar politics.

World War II left one other enduring legacy that permanently altered American politics: big government. Most histories trace the roots of big government to the New Deal, and correctly so. Notions about government's role and obligation did begin to change significantly in response to the Depression. But the federal government on the eve of World War II was still a relatively small enterprise that intruded, if at all, only at the margins of most peoples' lives. In 1939, for example, the federal budget was still under $10 billion, and federal employment, despite the perceived explosion in New Deal agencies, totaled less than 1 million, more than one-third of whom delivered the mail. Federal income taxes applied only to gross incomes above $5,000, and only 3.9 million people paid any federal income tax in that year.

The social security system had been put in place a few years earlier, but no one had yet received social security benefits, and social security payroll taxes were only charged at the rate of 1 percent on the first $3,000 of personal income. Although war had been imminent for some time, there were only 334,000 Americans in uniform, and none being drafted. There was no federal aid to education, no permanent program of federal support for the arts, no significant federal health care programs, no sizable American military presence outside the United States, no federal highway system, no comprehensive programs of environmental protection or occupational safety. Most Americans paid no direct taxes to the federal government, received no economic subsidy from it, and were unregulated by it. Only with the onset of World War II did big government become a permanent feature of American public life.

The New Deal bore the impression of transience and experimentation. Most Americans and most politicians anticipated that much of the New Deal, with the exception of such programs as social security and securities regulation, would disappear when the economic crisis had passed.

The bright young people who came to Washington to manage the New Deal agencies rarely thought of themselves as permanent government employees but rather as crisis managers who would fix things up and go back to the private sector. Irving Kristol called the 1930s "America's last amateur decade."[4] That is a description in which most New Deal leaders themselves would probably have concurred.

The war changed that perception about big government. For one thing, the war brought government more deeply into American lives than the New Deal had ever had. To feed the government's hunger for revenue, the income tax base broadened and deepened. In 1939, 3.9 million people paid income taxes; by 1944, 42.4 million were paying. In 1943, to get revenue sooner, the government began mandatory withholding from American paychecks. The Selective Service System was drafting men by the tens of thousands every month. Government contracts fueled the economy. The Office of Price Administration took charge of the distribution of scarce commodities such as gasoline, rubber, and meat. In the name of national security, blackouts were imposed, films were censored, mail was read, and wires were tapped. Those who were shocked when the federal budget reached the astronomical sum of $9.5 billion in 1940 had probably become hardened to the new realities by the time it climbed to $92.7 billion in 1945. For most Americans, for the first time in their lives, there was no escaping the looming presence of the federal government.

The end of the war did not bring an end to big government. Demobilization of the armed forces never approached prewar levels. In 1935 there had been 252,000 Americans in uniform; After World War II, the number never fell below 1.4 million; from 1951 to 1990 it stayed above 2 million. In many ways, in fact, government continued to grow after the war. The construction of the Pentagon and the creation of the Department of Defense and the Central Intelligence Agency certified the permanence of large military and intelligence establishments. The new Veterans Administration quickly became one of the largest and most expensive agencies of government. At the behest of President Truman, Congress in 1946 passed the Full Employment Act, which stated unequivocally that "it is the continuing policy and responsibility of the Federal Government . . . to promote maximum employment, production and purchasing power." In signing the law, President Truman said it was "not the end of the road, but rather the beginning."[5]

Big government took root during World War II for two reasons above all. One was that the war wrought a significant change in America's place and role in the world. In 1940 America had the world's nineteenth largest army. By the end of 1945, America had the most powerful military force the world had ever seen—including a new weapon of demonstrated and unprecedented capability for mass destruction—and it produced half of the world's GNP. To most Americans of the time, World War II was a lesson in the cost of unpreparedness. There could be no turning back to isolationism and withdrawal from the affairs of the world.

The second reason big government took such firm root is that it was working, or so a majority of the American people thought. Most people had never had it so good. Per capita gross domestic product (GDP) was up from $693 in 1939 to $1,523 in 1945. There were more good jobs available to more people than ever before. A good education was in almost everyone's sights. Home ownership was a real option for many who could not have afforded a home before the war. New government programs were easing the difficulties of the poor, the sick, and the aged. Even those at the bottom of the economic ladder were better off than they had been previously. If the war brought no massive redistribution of income, it had certainly brought an almost universal elevation of personal wealth. The Americans who saw government as the source of this substantial improvement in fortune—and most Americans did—were not anxious then to reverse direction.

AMERICA ON THE MOVE

After World War II, Americans hit the road. Some had started earlier: the Okies and Arkies who had headed west to escape the Dust Bowl of the 1930s and the blacks who had left the South in search of northern industrial jobs during the war. But the most significant movement of the population took place after the war ended. Americans moved to the suburbs.

During the war, the constant need for new housing in and around military installations had inspired a revolution in home building techniques. Before the war, skilled carpenters built most homes to suit individual owners. There was no time for that during the war, and many of the carpenters had been drafted anyway. To fill this need for hurry-up, low-skill housing construction, contractors began to develop designs and materials that were innovations in residential construction. One of these contractors was a young man named William J. Levitt, who made a name for himself by constructing twenty-five hundred new housing units in Norfolk, Virginia, in the year and half after Pearl Harbor. Levitt and others continued to refine their mass production techniques throughout the war.

When the war ended, millions of mustering-out veterans craved housing of their own. The existing housing stock could not begin to meet the demand, and most veterans could not afford the cost of a traditional new home. Into this vast new market stepped William J. Levitt and others like him. They bought up huge plots of land near metropolitan areas, cleared away all the trees, sketched out a few roads, and began to throw up inexpensive houses at unprecedented rates. Levitt houses were typically boxy rectangles with two or three bedrooms and an unfinished basement on a tiny lot. But they were cheap, and they were available, and home-hungry veterans gobbled them up.

Levittowns began to appear everywhere as Americans in droves packed up and headed to the suburbs. Pretty little country towns like Falls Church, Virginia; Wellesley, Massachusetts; Denton, Texas; and Whittier, California, were soon latticed with subdivisions and row upon row of simple, undormered Cape Cods and low-slung ranch houses. Wetlands were filled, forests were cut down, and pastures and groves became neighborhoods. On Long Island, in Hempstead, four thousand acres of potato farms were turned into more than seventeen thousand new houses for eighty-two thousand residents.[6]

By the late 1940s, Levitt was selling more than four thousand houses a year.[7] He had many imitators, and new developments of one thousand houses or more sprung up all across the country. These were communities in name only. The builders had little interest in schools or parks or other public facilities. Social infrastructures—churches, community centers, the local Young Men's Christian Association—were left to chance. For many residents of these new developments, life was sterile and isolated, despite the proximity of neighbors. Residents had little shared history and few ethnic or religious connections. They also lacked any collective political history or tradition.

The move to the suburbs had slowly got under way in the first half of the twentieth century, but as late as 1940 only 15.3 percent of the population lived in suburbs. America was still a vast rural landscape dominated socially and politically by its large urban centers. In the 1944 presidential election, for example, 7 percent of the nation's popular votes were cast in New York City.[8] No city would ever again loom so large in the political calculus.

It was only after the war that America became a suburban nation. The suburbs grew faster than the cities in each of the postwar decades: three times faster in the 1940s, four times faster in the 1950s, and more than five times faster in the 1960s. By 1970, for the first time, there were more people living in the suburbs than in the cities; by 1990, 46.2 percent of the American people lived in the suburbs.[9]

The service economy of the late twentieth century and advances in communications and computer technology no longer required steadily growing metropolitan industrial centers. So for the first time since the onset of the Industrial Revolution, population grew faster outside the metropolitan centers than inside them.[10] Americans were not just moving a few miles from downtown to a nearby suburb. Many were packing up and moving to different counties or different states entirely. Massive population shifts were occurring from some sections of the country to others. The demographic profile of the states was experiencing a significant rearrangement.

At midcentury America still conformed closely to the economic pattern that had resulted from industrialization. Much of the country was still engaged in various forms of agriculture. Heavy industry was still concentrated along the shores of the Great Lakes, in southern New England, and down through the Middle Atlantic metropolitan complex. As late as 1957, these areas still contained 46 percent of the American population, only a slight decrease from the percentage they had held at the beginning of the century. These same states, according to a study by William Issel, generated 53 percent of the country's personal income and provided 64 percent of its manufacturing employment.[11]

Since then, however, people and jobs have been moving away, moving south and west. Another new technology, air conditioning, made places that had once seemed uninhabitable not only inhabitable but also inviting. For the first time in America's history, the North and the East lost their dominance of the economy and the population. And when that happened, of course, they began to lose their dominance of politics as well. From 1970 to 1990, the American population grew by 45 million people. As a whole, the South and West accounted for 90 percent of the nation's population growth during those two decades. The three states of Florida, Texas, and California accounted for almost one-half of that growth.

In the 1980 and 1990 reallocation of congressional seats, Florida gained a total of eight, Texas gained six, and California gained nine. When the 103rd Congress convened in 1993, California alone had 12 percent of the seats in the House. California, Texas, and Florida combined had almost 25 percent of the total. In 1982, for the first time in American history, states in the South and West held a majority of the seats in the House. That advantage grew after the 1990 census, and all indications are that it will continue to grow in the decades ahead.

This population movement represents a shift not only in where the votes are located but also in how they are organized. Embedded in these data is an important postwar political trend: a movement of political power away from those states and cities with the longest history of effective party organization to those states, such as Arizona and Oklahoma, with no such history or those, such as Louisiana and Florida, with political histories rooted in the single and now largely irrelevant political issue of racial segregation. Even were the great political machines of David Lawrence and Richard Daley and Carmine DeSapio still operating—and we look in more detail later at why they are not—they would no longer control enough electoral votes and members of Congress to afford them anything like the influence they once wielded in American politics. And

most of the areas newly empowered by population growth never had political organizations of sufficient strength to turn those votes into consistent, deliverable political power—certainly not after desegregation
knocked out the racial underpinnings of southern Democratic hegemony.

The evidence that mobility seems to have become a normal condition
of the American people further confounds the political impact of the postwar population movement. Americans keep moving. In a sense this is a
familiar American tradition. Alexis de Tocqueville noted in his travels
here in the 1830s that "an American will build a house in which to pass
his old age and sell it before the roof is on; he will plant a garden and rent
it just as the trees are coming into bearing; he will clear a field and leave
others to reap the harvest; he will take up a profession and leave it, settle in one place and soon go off elsewhere with his changing desires."[12]

After World War II, Americans moved more than ever. In no postwar
year has the percentage of American households that moved fallen below
16 percent; some years it has been well over 20 percent. From 1960 to
1989, more than 91 percent of all households moved. From 1985 to 1989
alone, nearly 50 percent of the population moved. In 1989, 18 percent hit
the road.[13]

The enormous postwar population movement had many causes. One
was simply that by 1990 there were 110 million more Americans than
there had been at the end of World War II. They had to go somewhere.
Steady growth in personal income and the GI Bill and other government
housing subsidies encouraged growing levels of home ownership. Most
of the new homes needed to meet that demand were built in the suburbs.
The accelerating growth of national corporations and markets after World
War II meant that job transfers and promotions were a common impetus
to move. As the South and West expanded and prospered, they lured
workers and retirees from the North and East, where industries were
dying and winters were cold.

The growing centrality of the automobile in American life accounts for
much of this mobility as well. In 1948 there were 41 million motor vehicles on the road, and 54 percent of all families owned one. By 1990 nearly
88 percent of all families owned a total of more than 148 million motor
vehicles. After World War II, public policy encouraged automobiles over
other forms of land transportation. Mass transit ridership reached its all-
time peak in 1948.[14] In 1956 Congress created the federal highway system.
And in the decade that followed, more than 225,000 miles of new highways were built, with the federal government paying 70 percent of the
cost.

With the highways came many changes in American life: ready access
from suburb to city and the phenomenon of "bedroom communities," the
emergence of the shopping mall as the principal consumer marketplace,

the development and spread of national franchise outlets for fast food and many other commodities, the constantly moving family vacation, and ultimately a profound homogenization of American culture. The availability of the automobile and ready access to interstate highways spurred the American propensity to move and set the population freer than it had ever been before from its geographical anchors.

Sustained high levels of population mobility pose genuine problems for political organizers. People who do not plan a long stay in a community are unlikely to invest much of their time or interest in its politics or problems. Local organizations are in constant flux as their membership regularly turns over. And since census data show that the propensity to move is highest among the best educated and most affluent Americans[15] —precisely the group from which a community's political leaders are most likely to come—leadership recruitment is confounded as well.

BABY BOOM

Although not much noticed at the time, 1947 saw the beginning of a demographic development that would deeply influence American life and politics for most of the century that followed. Americans began to have babies—by the millions.

In 1940 the median marriage age had been 24.3 for men and 21.5 for women. By 1947 the medians had dropped to 23.7 and 20.5, and in 1956 they bottomed out at 22.5 and 20.1. With the marriages—and, increasingly as well, without them—came babies. In 1940, 2.6 million babies had been born in the United States. In 1945 there were 2.9 million. By 1947 the number of births grew to 3.8 million, and it never fell below 3.6 million in any year again until 1967. From 1953 through 1963, an average of 4.2 million babies were born every year in the United States.

This was the baby boom, and it produced the largest generational population cohort in American history. The effect on public life was dramatic. As the baby boomers started to reach school age in the early 1950s, an unprecedented wave of new school construction began, with attendant impacts on public budgets and tax rates. By 1965 the pressure of local school budgets had grown so great that the federal government began to provide aid to local education for the first time. By 1979 a new cabinet-level department of education had been created to supervise the myriad programs that had grown up in the wake of that initial decision.

As family size grew in the 1950s and 1960s, the demand for more and larger houses grew as well, accelerating the move to the suburbs. Not only were there a lot of baby boomers, but they also had access to more disposable income than any previous generation. Those with products to sell took notice. As the baby boomers passed through puberty and early adulthood, they quickly became the favorite target of mass marketers, inspiring fads such as hula hoops and coonskin caps and trends such as rock and roll music, informal dress, and a preference for television over books.

As the baby boomers passed through the crime-prone years of early adulthood, crime rates shot up. As they finished high school in record numbers, they inspired unprecedented demands for college education. As they reached working age, they required more new jobs than the economy had ever before produced. As their incomes grew to the highest levels in history, they created a vast new market for consumer electronics, luxury cars, pricey restaurants, and other amenities of the good life. As the baby boomers age, they will blaze yet another trail into the golden years. By the year 2030, under current projections, 22 percent of the American population will be over the age of sixty-five—nearly double the current percentage. The demand for retirement housing, medical care and the other perquisites and needs of old age will grow apace.

By 1968 the first of the baby boomers were eligible to vote. (The voting age at the time was still twenty-one.) Baby boomers represented less than 10 percent of the potential electorate in that election. By 1972, however, with the voting age lowered to eighteen, baby boomers composed more than 20 percent of the potential electorate. By 1976 their percentage had grown to more than 33; by 1984 to 50, and by 1988 to almost 60.

By virtue merely of their strength in numbers, baby boomers have had the potential to be the controlling force in American politics. But they have not been because they have resisted traditional forms of political organization, especially deep commitments of party loyalty. To date, baby boomers have been less likely to vote than members of other generations and less likely to identify strongly with either major political party. This generation, noted Paul Light in his book on the baby boomers, has been "less a kingmaker than a heartbreaker,"[16] a reliable source of support for no party or candidate or broad-based political movement.

To an extent rarely encountered before in American politics, the baby boomers went their own way. Probably it is not surprising that a generation so large would be so full of diverse impulses. This was not only America's largest generation but also its freest: free from the pressure to conform that had characterized the generation of the two world wars, free—because of the invention of the birth control pill and the availability of abortion—from the tyranny of unwanted children, free from the need so common to earlier generations to help support a financially marginal family, and free from the need to participate in politics to acquire life's necessities. The baby boomers forged their own diverse identities. Some fought in the war in Vietnam; others protested against it. Some joined in the fruits of the black liberation movement; others rioted in urban ghettoes. Some chose to be the first in their families or race or gender to go to the best colleges or work in the best law firms or own their own corporations. Others chose to follow the traditional lifestyles of their parents as homemakers or farmers or factory workers.

Whatever the baby boomers were, they were not a cultural or economic monolith. More than any previous generation, they had the power, means, and opportunity to make their own life choices. And they made them. They were not a political monolith either, for the same reasons. Their political diversity reflected their cultural and economic diversity. And they became a great frustration to national and local political leaders, even as they themselves became those leaders. There was no herding, and often no leading, the baby boomers. They resisted traditional calls to political action and political loyalty. They turned inward, to their own cultural, racial, and economic groups, and found little reason to work hard at bridging the differences—and sometimes the hostilities—among those groups. When the baby boomers came of political age, America became a more difficult country to govern than it had been at any time in the twentieth century.

THE EDUCATION COLOSSUS

In the decades following World War II, education became America's biggest industry. Table 2.1 indicates the escalation in public school growth and costs after World War II. All of this produced the most massive of all the social changes in the postwar American population: the growth in education levels of the people. Especially notable is the extent to which American citizens have accessed higher education.

Before World War II, it meant something quite special to be a high school graduate. In 1930, for example, only 29 percent of the total post–school age population had graduated from high school. As late as 1952, 41 percent of adults had not gone beyond grade school in their educations.[17] The 1980 census was the first ever to report that a majority of adults in every state were high school graduates.[18] The absence of a high school diploma was the norm for the majority of adult Americans before World War II.

College experience was even rarer. In 1940 only 10.3 percent of the population had completed at least one year of college, and only 5.4 percent were college graduates. After the war, with the impetus of the GI Bill, Americans began to attend college in larger numbers than ever before. Nearly 7.8 million World War II veterans took advantage of their GI Bill education benefits. By April 1947 the number of veterans enrolled in colleges and universities nearly equaled the total enrollment in 1940.[19] College enrollment never again fell back to its prewar levels. In fact, from

TABLE 2.1
Growth in Elementary and Secondary Education, 1920–1990

Year	Total Enrollment (public and private, in thousands)	Receipts ($ million)				Teachers (in thousands)
		Total, All Levels	Local	State	Federal	
1920	23,278	971	808	160	3	680
1930	28,329	2,088	1,727	354	7	854
1940	28,045	2,260	1,536	684	40	875
1950	28,492	5,437	3,115	2,166	156	914
1960	41,762	14,677	8,257	5,768	652	1,387
1970	51,319	40,268	20,985	16,063	3,220	2,131
1980	46,208	97,635	40,686	47,929	9,020	2,211
1990	46,221	206,753	92,930	100,546	13,277	2,365

NOTE: Data on student enrollment include private secondary and elementary schools; data on receipts and teachers include public schools only.

SOURCE: U.S. Dept. of Commerce, Bureau of the Census, *Statistical Abstract of the United States, 1992* (Washington, D.C.: GPO, 1992), pp. 138–154; U.S. Dept. of Commerce, Bureau of the Census, *Historical Statistics of the United States: Colonial Times to 1970* (Washington, D.C.: GPO, 1975), pp. 370–375.

1946 on the number of colleges and universities and the number of students enrolled in them took off on a steady escalation that continues today.

Before long, a high school diploma came to be seen not as a mark of educational distinction but as little more than a ticket of admission to college. At midcentury less than one-half the American people had completed high school. By the end of this century, nearly one-half of American adults will have had the benefit of training or education beyond high school. Median years of education completed grew from 8.6 in 1940 to 12.7 in 1991. That is a remarkable change in the educational profile of the American people.

This change has had at least two significant political impacts. First, it has converted the United States into a society run by those with college educations. A survey of most large American enterprises at midcentury—corporations, unions, legislatures, executive agencies—would have turned up a substantial percentage of noncollege graduates in leadership positions. The president of the United States, Harry Truman, would have been one of those. Today, however, people without college degrees are rarely found in any of those leadership positions. When the 103rd Congress convened in 1993, for example, it had among its 535 members only 36 who lacked a college degree. In fact, 67 percent of its members had not only a bachelor's degree but also a graduate or professional degree.

Increasing educational levels—especially, increasing percentages of the population with college degrees—have altered the face of politics. Politics has become the province of the educated. Those who legislate, those who arbitrate, and those who administer are college graduates. So, too, is the vast majority of those who seek to influence their decisions. As a result, the majority of Americans who are not college graduates are increasingly forced to the periphery of public life. Their participation is invited, and tolerated, only at election time, when the educated seek to manipulate their votes, often with simplistic messages delivered through the mass media.

A second impact of the postwar education explosion is that teachers have become a potent new force in American political life. In 1990 there were more than 2.3 million public school teachers in America, almost all of them members of one of two large labor unions: the American Federation of Teachers and the National Education Association. In 1968, 8 percent of the delegates to the Democratic National Convention were teachers. By 1984 the percentage had doubled to 16 percent. Teachers—increasingly strong in numbers, well educated and active, better organized than ever—have been a force to reckon with in postwar American politics.

THE CHANGING WORKPLACE

On the eve of World War II, the vast majority of American workers were men. Most jobs were located either on farms or in the country's few large urban centers, and muscle was still the primary requirement for many of those jobs. A majority of the workforce wore blue collars, and labor unions were growing rapidly in membership

Farming was still a major American occupation in the years before World War II. In 1920 nearly 33 percent of Americans lived on farms, and 26 percent of the workforce was employed in agriculture. By 1950 the percentage of people living on farms had dropped to 14 percent, and only one worker in eight was employed in agriculture. The decline continued through the rest of the century. By 1991 fewer than one American in fifty lived on a farm, and agriculture accounted for less than 3 percent of all employment. The twentieth century has seen America change from an economy in which the predominant form of work was agricultural to one in which farmers compose only a tiny segment of the workforce.

Labor union membership has followed a different pattern, starting out low, escalating rapidly in the middle decades of the century after bruising battles for management recognition and government protection, and shrinking again toward the end. Only 7 percent of the civilian workforce were labor union members in 1933. That grew to 15 percent in 1939 and to 27 percent in 1944. Membership reached a high of 28 percent in 1956 but then began to fall. Union membership was under 20 percent by 1980 and had fallen to 16 percent by 1991. This was not solely the result of rapid growth in nonunionized segments of an expanding labor force. Union membership was declining in absolute numbers as well, from a high of 22.2 million members in 1975 to 16.6 million in 1991. Figure 2.1 indicates the pattern of labor union membership from 1920 to 1990.

Farmers and labor union members had been two of the great political power blocs of the twentieth century. By the last decade of the century, one had passed into near oblivion, and the other was a shadow of its former self. No longer could any national candidate or political party build

FIGURE 2.1
Labor Union Membership, 1900–1990

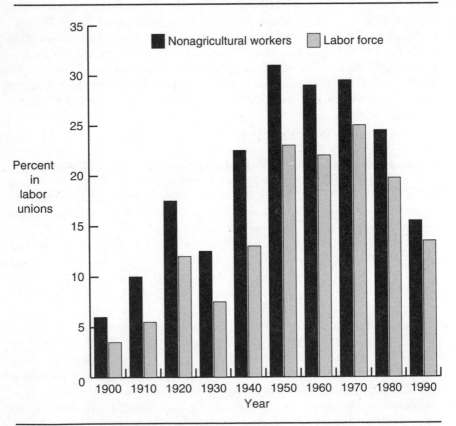

SOURCE: Prepared by author from data in Harold W. Stanley and Richard G. Niemi, *Vital Statistics on American Politics,* 5th ed. (Washington, D.C.: CQ Press, 1995), p. 176.

a successful campaign on the support of farmers or labor unions. And nothing similar had come along to replace these two great centers of political organization. Consequently, national political campaigns were more difficult to mount and sustain.

As the baby boom came to an end and the women's liberation movement took hold, women poured into the workforce in unprecedented numbers. Figure 2.2 indicates the pattern of change. By 1990 almost 40 percent of all workers were women, and 58 percent of women of working age were in the labor force. Even though some occupations, such as secretaries and construction workers, remained dominated by one gender or the other, women made heavy inroads after World War II in a number of jobs—the professions especially—that had previously been male provinces. By 1991 women composed 19 percent of all lawyers, 20 percent of physicians, and 41 percent of all college teachers; women were a steadily growing component of virtually every profession and managerial specialty.

Among the postwar data are two significant but little noted trends. One is that a larger percentage of all adults are working outside their homes than ever before. As farm employment has shrunk and as more women have moved into the labor force, the percentage of employed adults has grown from 53 percent in 1940 to 67 percent in 1990. A second is that Americans are spending more time on the job. At midcentury many futurists predicted that we were moving into a leisure age. Modern technology and higher wages would shorten the workday and the workweek. Quite the opposite has occurred. According to one recent study:

> Regardless of who they are or what they do, Americans spend more time at work than at any time since World War II. In 1950, the U.S. had fewer working hours than any industrialized country. Today, it exceeds every country but Japan, where industrial employees log 2,155 hours a year compared with 1,951 in the U.S. and 1,603 in the former West Germany. Between 1969 and 1989, employed Americans added an average of 138 hours to their yearly work schedules. The workweek has remained at about 40 hours, but people are working more weeks each year. Moreover, paid time off—holidays, vacations, sick leave—shrank by 15 percent in the 1980's.[20]

Political activists, indeed those who manage any kind of volunteer activity, have readily discerned the impact of more people spending more time at work: It is harder than ever before to recruit and obtain significant contributions of time from volunteers. Electoral politics and political activism have historically relied heavily on volunteers to do the "licking and sticking" and other routine tasks necessary to contact large numbers of people and persuade them to support a candidate or policy. But volunteers are harder to come by now, thus forcing candidates to rely more heavily on paid staff and consultants and forcing those who wish to in-

FIGURE 2.2
Female Participation in the Labor Force, 1920–1990

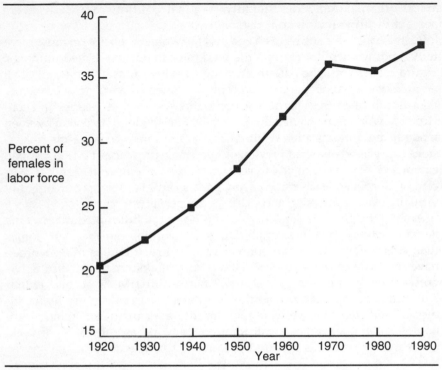

SOURCE: U.S. Dept. of Commerce, Bureau of the Census, *Historical Statistics of the United States: Colonial Times to 1970* (Washington, D.C.: GPO, 1975); U.S. Dept. of Commerce, Bureau of the Census, *Statistical Abstract of the United States* (Washington, D.C.: GPO, various years).

fluence public policy to spend large sums of money to replace the free volunteer labor that once fueled their activities. As the demands of the workplace grow, direct popular participation in politics has diminished.

WEALTH

In the second half of the twentieth century, America struck it rich. Rarely in the history of the modern world has a society experienced such long and widespread economic growth. From 1946 to 1990, the principal measure of that growth, the gross domestic product, increased at an average annual rate of more than 7 percent. Even with inflation controlled for, real GDP nearly quadrupled in the same period.

This economic growth permitted the United States to meet the formidable challenge of providing jobs for the millions of veterans who reentered the civilian workforce after the war and the tens of millions of baby boomers who came of age in the years after 1960. The number of employed Americans grew by an average of almost 1.5 million annually in the years from 1946 to 1990. Providing jobs for so many new workers was an extraordinary triumph for the American economy.

With economic growth and the attendant expansion of employment opportunities came great increases in personal income. Between 1946 and 1990, disposable personal income—adjusted for inflation—grew at an average rate of more than 3 percent a year. The products of this change included more millionaires and even billionaires, but what is more noteworthy is the extent to which economic growth benefited all segments of the population. The rich got richer, but working stiffs got richer, too, and the poor got a lot less poor, especially in the years between the end of the war and 1970. Nearly everyone's boat was rising on this economic floodtide, and the opportunities that wealth provides—to own a home, to send children to college, to start a new business, to invest for a prosperous retirement—became accessible after World War II to a broad range of Americans.

All of these developments had a number of important political consequences. The growth in national income produced in America a genuine middle class. That change began to be noted in the mid-1960s when for the first time white-collar jobs began to outnumber blue-collar jobs and most Americans began to tell opinion pollsters that they thought of themselves as "middle class" rather than "working class."[21] This new middle class was surprisingly affluent: Its members were well educated, most of them owned their own homes, and they were free from daily worries about economic survival. They were free as well to express concern about the less fortunate members of American society and to support government programs that aided those less fortunate at home and abroad. Members of the middle class also began to look to government to subsidize at higher levels those programs that benefited the middle class most directly: the arts and humanities, good schools, higher education tuition loans, tax deductions for home mortgages, highways and airports, to name just a few.

A second political impact of the growth in national wealth was that it provided government with the revenue to do things that it had never before done. The personal income tax had afflicted few Americans before World War II. Increasingly after the war, it became a commonplace of American life. Americans were paying more in taxes each year, but they were making so much more in personal income that they bore the rise in taxes without severe economic imposition. By comparison with the other industrialized democracies, American taxes as a percentage of personal income remained relatively low throughout the postwar period. They still are.

As a consequence, the federal government was able to sustain a steady increase in revenues without severely pinching the economic welfare of its citizens. Federal revenues grew from $38.5 billion in 1947, when the economy was beginning to settle back into civilian status, to $1.03 trillion in 1990. Americans could afford bigger government because national wealth had grown so dramatically in the postwar decades.

TECHNOLOGY

On February 14, 1946, a group of engineers, physicists, and mathematicians from the University of Pennsylvania invited two hundred dignitaries to a demonstration of the product of several years of their research. Their work, like that of so many scientists and inventors, was accelerated and funded by the rapacious needs of the armed forces trying to win World War II on the scientific front as well as the battlefield. In deepest secrecy, the team at Penn had labored to produce a machine that could calculate mathematical problems—like the trajectory of an artillery round—faster than a group of crack mathematicians.

The guests on that night were ushered into a room containing a peculiar looking machine one hundred feet long, ten feet high, three feet deep, and weighing thirty tons. It was composed of forty large, separate panels bunched in thirty different groups, each with a specific function. The machinery contained 17,468 vacuum tubes of sixteen different types, fifteen hundred relays, seventy thousand resisters, ten thousand capacitors, and six thousand switches. When the guests gathered round for a demonstration, the scientists instructed the machine to multiply 97,367 by itself five thousand times. The job was completed in less than one second. Other tests followed, concluding with a problem that would have taken a trained mathematician several weeks to complete. The machine printed out the answer in fifteen seconds.[22]

The machine was ENIAC, the Electronic Numerical Integrator and Computer, the most complex and sophisticated machine ever built. It was the world's first general purpose electronic computer. It launched the computer age—and a new revolution in American life.

America in the second half of the nineteenth century had been radically altered by the implementation of new technologies: the steamship, the transcontinental railroad, the telegraph and telephone, and electricity. America in the second half of the twentieth century was similarly altered by another technological explosion. In both eras politics and government quickly adapted to and were affected by these new technologies. They changed our capabilities for communicating with and understanding each other—the essence of politics—and in so doing, they altered the environment in which politics and government operate.

The mass marketing of the birth control pill that began in the 1960s gave Americans their most reliable form of artificial pregnancy prevention. Its appearance contributed mightily to the decline in family size that began at that time. The invention of new time-saving household devices—freezers, dishwashers, vacuum cleaners, food processors, microwave ovens—reduced the time and effort required to manage a household and permitted more women to return to the civilian workforce.

Jet travel, telephone networks, and fax machines facilitated the nationalization of economic markets. The salesperson based in Dallas could make a presentation to a client in Baltimore and be home for dinner. Revised bids and figures could be instantaneously communicated across country. Overnight deliveries of parts or products became increasingly common.

The modern computer became the very heart of late-twentieth-century business—and of politics and government as well. By the mid-1980s, computers were a familiar tool to most educated Americans and had taken their place in every business and profession in the country. In politics computers were used to analyze survey research, manage direct mail, track fund-raising efforts, schedule candidate appearances, and generate speeches and position papers. In government computers have become the essential tool of legislative redistricting, government's primary record keeper, a device for modeling the economic impact of proposed new programs, and a text scanner that permits rapid identification and updates of legal precedents and administrative regulations.

Perhaps no technology of the postwar period has had so deep and sweeping an effect as television. Within a decade of its first commercial appearance in the late 1940s, more than three-quarters of American homes had a television set. By 1990 television had become the most common home appliance in the land. There were almost 200 million television sets in operation, and more households had televisions than telephones.

The technology of television continued to change throughout the postwar period. Black and white gave way to color. The large clunky wooden set in the corner quickly became a dinosaur; today a television set can be carried in a shirt pocket. The hegemony of the national networks came to an end as cable reception spread through American communities in the 1980s. Cable offered more choices—and more news and public affairs. Other technologies, such as interactive and high-definition TV, are in development.

It is hard to measure the full impact of television on American life and politics because the independent variable, television itself, keeps changing. We do know that Americans rely on television for news and information more heavily than on any other medium. We also know that television has created an entirely new set of incentives for political leaders to emphasize certain activities—those that generate publicity and good theater—over others. Television favors certain kinds of candidates over others, certain kinds of messages over others, and certain kinds of political strategies over others. And what is good for TV is not necessarily what is good for the construction and nurturing of enduring political coalitions.

FAMILY

The American family survives into the 1990s, but it is a changing institution. Most Americans still marry and most married couples still have children. But the extended nuclear family and what came to be known at midcentury as the "traditional family" are declining archetypes.

In fact, the traditional family of the father who worked outside the home and the mother who stayed home to raise two or three children was a commonplace only in the middle decades of the twentieth century. For most of American history before that, families had tended to be larger, more often composed of three generations living in the same household, with multiple income earners, and frequently splintered by the early death of a parent. Typically as well, given the prevalence of agriculture, families were important economic units, heavily dependent on the physical labor of all their members. Postwar advances in personal income, education, and home ownership, followed by the baby boom, altered for a few decades what had been the historical norm and created an approximation of the kind of family life represented in the televised situation comedies of the 1960s. But the image of the traditional family was fleeting and no longer describes a majority of American households.

Today four household types prevail. One is the married couple with or without children present. The 1990 census found that this model accounts for 56 percent of all American households (and in less than half of these are there children under the age of eighteen). Another is the single-parent family. In 1990, 13.8 million households—nearly 15 percent of all households—fit this model. A third is the nonfamily, multiperson household; in 1990, 5 percent of all households fit this pattern of unrelated people living together. A fourth is the household occupied by one person only. In 1990, 23 million Americans lived alone, accounting for nearly 25 percent of all households.

Even though Americans are getting married in roughly the same percentages as they have throughout the second half of the twentieth century, typically they are marrying at a later age than they did at midcentury, and they are less likely to stay married. The frequency of divorce is the most dramatic change in family lifestyles in the past half century. The impact of divorce on family structure is equally dramatic. More than half of all children born in the 1980s will become part of single-parent households at some time before they reach their eighteenth birthday.[23]

The traditional family is passing into history. Nearly 67 percent of mothers who are married and living with their husbands now work outside the home. Fifteen percent of all households have only a single parent present. Only a small minority of American children are now in families where both parents live in the same household and only one works outside the home.

Changes in the character of the American family have significant political consequences. One of the central findings of postwar research on political socialization—the way in which Americans acquire their understanding of the political world and locate themselves within it—was that the family was a critically important socializing agent. Much of our initial political learning took place within the family, and our parents substantially shaped our acquisition of political values and preferences. As the leading study of its time noted in the early 1960s, "An orientation toward political affairs typically begins before the individual attains voting age and . . . this orientation strongly reflects his immediate social milieu, in particular his family. . . . For a large portion of the electorate the orientation toward politics expressed in our measure of party identification has its origins in the early family years."[24]

Historically, families tended to possess stable political views and loyalties, which they passed on to succeeding generations. Families played the primary role in teaching children to comprehend and cope with the perplexities and conflicts of the political world. But as the character of families has changed, as they have become increasingly mobile, more unstable in composition, and less dominant of children's attitudes, they have declined as units of political importance. Political learning is less likely to take place in the bosom of the family; lasting political attachments are less likely to be formed there. This dynamic contributes to the political rootlessness and lack of interest that are widely noted characteristics of the generations that have most recently come of age in American politics.[25]

CONCLUSION: GOVERNING
ON THE NEW LANDSCAPE

The broad and bold changes just described have produced a different country than the one that entered World War II. Its population has doubled. Its people are wealthier, better educated, and more mobile. A middle class has emerged and grown to social and economic prominence. A new service economy has been replacing the old economy based in agriculture and heavy industry. More women are working, and more people work in white-collar than blue-collar jobs. An enormous baby boom generation sits now in the middle of the age distribution. Soon its members will begin retiring and forming the largest cohort of elderly people the United States has ever seen.

These changes have significantly altered the environment in which Americans govern themselves, diminishing or destroying old organizing principles and political bases, creating new opportunities and constraints. Farmers and labor union members are no longer the great political forces they once were. The population has shifted away from the areas where political parties were most effectively organized, where the machines and bosses governed. Those machines and bosses were losing out to new technologies and new forms of political organization in any case, even as their geographical base was shrinking.

Changes in the character of American families, increasing education levels, new forms of communication—all of these have changed the ways that Americans gather political information, form loyalties, and respond to political appeals. Increases in the percentage of the adult population that works outside the home and simultaneous increases in the amount of time Americans spend at work have reduced the volunteer pool on which politics in America so long relied. The mobility of the population has further complicated political participation because fewer and fewer Americans have deep and lasting ties to the communities or states in which they live and work.

Changes in the landscape of American politics have been so profound that they have posed enormous challenges to American political processes and governing institutions. The United States could not possibly govern itself at the end of the century in the same way that it did at midcentury. Too much has changed. The second half of the twentieth century has thus posed a stiff and unrelenting test for the American experiment in self-government. It is to the nature of that test, and the responses of the political system, that we now turn.

THE POLITICS THE
REFORMERS MADE

On June 30, 1972, in Miami Beach, Florida, the Democratic National Convention's Credentials Committee refused to seat a delegation of Illinois Democrats chosen in a primary election and headed by the party's leading grandee, Mayor Richard J. Daley. Instead, the committee awarded the right to represent Illinois at the convention to a delegation that was more representative of women, minorities, and young people. In so doing, the Credentials Committee followed the new rules of the Democratic Party—and turned the political world on its head.

When the most visible and powerful political boss in the country could not get seated at his own party's national convention, something significant must have been happening to the character of American politics. Indeed, it was. The events in Miami Beach certified what many observers had already suggested: A new politics with new rules, new processes, new people, and new outcomes—a new politics that radically alters the way in which Americans select and influence their leaders—was coming to life. The old politics, after prevailing for almost a century, was vanishing. This change was a political revolution.

But no one had planned this revolution. No one seemed to be leading or guiding it. And no one was very sure where it would lead. With the new politics having taken hold during the years since 1972, its direction and implications are subjects of constant debate. On one point, however, consensus has emerged: The new politics has dramatically changed the calculus of power in the United States.

THE CHANGING AMERICAN ELECTORATE

At the beginning of this century, barely 25 percent of American citizens were eligible to vote in national elections. The voting age was twenty-one. Women had no constitutional right to vote. After the Civil War, the Fifteenth Amendment had granted black citizens the right to vote. But throughout the South, where most blacks lived, and in other places as well, the exercise of that right was impeded by poll taxes, literacy tests, "whites only" primaries, and violence or threats thereof. Few blacks voted. Many states also had rigid registration requirements that hindered even those who were eligible to vote in doing so.

Fewer political trends are clearer in the twentieth century than the expansion of the franchise. The ratification of the Nineteenth Amendment in 1920 granted women the right to vote. The elimination of the poll tax by the ratification in 1964 of the Twenty-fourth Amendment, the Voting Rights Act of 1965, and courageous action by many individuals undermined most of the formal and informal impediments to black voting. The Twenty-sixth Amendment, ratified in 1971, lowered the voting age to eighteen. The liberalization of voter registration laws in many states and the federal government's Motor Voter Law have made it possible for even the most forgetful or procrastination prone to vote on election day.

Opportunities to cast ballots have also expanded remarkably. The trend throughout this century has been to expand the number of officeholders selected by popular vote. In 1912 U.S. senators were popularly elected for the first time. In many states and municipalities, the number of positions filled through the ballot has steadily grown. The widespread use of direct primaries—a device to which virtually no Americans had access at the beginning of the century—now affords voters everywhere an opportunity to participate directly in nominating party candidates. The initiative, referendum, and recall—legacies of the Progressive movement at the beginning of the twentieth century—permit voters ample opportunity not only to remove officials who have fallen out of favor but also to vote directly on policy matters. In California in 1992, for example, voters were able to indicate their preferences on thirteen initiative and referendum questions.

As the twentieth century ends, Americans are unique in the world in the frequency with which they are able to vote and in the scope of offices and issues their votes can shape. It is, therefore, a powerful and peculiar irony that among the citizens of all the countries of the world, Americans rank seventy-third in voter turnout.[1] In the country where elections are most common, a majority of those eligible to vote usually do not.

This irony is compounded by yet another significant twentieth-century trend: the escalating educational levels of American citizens. As noted in Chapter 2, more Americans have more education than ever before. Among those of voting age in 1940, for example, the median number of years of school completed was 8.4; for the equivalent group in 1990, the median was 12.4 years.

Every bit of political intuition and most scholarly analysis find a strong correlation between education and political participation. The greater the number of years of school completed, the higher the level of participation is likely to be. In recent years, however, even among the best educated, there have been declines in electoral participation. The better educated are still more likely to vote than those with less education, but across all education levels voter turnout is in decline.[2]

Two developments are at work here. One is the spread of a general and penetrating disaffection, a dissatisfaction with mainstream politics, that has permeated American public life since the mid-1960s. A series of shocks jolted the political system—the assassinations of John and Robert Kennedy and Martin Luther King Jr., the failure of the American effort in Vietnam and the protests it generated, Watergate and the resignation of Richard Nixon, constant reports of other political scandals, the enlargement of the role of money in electoral politics, unprecedented budget deficits. These eroded public trust and steadily swelled public doubts about the efficacy of traditional politics, the value of voting, and the competence of the American government.

Americans are voting less for another reason as well. Many of them have come to believe that elections do not really matter very much. Forty-seven percent of nonvoters in 1990 agreed that "things go on as before no matter who is elected."[3] An inability to perceive significant differences between parties and candidates, a feeling that government rolls along undiverted no matter who wins elections, and a growing sense that the real action in public life is occurring somewhere other than the electoral process all encourage the disinclination to vote.

These perceptions are entirely rational, for all of the evidence suggests that elections do matter less as determinants of the direction of government and the shape of public policy. Those who refrain from voting because they think it an inconsequential act are on to something quite significant. Electoral politics has changed not only in style and form but also in impact.

THE PARTY IS OVER

No recent political trend has been more fully studied or convincingly demonstrated than the postwar decline in the importance of American political parties. Since their emergence in the first decade after George Washington's inauguration and until that decline, political parties performed four important democratic functions:

- They maintained links between the American people and their government and provided a reliable mechanism for sounding out and organizing public opinion.
- They mobilized large coalitions to compete in elections and possessed the skills and experience required to manage successful political campaigns.
- They filled the personnel needs of government.

- They organized the operations of the legislature and its interaction with the other branches.

The parties that performed those functions were always something of a mess. They rarely possessed much ideological coherence. Their leadership was constantly shifting and widely shared. They were often less interested in issues than in winning. As a practical matter, the national parties were little more than federations of the state political parties. It might have been more accurate to note, as some commentators did, that America had not two parties but one hundred: two in each state.

For most of the century that followed the Civil War, material rewards fueled the operation of the parties. Party leaders paid lip-service to ideas—and sometimes even meant what they said—but their real objectives were the practical fruits of victory: contracts, bureaucratic assistance for party loyalists, and, most of all, jobs. Power in the parties rested in one or a few sets of hands in each state. The task confronting candidates for the presidency was to cobble together a coalition of state party leaders large enough to ensure the support of a majority of the convention delegates. Since party leaders often played politics the way they played poker, early commitments were hard to come by. Many state delegations went to their national convention supporting a favorite son. This was a holding action designed to increase the leverage of that delegation on the nomination—and later, of course, to bring it a larger share of the fruits of office.

An important consequence of this party system was that the quadrennial conventions were important political events. They actually chose nominees. In many years the nomination was in doubt when the convention began, and often many ballots were required before a majority coalition of balky state bosses coalesced around a single candidate. The worst case was 1924. One hundred three ballots and seventeen days were necessary for the Democrats to settle on John W. Davis of West Virginia, a candidate who, for all of the care of selection, was clobbered by Calvin Coolidge in November.

Members of Congress, like presidents, usually owed a substantial debt to their party for the office they held. In most places parties "slated" congressional candidates. As a practical matter that meant that state and local leaders controlled nominations. And typically those nominations went to people who had demonstrated their loyalty to the local party or machine through years of political work. These were not always the brightest or most energetic people in the country, but they were reliable. And in a system driven primarily by material rewards, reliability and predictability were valued assets.

When difficult policy choices confronted Congress, members were most likely to take their cues from party leaders at home. Knowing this, presidents and congressional leaders often sought to build majorities not by lobbying individual members directly, but by seeking the support of state and local party leaders, who would then "deliver" the votes of their members in Congress. It was a messy system, to be sure, but parties provided a valuable and often effective lubrication for the machinery of government. The party bosses were often callous, not infrequently corrupt, and more democratic in rhetoric than reality. But they brought one trait of great value to the political arena: They could boss. They could get things done. They could make the deals and construct the coalitions necessary to produce working majorities.

That party system is not so ancient as it might seem. It remained largely intact throughout the 1950s, and some of its specimens were still breathing in the late 1960s. Most of the commentary on John Kennedy's capture of the Democratic nomination in 1960 focused on his success in the primaries. But Kennedy actually competed in only seven primaries, which determined only 10 percent of the delegates at the Democratic convention. In fact, he used the primaries as a showcase to demonstrate to the party leaders—who would really determine the nomination—that he was electable in spite of his youth and Catholicism.

As recently as 1968, Hubert Humphrey won the nomination of the Democratic Party without contesting a single primary. That campaign seems rather quaint now, a museum piece in which Richard Daley of Chicago, John Bailey of Connecticut, David Lawrence of Pennsylvania, and the other surviving bosses are the major fossils. It was the last election in which the old party system—which had dominated American politics for more than a century—still mattered.

The fissure lines in the old system began to appear clearly in the 1950s. The 1956 presidential election produced an outcome that had occurred only once before, in 1848:[4] The American people elected a president of one party and a House and Senate controlled by the other. The phenomenon that produced this outcome came to be known as "ticket-splitting," and in most of the commentaries on the 1956 election it was treated as an aberration. Voters, who were predominantly Democratic, had split their tickets to vote for Democrats for Congress and the very popular Dwight Eisenhower for president. "I vote the man not the party" became the voters' justification and the analysts' explanation for the peculiar outcome of the 1956 election.[5]

With the election in 1960 of a Democratic president and a Democratic Congress, political life seemed back to normal. A seminal study published that year, *The American Voter,* argued convincingly that most American adults identified with one of the two major political parties and that this "party identification" was the dominant factor in their voting decisions. Typically, they would vote for the candidate nominated by the party with which they identified. In other words, parties mattered. "Few factors," the authors wrote, "are of greater importance for our national elections than the lasting attachment of tens of millions of Americans to one of the parties. These loyalties establish a basic division of electoral strength within which the competition of particular campaigns takes place. And they are an important factor in assuring the stability of the party system itself."[6]

The two decades that followed sorely tested that simple proposition. Americans watched as five consecutive presidencies failed or came to unnatural ends. They saw the disintegration of the New Deal coalition that had held the Democratic majority together for two generations. They watched the Republicans nearly drown in a scandal called Watergate. They adjusted to changes in political technology, legislative organization, and party rules. And, as already noted, they became better educated.

Parties declined in importance through this period. Fewer Americans identified strongly with the Democrats and Republicans. As Table 3.1 demonstrates, voters were not shifting their loyalties from one party to another as they had in previous periods of change. Instead, they were abandoning or weakening their attachments to either party. Independents (the nonpartisan form of registration) and independence (the political behavior) were the growth sectors in American politics in the 1960s and 1970s. When the baby boomers began to show up on the voting rolls in the late 1960s, they accelerated this trend away from party attachment. No generation in American history has been so reluctant to acquire party loyalties. And this was the biggest generation in American history by far. By the time the baby boomers became a majority of voting age adults in 1984, their lack of interest was the dominant melody in the swan song of American political parties.

What accounts for the ebbing importance of political parties? This is not an easy question, but some excellent analysis by scholars and journalists allows us to identify the principal answers. Let us recall that Americans always had ambivalent feelings about political parties and thus that some of the seeds of their recent demise were always present. But parties were useful devices for much of our history, and Americans hitched their destiny to parties because there were few alternatives. For winning elections, influencing public policy, and obtaining the material rewards of government, parties were the only game in town. They controlled nominations, had a corner on the market of campaign skills and campaign funds, distributed the rewards when their candidates won, and provided outlets for opinion and avenues to power for those who were weak, unorganized, or newly immigrated.

In the postwar period, the foundations of party strength deteriorated rapidly. The direct primary had first appeared early in the century, but its prominence in congressional and presidential nominations is a recent

TABLE 3.1
Party Identification Among Americans of Voting Age, 1952–1992

Party	1952	1956	1960	1964	1968	1972	1976	1980	1984	1988	1992
Democrat	47	44	45	52	45	41	40	41	37	35	35
Independent	23	23	23	23	30	34	37	34	34	36	39
Republican	28	29	30	25	25	23	23	23	27	28	26
Apolitical	3	4	2	1	1	1	1	2	2	2	1

SOURCE: Adapted from Harold W. Stanley and Richard G. Niemi, *Vital Statistics on American Politics*, 4th ed. (Washington, D.C.: CQ Press, 1994), p. 158.

phenomenon. The spread of direct primaries cost the parties their hegemony over the nominating process. And when parties lost control of nominations, they lost a substantial measure of control over public officials. Acutely sensitive to that change, public officials quickly took command of their own campaigns, bearing a party label but feeling little loyalty to or dependence on party organizations.

Parties also lost their monopoly on campaign skills and campaign funds. A significant new industry—the campaign consultants—emerged after 1960. There had always been Americans with extensive campaign experience and knowledge, but their primary attachment had typically been to parties, not individual candidates. That has changed in recent decades. Campaign consultants are independent entrepreneurs. Candidates pay them for their services. The consultants' loyalties are to their clients, not to a political party.

The financing of campaigns has undergone two dramatic changes in the postwar period. One, as Table 3.2 indicates, is an extraordinary escalation in the costs of campaigning, an escalation driven by such factors as a growing electorate, the need to hire campaign consultants, and the costs of television advertising and public opinion polling. Because campaigns cost more, candidates have to compete aggressively for funds outside the political parties because parties simply cannot meet the financial needs of all the candidates who bear their label.

The campaign finance laws that govern the competition for funds are the other major postwar change. The effect of those laws has been to diminish even further the role of parties by encouraging other sources of money, particularly direct individual contributions and donations from the political action committees of a wide array of nonparty organizations.

So parties have declined on all fronts. They have lost their hold on the loyalties of a substantial portion of the electorate. They no longer control nominations. And their monopoly on the skills and materials of politics has vanished. The impact of this decline has altered the face of American

TABLE 3.2
Campaign Expenditures by Candidates for House,
Senate, and President, 1972–1992 ($ millions)

	Year									
	1972	*1976*	*1978*	*1980*	*1982*	*1984*	*1986*	*1988*	*1990*	*1992*
Presidential[a]	138	160		275		325		500		550
Senate[b]		38	65	74	114	142	190	185	173	272
House[b]		60	86	112	175	177	210	222	238	407

[a]Presidential expenditures include prenomination, convention, and general election costs.

[b]Congressional expenditures include primary and general election expenditures for general election candidates only.

SOURCE: Nelson Polsby and Aaron Wildavsky, *Presidential Elections* (New York: Free Press, 1991), p. 64; Norman J. Ornstein, Thomas E. Mann, and Michael J. Malbin, *Vital Statistics on Congress, 1993–1994* (Washington, D.C.: CQ Press, 1994), pp. 75, 79. Data for 1992 are from Herbert E. Alexander and Anthony Corrado, *Financing the 1992 Election* (Armonk, N.Y.: M. E. Sharpe, 1995).

politics and begun to evoke major changes in the way Americans govern themselves.

What does it matter that political parties have become more shadow than substance? In fact, it matters a great deal and in several ways. For one thing, the end of the party monopoly on politics creates a vacuum into which into which all sorts of organizations have poured: special interest groups, public interest groups, trade associations, political action committees. These organizations and their members now compete for political influence through no structured channels, without effective brokers, and with few recognized rules of engagement. The result is a recipe for chaos and the disintegration of the policymaking process, which will lead inevitably to immobility and inaction. No political system moves forward without leadership, organization, and direction. Politics without effective parties lacks all of those ingredients.

The decline of political parties also disconnects voters from their elected leaders and political institutions. Party loyalty has been a very important political bond for Americans, clarifying their support and opposition and encouraging their participation to strengthen their own party's chances to govern. As party loyalty diminishes in importance, the bond weakens, and Americans lose interest—and faith—in government and politics.

The decline of parties attenuates the connections between politicians and institutions. In the American system of separation of government powers, mechanisms that bridge the distance between institutions are critically important. Political parties, though always imperfect, have been the most important of those bridges. Parties were the one filament of shared purpose that held together the fate of presidents and members of the two houses of Congress and encouraged them to work together—even in the face of substantive differences—to accomplish policy goals. As the party connection deteriorated within Congress and between Congress and the president, multiple, self-interested patterns of behavior emerged in its place. These impeded the achievement of substantive consensus in Washington. Even though the forms of democracy survive, as political scientist Martin Wattenberg notes, its substance is negated.[7]

A politics in which candidates are more important than parties—which is the direction in which American politics has tended in recent decades—undermines accountability. When no party appears to be in charge, and neither party seems to have a definable record or coherent program, how can voters assess blame and award credit? Whose failure of vigilance permitted the savings and loan scandal? Who caused the addition of $2.4 trillion to the national debt between 1980 and 1990? Whose policies led to a happy conclusion of the cold war? In the absence of strong parties, questions like these befuddle voters. They have no reliable way to use their vote to reward satisfactory performance or sanction failure. Not surprisingly, since the vote has become so ineffective an instrument of political expression, fewer people are choosing to use it.

Most important, the shrinking significance of political parties has yielded a rearrangement of power in American politics. As political scientist Walter Dean Burnham correctly noted years ago, "Political parties, with all their well-known human and structural shortcomings, are the only devices thus far invented by the wit of Western man which with some effectiveness can generate countervailing collective power on behalf of the many individually powerless against the relatively few who are individually—or organizationally—powerful."[8]

The New Deal coalition and its demise are prime evidence of this change. When one party, in this case the national Democratic Party, provided a political vehicle and a policy agenda for the have-nots in American society, government responded with jobs and job training. Government also subsidized education and health care, provided minimum wage guarantees, protected the right to organize and bargain collectively in the workplace, enforced desegregation, and instituted a host of other programs that contributed to dramatic increases in national income and standards of living. When that coalition fell apart and parties lost their hegemony on politics, the policy pendulum changed direction. It is not mere accident that Reaganomics, decreases in the tax burden on the wealthiest Americans, stagnant incomes for the working class, relaxed enforcement of antitrust and civil rights laws, and hard times for American labor unions and public schools all occurred in the 1980s, when American political parties reached the nadir of their influence in this century.

American government can probably function without dominant political parties. Indeed, it has been acquiring that knack now for several decades. But politics without parties is very different, in form and outcome from politics in which parties matter. With parties in repose, Americans are less connected to the people and institutions that govern them, the chasm between those institutions broadens, accountability is harder to affix and enforce, and influence in policymaking inevitably shifts from the many who are poor and marginal to the few who are rich.

PRESIDENTIAL NOMINATIONS

The one arena of American politics in which parties still appear to play a major role is in the selection of presidential candidates. The notable but unsuccessful candidacies of George Wallace in 1968, John Anderson in 1980, and Ross Perot in 1992 only remind us that there is no viable route to the White House without the nomination of one of the two major political parties. But closer examination of recent events quickly reveals that here, too, the parties have become shells of their former selves. Parties are no longer oligarchies of local potentates who gather to designate a national standard-bearer. Instead, they have become little more than referees who impose rules of procedure on an open competition among independent entrepreneurs seeking to accumulate enough delegates to win the party's nomination.

The first clear set of fissure lines in the old oligarchic model appeared in the Republican Party in 1964. The party's nomination that year was captured—and captured is the right word—by Barry Goldwater, the darling of its right wing. Goldwater's delegates were not typical of the people who usually attended national party conventions. What principally set them apart from the norms of the breed were their priorities. Issues and ideology were more important to them than winning. Goldwater's statement that he would "rather be right than president" perfectly captured their spirit. To adherents of the old party system—for whom winning was everything—that attitude was heresy squared. To Goldwater's supporters, it was exactly the point.

To no one's surprise, Goldwater lost badly in 1964. But the new politics that his nomination represented gained a toehold that would grow stronger in the years ahead. Its strength became manifest, however, not in the Republican but in the Democratic Party. For the Democrats—and for America—1968 was to be the political crossroads of the century. At the Chicago Democratic Convention of that year, the old politics heading to oblivion passed the new politics coming to life.

There is a long tradition in American public life of tinkering with the rules. Although our Constitution is now in its third century, we are constantly looking for ways to perfect it. The Progressives sought to establish direct primaries and to take the selection of U.S. senators from the state legislatures. The Twenty-second Amendment originated in the Republican-controlled Eightieth Congress to ensure that no president would ever again hold office for as long as Franklin Roosevelt had. Our tax laws, as any taxpayer knows, are in constant flux: They are never the same from one year to the next.

Our political processes as well go into the shop for an overhaul after every presidential election. What drives this tinkering is the widespread understanding that rules are not neutral. They inevitably advantage some people and disadvantage others. Changing the rules, therefore, is one way to improve one's lot. Those who lose under existing rules have powerful incentives to change them. And they do, in one of the great eternal dynamics of politics in America.

So it was after the 1968 election that a group of activists in the Democratic Party sought to change the rules that governed the nominating process and determined the criteria for participation in the party's convention. They persuaded party leaders to form a commission headed by Senator George McGovern of South Dakota and Representative Donald Fraser of Minnesota to review and recommend changes in the party's rules. Although not fully realized at the time, the McGovern Fraser Commission was a watershed in the history of the Democratic Party and in the twentieth-century development of American politics.

The commission went to work at one of those points in American history when many new ideas seemed to be coming of age. The civil rights movement had recently reached its zenith. A burgeoning new movement for women's rights was beginning to gain strength. All over the country, traditional institutions of authority—the church, universities, corporations, the military, government—were being challenged as never before. And even if these movements for minority and female rights and the challenges to traditional institutions did not directly affect every American, they began to create a widespread interest in institutional rules and processes, especially those of government. As Michael Barone recently pointed out, Americans "who had once been concerned mainly with results and substance were now increasingly concerned with methods and process. Not only must ends be good but so must means."[9]

The implications of this growing concern, as it filtered through the work of the McGovern-Fraser Commission, had a dramatic impact on the Democratic Party. Among many recommendations, the commission banned proxy voting, the "unit rule," and ex officio delegates. The commission also limited to 10 percent the proportion of any state delegation that the state party committee could choose directly. It opened up the delegate selection process, imposed the national party's antidiscrimination policies on each of the state parties, and mandated the inclusion in each state's delegation of minority group members, women, and young people "in reasonable relationship" to their share of the state's population. Many state party leaders disapproved of the McGovern-Fraser changes, but by July 1972 all but a few state Democratic organizations were in compliance with the new rules.

The Democrats were being introduced to something quite unfamiliar to the recent operating traditions of that party: democracy. It was a change with two potent implications for that party and eventually for all of American politics.[10] First, the reforms undermined the position of the remaining party bosses by removing their dominance of the delegate selection process and by ending the unit rule that had allowed them to deliver their state delegations as a bloc to the highest bidder. Second, as a consequence of the weakened position of the bosses, the party convention became much more permeable than it had been. By following the new rules, almost anyone could become a delegate. It was no handicap—indeed, in some places it was an advantage—to lack political experience. The change was remarkable. At the 1964 Democratic Convention, 46 percent of the delegates had also been delegates at a previous convention. At the 1972 Democratic Convention, the comparable figure was 17 percent. Delegates participating in their first national Democratic convention composed 83 percent of the delegates in 1972, 80 percent in 1976, and 87 percent in 1980. First-time Republican delegates went from 66 percent in 1964 to 78 percent in 1972, 78 percent in 1976, and 84 percent in 1980.[11]

And who were these first-time delegates who began to penetrate both political parties in the years after 1968? They were, in a term coined by Jeane Kirkpatrick, a "new breed" of American political activists.[12] They were demographically diverse in a way that their predecessors had never been: More of them were women and members of minority racial and ethnic groups. Women, for example, were 13 percent of Democratic and 16 percent of Republican delegates in 1968. By 1988 women composed 48 percent of Democratic and 33 percent of Republican delegates. Five percent of the Democratic delegates in 1968 were black; 23 percent were black in 1988.

As a group, the Democratic delegates hatched by the McGovern-Fraser reforms also had less political experience than the typical delegate of previous generations. Journalists at the 1972 convention, for example, quickly noted the absence of members of Congress: Only 35 percent of Democratic senators and 15 percent of Democratic House members were in attendance compared to 67 percent of the former and 36 percent of the latter in 1968. The new delegates were less likely to be professional politicians or public employees.[13] By and large, new delegates were not seeking the material rewards of politics. Most of them were reasonably well off economically and their economic well-being was not directly reliant on the outcome of the next election. The standing political bargain that had sustained the bosses—you give me your vote, and I'll give you a job—was not much in evidence at Democratic conventions after 1972.

These new delegates were also much more interested in national politics than their predecessors. Their participation in politics was not motivated primarily by a desire to maintain local practices, such as racial segregation, or to secure localized benefits, such as public works. Instead, the new breed of delegates was driven by a genuine, substantive interest in issues and ideology. They were, in fact, often much more interested in where the party stood than in how it fared. Like the people who had supported Barry Goldwater in 1964 and George Wallace and Eugene McCarthy in 1968, the delegates who came to dominate the party conventions in the 1970s and 1980s were issue oriented and candidate connected. Many of them cared more about party platforms and candidates' policy views than about party maintenance or the winning of elections. Many of them, like Goldwater, would rather be right than victorious.

Occurring simultaneously with these reforms in party rules on delegate selection and convention procedures were two other significant changes in presidential nominating process. One was a broad increase in the number of presidential primaries. In 1964 each party held seventeen state primaries; in 1992 there were forty Democratic and thirty-nine Republican primaries. Neither the national parties nor federal law mandated this increase. It was the product primarily of decentralized decisions made by state parties and state legislatures in response to local desires for alterations in how and when delegates to national party conventions would be selected. Because these decisions were decentralized, no logical pattern of nominating devices or any logical schedule of state decisions has emerged. Randomness and the irrationality it breeds prevail. How else can one account for a nominating process in which the citizens of New Hampshire, the country's fortieth largest state, have far broader candidate choices and their votes receive infinitely more media coverage than those of the citizens of California, the country's largest state. An accumulation of decentralized state actions produced in the brief period from 1968 to 1972 occasioned a major change in the way national convention delegates were chosen. No one ever planned that system, and there are few respected advocates of its wisdom.

In 1974 another profound change unfolded. In response to the extraordinary sums of money that incumbent Richard Nixon had raised for his campaign in 1972—and to subsequent revelations of the shady ways in which some of those funds had been solicited and given—the Democratically controlled Congress enacted the Federal Election Campaign Amendments Act. The largest impact of this legislation resulted from its provision, for the first time, of public funds for presidential campaigns, including nominating contests, and from the permission it granted to the members of special interest groups to make campaign contributions through the device of PACs. It is ironic in retrospect to note that the PAC provision was intended to limit the impact of special interest contributions by prohibiting direct contributions from businesses, unions, and interest groups and allowing their members or employees to form and make voluntary contributions to a political action committee.

The impact, of course, has differed broadly from the intent. Instead of limiting special interest influence through campaign contributions, the legalization of PACs has encouraged and enhanced it. PACs have grown remarkably in number and impact since their immaculate conception. Even in general election campaigns where the acceptance of public financing requires candidates to decline to accept private funds, PAC funds have recently flooded through the loophole in campaign finance laws that permits "independent expenditures" in support of preferred candidates.

What a difference a couple of decades have made. In 1968 there were just a few political action committees, state and local potentates still dominated the parties, less than 45 percent of the delegates in either party were chosen in primaries, and Hubert Humphrey could obtain the Democratic nomination without contesting a single one. In the current presidential nominating process, primaries are dominant, and the earliest primaries dominate most of all; special interest funds course openly through the veins of the system; a new breed of independent delegates often more interested in issues and ideology than in winning elections has supplanted the bosses; and party conventions have become media events with minimal impact on the selection of nominees.

A new system has replaced the old, but it did so largely by coincidence and inadvertence. This new system is the product of no careful and comprehensive study or planning. In its totality, it never passed the review of any representative body of Americans or party figures. It is the result of little more than a set of disconnected, decentralized, and narrowly focused decisions. But those decisions add up to a presidential nominating process that is widely despised by professional politicians, leading journalists and academics, and the American people, who have responded to the new democratic opportunities this process is reputed to provide with deafening lack of interest and nonparticipation.

Any nominating process offers a particular set of incentives and opportunities to potential presidential candidates. It shapes their strategic calculations. When the process is altered, so, too, are its inherent incentives and opportunities. The principal difference between the new presidential nominating process and the one it succeeds is that the old system emphasized the formation of broad majoritarian coalitions, whereas the new emphasizes the identification of coherent, minority factions.[14]

In the old system, dominated largely by strong state and local leaders and peopled by practical delegates whose primary objective was electoral victory, a candidate's best chance for success was to demonstrate electability. The candidate who could pull together the different elements of the party and even offer the potential to reach out to independents and pluck away some of the opposition was most likely to attract the support of the party potentates. Wise candidates recognized that their primary objective had to be the demonstration of broad appeal.

Under the new system, the incentives are quite different. A candidate's goal in the current nominating process is simply to survive, for nominations go to the last candidate who is sitting when the music stops. Where candidates under the old system were encouraged to build broad coalitions, candidates under the new system need only take command of a faction of the party that is large enough and intense enough to guarantee a plurality of votes in a plurality of primaries, especially those scheduled at the beginning of the campaign season.

Jimmy Carter, who played the new system like a Stradivarius, for example, became the front-runner among the nine Democratic candidates in 1976 by winning the New Hampshire primary. But "winning" in that case required only a small plurality in a multicandidate primary. Carter received 28.4 percent of the vote—23,373 votes in absolute terms—and he was not the first choice of 72 percent of the Democratic voters in that primary. But the numbers mattered little. What mattered was carving out a faction larger than anyone else's. When that happens, the media soon come along to magnify a small plurality into a major victory, and funding begins to dry up for other candidates. A little plurality here, a little plurality there, and suddenly the cheese stands alone: the nominee by default of one of the major political parties.

Factionalism is a natural result and a prime cost of weak party organizations. In recent decades the momentum of factionalism has been accelerated by the emergence of a nominating process that creates incentives for such factionalism and rewards those who are most successful at forging a faction that can serve as their ticket to nomination. An important consequence of that development is that the two major parties no longer do well what they once did best: aggregate a diversity of interests into broad electoral and governing coalitions. The nominating process is now populated by people whose primary interest is not always victory and who are indisposed to compromise. To them, getting the right candidate—right on the issues, right on ideology—is often more important than holding the party together or broadening its appeal. That is no recipe for interest aggregation; quite the opposite, in fact.

As the process of winning the nomination has grown increasingly distanced from the task of winning the general election, so, too, has it grown apart from the task of governing when the elections are over. This is the greatest concern of all. The new process discourages the construction of broad coalitions. It provides little opportunity for involvement of the people, especially members of Congress, who will matter most when it comes time to lead the government in Washington. This process has a strong tendency to promote the candidacies of outsiders who have little or no Washington experience and who are often strangers to the leading members of their own party. And the process of seeking the nomination provides little opportunity for candidates to broaden the base of their support or to swim in the ideological mainstream of their party.[15] Whatever the virtues of the new electoral process might be, it contributes little to the task of governing a complex country when the election is over.

PRESIDENTIAL CAMPAIGNS

The first presidential campaign of this century was also the last in which candidates stayed on their front porch and left the corralling of votes to surrogates and party leaders. When in 1904 Theodore Roosevelt began what many regarded as the unseemly practice of traveling about and speaking directly to voters, he initiated a long evolution in the nature of presidential campaigns.

As political parties faded in importance, especially after World War II, campaigns became increasingly candidate centered. By the 1970s the political parties had no meaningful presence in the higher levels—or much in the lower levels—of presidential campaigns. Candidates and their personal advisers now shape their own message, devise their own strategy, spend their own (not party) money, and deploy their own field organizations.

In earlier times parties managed the campaigns for their nominees. This is not so anymore. In 1992, for example, incumbent George Bush built his own campaign organization, Bush-Quayle '92, independent of the Republican Party. When he hired Mary Matalin as political director, she left her job as chief of staff of the Republican National Committee to work for the Bush campaign. This was merely the continuance of a pattern that had been in effect for several decades, one established most markedly in 1972 when an independent Committee to Re-Elect the President, not the Republican Party, managed incumbent Richard Nixon's campaign.

These candidate-centered presidential campaigns are unhinged not only from the national party but also from the state party organizations and from many of the leading political figures in the candidate's party. The campaigns' objective is a single-minded one: to get their candidate elected president. All other objectives, including the election of other members of the candidate's party, are of relative inconsequence. This is not surprising in view of the changes in the nominating process just described. Candidates believe that they have gone out and won the nomination on their own; no one gave it to them. So they feel no indebtedness to their party or to most of its other candidates. They are free agents in pursuit of a single objective. Since the nominating process at the state level operates in much the same way, many candidates for Congress have the same perception of themselves as self-made and unindebted.

Once under way, modern presidential campaigns quickly come under the sway of two recent and now dominant developments: technology and professional managers. Technology is everywhere in modern campaigns: computer-generated direct mail, telephone banks, jet travel, public opinion polling. But the technology that has most significantly changed the face (and the soul) of presidential campaigns is the broadcast media.

Modern presidential campaigns are little more than a traveling backdrop for TV cameras. If a candidate goes to a flag factory, it is not to get the seamstresses' vote; it is to convey a symbolic message when the president later appears on the evening news standing in front of a giant American flag. Using pollsters to identify "wedge" issues and shape strategies, hopping from place to place in a chartered jet, seeking to wrest maximum symbolic expression from television coverage, contemporary presidential candidates rarely have any meaningful contact with voters or with state and local political leaders. The twelve-second snippet that shows up on the evening news is far more important to the candidate than a half-hour conversation on the campaign trail with a senator who may chair a key congressional committee. Media coverage is the driving rationale of modern presidential campaigns.

There have always been professional managers in American politics, the campaign perennials whose skills, accumulated experience, and contacts made them valuable resources for presidential candidates. But for most of American history, those people were associated with and often employed by (sometimes indirectly through a government payroll) one of the political parties. They had names such as August Belmont, William Barnum, Mark Hanna, and James Farley, and they were real powers in American politics. They played large roles in the selection of the party nominees, and they quickly assumed commanding roles in the general election campaign even if they had had no previous close relationship with the candidate.

Mark Hanna, for example, was the supreme power in the Republican Party at the beginning of the twentieth century. He had little affection for Theodore Roosevelt, whom he called "that damned cowboy," but Hanna engineered Roosevelt's selection as the party's vice-presidential candidate in 1900 so that Roosevelt's war record would enhance William

McKinley's chances of winning the White House. When McKinley was later assassinated, Hanna's damned cowboy became president. In 1904 Hanna was a major figure in Roosevelt's campaign for reelection.

Such scenarios all seem very foreign now. Contemporary campaigns are still run by professionals, but they are of a very different breed. Although these new campaign professionals had been appearing here and there on the political landscape for a decade or more, their presence had its first dramatic impact in 1968. It is hard to imagine a more daunting challenge for any campaign manager than to get Richard Nixon elected president in 1968. Widely derided during his years as Dwight Eisenhower's vice president, unsuccessful in the presidential campaign against the less experienced John Kennedy in 1960, defeated badly in the race for governor of California in 1962, and out of politics after that, Richard Nixon seemed a very long shot for the White House in 1968. But Nixon put together a team dominated by media specialists and public relations professionals who mounted a campaign that tightly controlled his appearances, skillfully manipulated his image—recall the "new Nixon"—and created the one center of calm and stability in the chaos of that year.

The lessons of the 1968 Nixon campaign revolutionized presidential campaigns in America. And one of the principal impacts of that Nixon effort was to enhance the stature of this new kind of campaign operative. Most of these new professionals earn their incomes not from party salaries or government jobs but from fees they charge to the candidates who become their clients. Some have worked on many political campaigns; others have not. Their backgrounds are in scientific opinion polling, public relations, or television. Some of them, when not working for political candidates, help corporations market their products. These are people who typically have little deep interest in the long-term maintenance of political institutions such as parties (which, in fact, some of them see as competitors) or in the building of broad governing coalitions. They are hired to do a job, and that job is to destroy the credibility of the opposition and obtain a plurality for their client.

The changes that have overtaken presidential campaigns in the past few decades emerged from no grand design. They were not the product of some thoughtful group of reformers trying to fix a broken system. Instead, these changes were wrought by the unrelenting force of modern technology, by the entrepreneurial efforts of a new class of independent campaign professionals, and by the early successes of candidates, such as Richard Nixon and George McGovern, who chose to go it alone in pursuit of the presidency.

Because these changes sprung from no single source or motivation, they emerged without any clear intent beyond improving the electoral chances of individual candidates. They were certainly not designed to improve the voters' ability to make wise choices or to enhance the capacity of the government to function effectively after the election. In fact, the character of contemporary elections makes intelligent voter choice and effective government performance less, not more, likely.

National elections have become more atomized as their character has changed. The vacuum left by declining parties has been filled by candidate-centered presidential and congressional campaigns that are connected only by coincidence. In 1964 there was compelling evidence that support for Lyndon Johnson and popular repudiation of Barry Goldwater brought a tide of new Democrats to Congress. The ebbing of that tide—and a Republican net gain of forty-seven House seats two years later—strengthens the case for a connection between the Johnson victory and the outcome in many congressional races. Since then, however, there has been no similar connection between the presidential and congressional election outcomes. Only the election of Ronald Reagan in 1980 altered the partisan makeup of Congress in any notable way, and even that change was well below pre–World War II norms.

Presidential coattails have gone out of fashion. Presidential and congressional elections are now independent enterprises, run by different people, emphasizing different issues, paying little more than lip-service to the need to build national coalitions. The churlishness that now passes for campaign debate turns voters off, not on. Modern campaigns inspire little durable support for new presidents, in part because the campaign tone is often so negative, voters are rarely offered an exciting substantive agenda for the future, and voters have been asked for little more than their vote. Voter investment is small, and so, therefore, is the longer-term need to protect that investment.

Presidential campaigns, like the presidential nominating process, have driven a deep wedge between the electoral process and the governing process. The skills and qualities needed to become president rarely match the skills and qualities needed to succeed as president. In fact, the nature of the electoral process increasingly guarantees the re-creation every four years of a government led by individuals who are strangers to each other, who share no substantive program for progress, and who have already earned the skepticism of the American people.

MADISON'S NIGHTMARE:
THE INTEREST GROUP EXPLOSION

Politics abhors a vacuum. A democratic people have interests that require an outlet. When a traditional outlet shuts down, another emerges to take its place. When one interest emerges as a public entity, a counterinterest usually follows. The process of interest formation is shaped by the formal channels of politics but is not limited to them. In a dynamic society, interest emergence is relentless.

Americans have always been joiners. The First Amendment to the Constitution esteems and protects this habit in its guarantee of freedom of speech but also of the rights to peaceably assemble and petition the government for redress of grievances. These are rights that Americans have exercised with vigor. Alexis de Tocqueville noted in his visits here in the 1830s, "Whenever at the head of some new undertaking you see government in France, or a man of rank in England, in the United States you will be sure to find an association."[16] He further observed, "In no country in the world has the principle of association been more successfully used, or applied to a greater multitude of objects, than in America. . . . In the United States, associations are established to promote the public safety, commerce, industry, morality, and religion. There is no end which the human will despairs of attaining through the combined power of individuals united into a society."[17]

The associations of which Tocqueville wrote have usually been called interest groups, and they have been a continuing and important feature of American politics. It was, after all, the Sons of Liberty that instigated the Boston Tea Party, the Abolitionists whose antislavery fervor helped push the country into the political morass that resulted in the Civil War, the Ku Klux Klan that fought to prevent racial and ethnic integration, and the America Firsters that resisted national calls to prepare for a second world war. In every era of American history, interest groups shaped, and often dominated, political debate.

The emergence of interests and the filling of political vacuums are part of the long swell and sway of American history. But America has never seen anything like the interest group explosion that occurred after World War II. In earlier times politically active interest groups were few in number, usually highly focused, typically transient, and often suborbitals within the political party system. A few groups endured through the generations either as large confederations of broad interests (the Grange, "labor," the railroads) or persistent voices for groups of people who lacked full representation in politics (the NAACP, the Suffragettes). The most common pattern was for an interest group to form around a specific policy concern, exert itself energetically in pursuit of a particular policy change, and then to fade away when the mission was accomplished.

The postwar pattern is dramatically different in almost every way. One measure of that difference is the extraordinary proliferation in American interest groups in recent decades. There is no standard definition of an interest group or central registry to certify its existence. Like insects, interest groups take many forms, constantly mutate, and do a good deal of breeding. They are not simple to count. But the accumulation of evidence and impression is compelling. In 1929 political scientist Pendleton Herring counted 500 organizations with direct political interests. Oliver McKee Jr., in the same year, counted 300 "effective lobbies." During World War II the Temporary National Economic Committee set the number of Washington lobby groups at 400.[18] There is no certainty about the right number of such politically active interest groups, but neither is there any doubt that their number was quite small.

After the war the number of interest groups and the number of people representing those groups in Washington began to swell steadily. The *Encyclopedia of Associations* identified 10,298 organized groups of all kinds in 1968. By 1980 the number had grown to 14,726 and by 1988, to 20,643.[19] Not all of these groups were politically active, but the pattern of growth surely indicated what was happening in politics.

A 1946 law required individuals who spent a majority of their time lobbying the federal government to register as lobbyists. The total of registered lobbyists hardly measured the lobbying universe because many who did some lobbying did not register. By the early 1960s, however, several studies had found that there were more than one thousand registered lobbyists in Washington, presumably reflecting a cohort of lobbyists of even greater number.[20] Then the real growth began.

The greatest escalation occurred from the late 1960s on. Hedrick Smith identified 5,662 registered lobbyists in Washington in 1981 and then noted that the number had grown to 23,011 by 1987. In 1977 came the first annual issue of a reference volume, called *Washington Representatives*, that sought to list every person representing a political interest group in Washington. Figure 3.1 shows that the number of such representatives nearly quadrupled in fourteen years.

By the early 1990s, Washington was awash with interest groups and their representatives. More than fifteen thousand groups were represented there. The number of employees of these groups exceeded one hundred thousand, including nearly twenty-five thousand registered lobbyists. The number of lawyers in Washington totaled more than forty-five thousand compared to fewer than ten thousand there in 1970. Most of the law practiced in Washington is special interest representation; the extraordinary growth in the number of Washington lawyers is simply another measure the growth in interest group activity. In addition, more than ten thousand public relations specialists and public affairs consultants had set up shop to serve the needs of the special interests encamped there.

In Washington the evidence of this growth is everywhere: in the K Street canyon where new office buildings bustle with the activity of thou-

FIGURE 3.1
Growth in the Number of Washington Representatives
of Interest Groups, 1977–1991

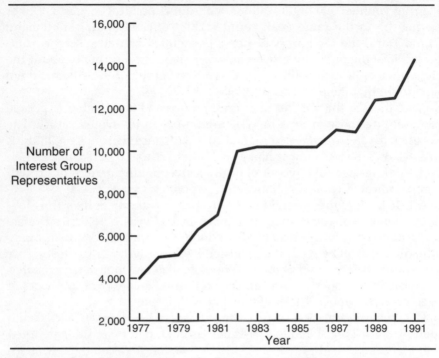

SOURCE: Compiled from Arthur C. Close, ed., *Washington Representatives* (Washington, D.C.: Privately published, annual volumes 1977–1991).

sands of interest groups and trade associations; in the trade papers and magazines of government (Congressional Quarterly, National Journal, Federal Times), whose pages are full of advertisements for new fighter aircraft and praise for the benefits of rural electrification; in the "expense account" restaurants that now circle every government building; and in the lobbies of Congress, the fabled "Gucci gulch." Interest groups have colonized the nation's capitol, and in so doing, they have changed the way America governs itself.

The interest group universe changed in character as well as magnitude after World War II. There was a greater diversity in the kinds of interests expressed in policy debates. Groups that had previously been outside the orbit of effective representation were suddenly important players. As recently as the 1940s, there were few or no potent organizations representing the mentally ill, homosexuals, women, the physically disabled, people of color, or children. Who could have imagined a half century ago that in 1993 one of the most influential interest group representatives in the nation's capital would be a black woman heading an organization called the Children's Defense Fund?

The intergovernmental lobby has grown dramatically as well in the postwar period. A majority of states and many cities now have their own representatives in Washington. Organizations such as the U.S. Conference of Mayors, the National Governors' Association, and the National League of Cities have very active lobbying practices. Foreign interests also have established a powerful presence in Washington, one that extends far beyond the traditional activities of their embassies. Many foreign governments and commercial groups retain Washington lawyers and lobbyists to promote their interests and public relations firms to shine up their images. In 1990, for example, there were registered foreign agents in the United States for more than one hundred Japanese organizations—not only for electronics firms such as Mitsubishi and Toshiba but also for the Japan Whaling Association and the Japanese Tanner Crab Association.[21]

Even though virtually every interest in America is now organized and represented in Washington, business is the heavyweight of this recent development in both numbers and influence. That pattern is especially clear in the formation of PACs since they became the prominent vehicle for campaign contributions in 1974. The number of PACs grew from 608 in 1974 to 4,195 in 1992. Corporate PACs grew from 89 in 1974 to 1,735 in 1992.

The most notable change in the character of interest groups in postwar Washington has been the emergence of a new species known as "public interest groups." It is a term that brings to mind images of Ralph Nader and blue-jeaned college interns, a handful of underfinanced, morally righteous Davids out to slay the corporate Goliaths. In the 1960s and 1970s, many of the public interest groups fit that image quite closely. Some still do. But the category of public interest groups has gotten larger, wealthier, and far more influential in the past twenty-five years. Recent studies count more than twenty-five hundred national organizations representing a wide range of interpretations of the "public interest": environmental protection, electoral reform, historical preservation, social justice, nuclear disarmament, and animal rights, to name just a few. Some of these groups have more than one hundred thousand members. Many—almost one-third according to some studies—have no "members" at all. But collectively these public interest groups are supported by the memberships and contributions of more than 40 million individuals, whose giving totals more than $4 billion annually.[22]

The vast majority of these public interest groups were formed after 1965. A study of a sample of public interest groups by the Foundation for

Public Affairs found that of those in existence in 1985, only 12 percent existed before World War II, and more than 70 percent were founded after 1965.[23] Once created, public interest groups tend to survive even after the passions inspiring their creation have dissipated. The Committee for a Sane Nuclear Policy was created in the 1950s as a counterweight to the massive nuclear armament inspired by the anticommunist hysteria of the time. Now known as Peace Action, the group is still in operation, with nearly eighty thousand members.

A steady centralization of interest group activities in Washington has accompanied this growth in the interest group universe. Each year more groups move their headquarters to Washington. Between 1971 and 1984, for example, the percentage of trade associations with headquarters in Washington grew from 19 to 31, and the escalation continued thereafter. The number of individual corporations with Washington offices has also grown steadily in the postwar period. A 1981 study of over four hundred corporations found that of those with Washington offices, more than half had opened those offices in the previous decade. There has also been steady growth in the size of corporate offices in Washington. The Washington office of General Motors, for example, grew from three people in 1968 to twenty-eight ten years later.[24]

The larger interest group universe has also become much more competitive. As more interests organize and establish outposts in Washington, they have to fight harder to get the attention and shape the decisions of government policymakers. This intense competition has produced an arms race of its own in the use of sophisticated techniques of expressing opinions and exercising influence. Skilled lobbyists remain essential weapons in the arsenal of many interest groups. The more effective the lobbyists are, the greater is their access to decisionmakers, and the more they cost. The best of them now earn annual incomes of several million dollars.

But skilled lobbyists are rarely enough, so groups have deployed the wonders of modern technology, especially computers, to generate massive outpourings of public opinion at critical points in policy debates. This is sometimes called "indirect lobbying" or "grassroots lobbying." It usually involves an effort directed from Washington to stimulate a group's members in congressional districts all over the country to communicate directly with their representative as a legislative vote is about to occur. Sometimes these are "shotgun" operations in which mail, faxes, or phone calls flood every congressional office. Sometimes they are "rifle shots" in which expressions of opinion are focused on subcommittee members or other critically placed members of Congress.

The level of technological sophistication and political savvy that supports these operations is enormous. The National Association of

Manufacturers, for example, has thirteen thousand member firms. Computers at the association's Washington headquarters can organize indirect lobbying campaigns based on geography, the manufacturing interest of particular firms, or any of a variety of other categories. The National Rifle Association claims it can generate a half million letters to Congress on gun control issues within three days of a directive from Washington. When President Reagan's proposal to cut the school lunch program was under consideration in 1981, members of Congress received 1.25 million letters, 800,000 postcards, 600,000 mailgrams, and 600,000 paper pie plates to protest the cuts.

Such campaigns are now a common tactic on the interest group battlefield, and they are deployed by groups of the Left and Right, by public and special interest groups alike. It is a far cry from the days before World War II, when Washington was a sleepy southern town and "the lobby," as it was then called, was composed of a few hundred good old boys whose connections and amiability (and whose liquor) were the principal weapons in their efforts to pry favors from their friends in Congress. One of those good old boys, brought back from the dead to visit contemporary Washington, would think he had been transported to another planet.

What caused the interest group environment to change so radically in the postwar period? There is no single or simple answer. The postwar interest group explosion resulted from a convergence of many factors, including the following.

- A well-educated middle class with disposable income and wide-ranging political interests was available for the first time to join and fund a broad array of groups, some pursuing the economic self-interests of their members, others committed to the public interest

- The declining effectiveness of and diminishing loyalty to political parties opened the way for new channels of political communication and new avenues of political influence. Interest groups rushed in to grab those opportunities.

- The civil rights, antiwar, and other social protest movements of the postwar period weaned the baby boom generation on a social activism that came to be institutionalized in interest groups seeking to change public policy. The protest movements changed venue by moving into the political system they had once challenged from the outside.

- Bigger government reached into more segments of American life than ever before. This begat a natural reaction. As interests came to realize that government policy directly affected their welfare, they formed groups to limit the regulations government imposed on them and to increase their share of government benefits. Vast expansions of group activity often followed major policy break-throughs such as the GI Bill, the Older Americans Act of 1965, and the National Environmental Policy Act. The conventional notion that pressure groups formed to change policy was often turned up-side down; policy changes stimulated interest group formation and activism.

- Many groups, especially public interest groups, found patronage in the postwar economic and social milieu that freed them from re-liance on the limited wealth (and sometimes limited number) of their supporters. Foundations, philanthropists, churches, trade unions, and business firms all contributed money to interest groups whose activities they supported. In many areas the greatest patron of them all was the federal government, which subsidized an ex-traordinary array of groups through formal charter, contracts, grants, and tax incentives.

- New technologies expanded the range of opportunities for interest groups. Television and ancillaries such as videotape and satellite transmission opened up whole new realms of persuasion. Computers enabled groups to raise funds more systematically through direct mail and to target their influence more directly through the techniques described previously. Jet travel ended the isolation of the federal government from the people affected by its decisions. And faxes, overnight mail, electronic mail, and the Internet made direct communications virtually instantaneous. Technology enabled organizations, for the first time in history, to mobilize large and dispersed groups of citizens with nothing else in common but a shared set of interests in specific policy decisions.

- Finally, there is the effect of contagion. Like-minded citizens and in-terests formed groups to influence public policy because everyone was doing so. Without an interest group, citizens and other interests were left out of the political equation. Without money to make a group effective, interests lost political battles. Without an office in Washington, interest groups were not playing where the action was. As interest group politics came increasingly after World War II to be the principal form of national politics, more and more people wanted in. They joined existing groups and formed new ones in a spiraling expansion that continues unabated into our own time.

The postwar interest group explosion has had profound impacts on American politics and government. It has caused some thoughtful polit-ical analysts to worry about a genuine crisis of participation. The politi-cal community in America became larger, more active, more organized, and more sophisticated all at the same time. Can any democracy tolerate

squabbling voices of the present. It becomes ever more difficult to or-
chestrate harmony from the din.

GOVERNMENT SUBVERSION OF POLITICS

The New Deal initiated the largest and most significant takeover of the
twentieth century. No one planned it, and it unfolded gradually over the
half century after Franklin Roosevelt's election. But the New Deal altered
the character and significance of political parties, inspired the interest
group explosion, and fundamentally redefined the relationship between
the American people and their government. The New Deal represented
the takeover of electoral politics by government.

Through Republican and Democratic administrations alike, the federal
government has been creating new programs that absorb and then insti-
tutionalize functions once performed by political parties and local politicians. When government was small and its responsibilities limited, the
local party leaders and political machines were the only public source of
jobs for the unemployed; they provided food for the hungry and care for
the sick and elderly. There was no illusion about the quid pro quo this involved: Support at the voting booth was the price of these benefits. It was
a good deal for those of the poor and the working class who had nowhere
else to turn, and it fueled the political parties with a reliable stream of
electoral support.

But the Depression overwhelmed the ability of the local political parties to meet the demands of their traditional constituents. The focus
turned to government and especially the federal government. And after
Roosevelt's election, government responded with jobs, new rights for
workers, protection for farmers, deposit insurance, and a national pension system for the elderly. In the years that followed, the federal government provided food stamps, school lunches, aid to local education,
Medicare and Medicaid, public works, veterans benefits, job training, rent
subsidies, and aid for dependent children. And it steadily increased the
size and coverage of these programs.

The federal government did more than just create these new benefits
for individuals; it embedded them in steel. Through technical legislative
devices such as permanent authorizations and permanent appropriations, many of the elements of the new welfare state were removed from
annual legislative review. They became ongoing government obligations
to which their beneficiaries were entitled by law. Then to ensure that the
value of these programs would not be eroded by inflation or political
sniping, the government "indexed" these benefits to the Consumer Price
Index or some other formula that provided for regular cost-of-living adjustments.

Budget makers came to call these programs "uncontrollables" because they were beyond the easy reach of annual budget decisions. Once in place, they quickly took root and sprouted. By 1993, 65 percent of the federal budget was composed of expenditures that the Office of Management and Budget had labeled "relatively uncontrollable under current law." Of these, 78 percent, or $766 billion, were expenditures for programs, such as Medicaid, Medicare, social security, Aid to Families with Dependent Children, and food stamps, that provided direct benefits to individuals.

The dynamic by which the welfare state was created had a profound effect on electoral politics. The fortification of these new welfare state programs protected them in a significant way from the impact of national elections. With permanent authorizations and appropriations, programs, once established, did not have to be rejustified every year. Changes in the cast of public officials would have little effect on the benefits provided by the welfare state because there were few annual debates on the continued existence or funding levels of those benefits. The beneficiaries could afford to be less attentive to politics—and less active participants in elections—because government had taken over control of the benefits that had once inspired so much political activity.

Gradually the base of the Democratic Party shifted from local party organizations to the federal bureaucracy and its patrons in Congress. What had long been the game of the political machines—the provision of material benefits in exchange for political support—soon became the game of government. And when it did, the machines ran out of fuel and shut down.

The formation of interest groups to represent the beneficiaries, or clients, of government programs accelerated the institutionalization of the service orientation of government. These clientele groups, such as the National Welfare Rights Organization, Disabled American Veterans, the Farm Credit Council, and the Shipbuilders Council of America, built enduring relationships with the agencies that served them and with the congressional subcommittees that had jurisdiction over those agencies. That symbiosis soon spread across the full range of government programs. It offered a direct and influential avenue to policymaking with which broad-based political parties simply could not compete. Thus, the parties and the traditional politics they represented began to wither.[29]

CONCLUSION

The purpose of elections is to form a government: to assemble and activate a majority coalition, to forge consensus around a substantive national agenda, to concentrate the political power necessary to implement that agenda. Since World War II American national elections have increasingly failed to secure these objectives. That failure has driven Americans and their public purposes away from electoral politics. The great mystic battlefields of national debate—where a democracy continually and necessarily redefines itself—have shifted from the electoral arena to other less visible, less open, and less effective forums. That change is deep and fundamental. And it is not without cost.

The sickness of electoral politics has caused a loss of accountability. Elections fail to provide adequate opportunities for Americans to comprehend or pass intelligent judgment on the current policies of their government. This yields increasing levels of frustration and anger and a broad, corrosive disaffection aimed at all incumbents regardless of party or culpability. Americans have always been ambivalent about politics. Recently, however, as E. J. Dionne argued persuasively, they have come to hate politics.[30] An important part of the reason for the emergence of this hatred is the failure of contemporary elections to offer the sense of control or direction over their government to which citizens of a democracy feel entitled.

An important and obvious result is that declining percentages of the American people are participating in elections. There is a raging debate among scholars and journalists about the consequences of diminished voter turnout. But one impact is undeniable: Americans who do not vote have made little investment in their leaders or their government. The bond between government and non-voting citizens is tenuous and fragile. Political support for incumbent presidential administrations is shallow and fleeting. The evidence of this condition is compelling. Indeed, one of the most striking characteristics of postwar politics has been the frequent abandonment of American presidents by the people who elected them, described in Chapter 5.

Because elections are no longer the place where major social conflicts are resolved (or, in many cases, even debated), potent new incentives have emerged for politicians and activists, and new forms of political organization and action have risen to prominence. Public relations techniques, the exponential multiplication of interest groups, direct mail, the growing reliance on the broadcast media, the burgeoning influence of professional campaign consultants, the permeability of party conventions, candidate-centered campaigns, and frequent public demonstrations are postwar phenomena that define the new American politics. And all of them, taken together, have consequences of great magnitude for the quality of American public life.

Principal among those consequences is the atomization, what Kevin Phillips called the "balkanization," of national politics.[31] The decentralizing forces of special interest have won out over the centrifugal lure of the national interest. *E pluribus unum*, "one out of many," no longer obtains. Today's currency, to be more accurate, should bear the motto *nemo e pluribus*, "none out of many," or *quisque pro sibi*, "every man for himself."

A political system that relies on so many disparate and often competing forms of political mobilization and expression cannot aggregate its component parts for collective action. Such a system is fated to have deep and persistent problems governing itself, for in a democracy collective action is the only effective route to progress. A democracy that cannot work together cannot work.

The changes that have overtaken American politics in the postwar period are the product of many separate, disconnected, narrowly focused reforms and of the secular impact of technology and demographic change. No comprehensive plan designed these changes. No party or group or leader sought the new politics they have created. Nobody much likes their overall impact. But they add up, however unintentional their formulation, to a profound alteration of the American political process. And they contribute—as we see clearly in the chapters ahead—to a striking transformation in the role and performance of the institutions of the federal government.

THE CONGRESS
WE LOVE TO HATE

Hubert Humphrey could not have been happier on the morning of November 5, 1958. As election results rolled in from across the country, it grew clear that a liberal tide of enormous proportions was coming to Congress: fifteen new Democrats in the Senate and forty-eight in the House. The new Congress, the 86th Congress, would have its crack at the backlog of pressing issues—civil rights, minimum wage, aid to education, health care for the elderly, and so on—that had danced for so long in liberal fantasies. "The 1958 election . . . changed the complexion of the Senate," Humphrey later wrote, "and we liberals were no longer an embattled minority."[1]

But Humphrey could not begin to imagine that the 1958 election would be more than just a swing of the ideological pendulum. It would, in fact, be a turning point: the beginning of an era in which Congress itself would be remade by its members, in which the character of that institution would be profoundly altered. For the Ed Muskies and Phil Harts and Gene McCarthys were different from so many of their predecessors. They were not coming to Washington to be mere cogs in a wheel. They intended to change the world, to do it from Congress, and to do it soon. They were ambitious; they were impatient; they were the harbingers of a new Congress whose time had come.

The Congress they joined in 1959 was not terribly different from the one that had emerged in the 1910s from a rebellion against the iron-handed rule of its party leaders. That "revolt against the Speaker" occurred in the House when power was stripped from the domineering "Uncle Joe" Cannon of Illinois. In the Senate at about the same time, insurgent members challenged the suzerainty of Nelson W. Aldrich of Rhode Island.

In the place of strong centralized leaders came what could only be called an oligarchy. A small clique of potentates—the party leaders and the chairs of the most important congressional committees—dominated each house. The selection of those chairs resulted from a simple, rigid process of seniority: The member of the majority party with the longest consecutive service on the committee automatically became chair and remained chair for the remainder of his time in Congress.

Party leaders such as Nicholas Longworth, Sam Rayburn, and Lyndon Johnson worked closely with committee chairs such as Carl Vinson, Richard Russell, and Clarence Cannon to determine the agenda of Congress, formulate legislation, negotiate with the president, and build coalitions to enact a legislative program. Organized in this fashion, Congress was a remarkably efficient American legislature, in spite of the absence of true party discipline of the European sort. In the quarter century from 1935 through 1960, Congress enacted an average of 919 new laws in each Congress, one-third more on average than in each Congress after 1960. Even the Eightieth Congress, which Harry Truman called the "do-nothing" Congress, passed 906 public bills. No Congress after 1958 ever passed as many.

To be a new member, a junior member, in the midcentury Congress was to experience obscurity, powerlessness, and humility—often for years on end. Endurance, not talent or ambition, was the road to influence in that kind of Congress. "To get along," Sam Rayburn often said to new members, "go along." Informal expectations constrained new members to serve a long apprenticeship before they introduced significant legislation or spoke on the floor of their house or won assignment to an important committee. A decade of service in the majority might yield a subcommittee chairmanship, but even then subcommittees were firmly controlled by the committee chairs. And few members made it to a committee chair in less than two decades.

Lyndon Johnson is widely regarded as one of the most skilled legislators of this century. His rise to influence in the Senate and his skillful use of that influence are legendary. But this same Lyndon Johnson spent eleven years in the House before he was elected to the Senate. And in the House, he never chaired a committee or subcommittee, never became part of the leadership, and never introduced a single piece of legislation that became law, except for two minor bills that affected only his own district.[2] The system served its leaders, not its rank-and-file members. Even skill and ambition as large as Lyndon Johnson's could not unbolt the doors to power.

The rigor of the old system looked like rigor mortis to many of the new Democrats elected in 1958. Its confining impact on their public lives was exacerbated at the time by two flukes of coincidence. One was a legacy of the 1946 congressional elections, in which the Democrats had lost their majority in both houses of Congress for the first time in a decade and a half. They won it back two years later and then lost it again for the first two years of the Eisenhower presidency. During that transition period, a number of senior Democrats from the North were defeated and replaced, first by Republicans, then by younger Democrats. Virtually untouched by the postwar elections were the southern Democrats in whose region no Republican Party had yet emerged.

When the dust settled in 1955, Southerners dominated the Democratic Party and controlled nearly all of the important committee chairs. Even after the 1958 elections, Southerners held nearly 50 percent of the Democratic seats in the House and 43 percent in the Senate. Their dominance of the committee chairs was even greater—more than 70 percent were filled by Southerners in both the House and the Senate.[3] The southern stranglehold on the only genuine positions of power in Congress would continue well into the 1960s.

Simultaneous with the southern power surge in Congress was the explosion of the civil rights revolution. By the end of the 1950s, the need for national legislation to protect the civil rights of black Americans was becoming increasingly clear. Liberal Democrats and many in the still sizable moderate faction of the Republican Party wanted to move quickly and dramatically to open public accommodations, schools, and voting booths to racial minorities. But advocates faced the obdurate obstacle of congressional rules that placed power in the hands of committee chairs and a political legacy that filled those chairs with conservative white Southerners who were truculent opponents of new civil rights legislation.

As the number of liberals in Congress grew after 1958, the battle lines between the old order and the new were drawn ever more sharply. What followed was an effort, which went on for almost two decades, to change the procedures and the organization of power in Congress to suit the needs of a changing membership and a changing country. What resulted from this period of change, and what survives today, was a Congress radically different from its 1958 counterpart.

I describe that new Congress in the pages ahead. And we see that the cumulative effect of the recent era of reform diverges widely from what many of the reformers sought. No one drew a blueprint for this new Congress. No one intended to create the brooding, overmuscled, under-coordinated legislature that sits on Capitol Hill today. Reform was necessary, for the old order was self-destructing. But the momentum of reform became a victim of its own acceleration and killed off the only people with the power to control it. The new Congress that emerged was, and is, many things, but above all it was the Congress that everybody loved to hate—and with good reason.

THE NEW CONGRESS

Congress has never quite figured out who should run the place. Sometimes it entrusted powerful individuals to do that. More often power resided with a small band of party leaders (not all of them members of Congress) or with the chairs of the standing committees. Occasionally, and briefly, during transitions between these two modal types the rank and file had some say in how Congress was run.

Every allocation of power seemed to possess the seeds of its own destruction, and eventually members without influence sought reforms that would provide them greater influence on the operations of Congress and the policies it produced. Often those reform movements were encouraged by demographic, political, or technological changes outside Congress that made the existing congressional order seem anachronistic. But never have the forces of change, internal and external, collided with such impact as in the years since 1958. And never has the character of Congress been so dramatically altered.

The contemporary Congress is a perplexing amalgam of incentives and constraints that often defies understanding even by its own members. Its collective identity differs deeply from the identities of its individual members. It performs some of the functions of a legislature exceedingly well and others not well at all. But more than anything, this is an institution out of control, a body without a cerebral cortex, a Congress that cannot think for itself. How did it get that way?

Members

When Alexis de Tocqueville visited the House of Representatives in the 1830s, he was not impressed:

> On entering the House of Representatives at Washington, one is struck by the vulgar demeanor of that great assembly. Often there is not a distinguished man in the whole number. Its members are almost all obscure individuals, whose names bring no associations to mind. They are mostly village lawyers, men in trade, or even persons belonging to the lower classes of society. In a country in which education is very general, it is said that the representatives of the people do not always know how to write correctly.[4]

Had he come a century later, he probably would have drawn much the same impression. Over the history of the House, it has been a place where some rare figures of distinction stood out in a sea of mediocrity. Membership in the House conferred no great status in life, no great wealth—as recently as 1954 the congressional salary was $12,500 a year—and, most important for most members, no great opportunity to affect the course of human history. Before World War II, service in Congress, and in the House especially, was not very taxing work. Members arrived in January and usually stayed in Washington until the weather became unbearable in late May. Then they returned to their districts, and often to their "real" jobs, for the remainder of the year.

In Washington the pace was rarely overwhelming. Members tended to live in hotels, take their meals together, and spend their evenings and weekends playing poker or golf, talking politics, and bending elbows. The federal government remained a relatively small enterprise even through the early years of the New Deal. It did *not* run a national pension system, provide for anyone's health care, regulate much of the private sector, shoot rockets into space, or serve as the world's policeman. It did few of the things we now regard as routine functions of the government in Washington, so there was often little for Congress to do. Representative Joe Martin of Massachusetts, who served forty-two years in the House, including two terms as its Speaker, recalled legislative life in the 1920s:

> The great difference between life in Congress a generation ago and life there now was the absence then of the immense pressures that came with the depression, World War II, Korea, and the cold war. Foreign affairs were an inconsequential problem in Congress in the 1920s. For one week the House Foreign Affairs Committee debated to the exclusion of all other matters the question of authorizing a $20,000 appropriation for an international poultry show in Tulsa. This item, which we finally approved, was about the most important issue that came before the committee in the whole session.[5]

Members rarely went home during the session, congressional staffs were tiny, few constituents visited in Washington, the mail was so light that many members answered it themselves, and there were few interest groups stirring up trouble in the capital. For most members, a seat in Congress was a reward for a career of party loyalty or lengthy service in local or state government. The only way to get to Congress was to be sent by somebody. Individual initiative and self-promotion were largely irrelevant. Members were not expected to be brilliant or articulate or inventive. Except for the handful who survived to become leaders, members were expected to do what they were told by their party leaders in Congress and their patrons back home. Members watched history being made far more often than they made it.

Few members risked losing their seats as long as they played by the rules. The principal rule was follow the leader. Turnover was higher than it is now, but, as now, it was mostly voluntary. Members departed when they lost interest and resigned or when they lost the support of their patrons and were not renominated. Few incumbents who stood for reelection were defeated in the general election.[6]

The character of congressional members began to change in the 1950s and 1960s when the selection process began to change. After World War II, the rapid growth in population and the movement of the population had a significant impact on the House of Representatives. The South and West were growing at a faster rate than the rest of the country. After the

1940 census, the sixteen southern and border states and the five western "rim" states (Washington, Oregon, California, Arizona, and New Mexico) held 42 percent of the seats in the House. By the 1990 reapportionment, their percentage had grown to 53 percent. Especially notable was the change in three states: Florida, Texas, and California. In 1945 the three combined held 11 percent of the seats in the House. After 1992 they combined for almost 25 percent of the membership of the House. By contrast, the three states of Illinois, New York, and Pennsylvania had 24 percent of House seats in the 1940s and only 17 percent after 1992.

But there was more to this change than the mere relocation of the population. The states that were losing seats in the House were those where party organizations and party bosses had traditionally been strongest: New York, Pennsylvania, Illinois, and the other highly urban, highly ethnic enclaves of the Northeast and Upper Midwest. The states that were gaining population most rapidly were those where parties had been less well developed or organized primarily around the increasingly irrelevant issue of race. The House reapportionments of the postwar years helped destroy the ability of the parties to determine who would serve in Congress.

Nor was that all. In 1964 in *Wesberry* v. *Sanders*, the United States Supreme Court reversed its historical aversion to interfering in the creation of congressional districts by the state legislatures. When the Court's new standard of "one man, one vote" was imposed on the process of congressional redistricting, yet another sweeping change took place. For decades many state delegations to Congress had been dominated by the upstate and rural members, who were the primary beneficiaries of malapportionment. They represented districts with much smaller populations than their urban counterparts, and they tended to be more conservative, especially about spending federal money.

Just as the Supreme Court was requiring the states to redraw congressional districts to equalize their populations, Congress passed the Voting Rights Act of 1965, which led in the following decade to a very substantial increase in black registration. From 1962 to 1970 the number of black voters in the South more than doubled, from 1.5 million to 3.3 million. In the seven southern states identified for special attention by the Voting Rights Act, black voter registration also doubled, from 30 percent of those eligible to almost 60 percent.[7]

Suddenly much had changed. The door had been opened to new members from places, mostly urban ones, that had long been underrepresented in the House. Many of the new districts that resulted from the 1970 redistricting were substantially more heterogeneous in character than the districts they replaced, combining, rather than separating, urban, rural, and suburban populations. The electorate, too, especially in the South, was growing increasingly diverse. And when the voting age was lowered to eighteen in 1971 just as the huge wave of baby boomers was reaching that age, members of Congress found themselves representing many more potential voters than before.

All of this encouraged members' interests in a wider range of policy questions because the districts they now represented included a broader array of people and economic concerns. Members found themselves increasingly restive in a committee-dominated Congress where they were pigeonholed in a single committee. For most of them, there was little opportunity for influence beyond the committees on which they served—and for junior members there was little opportunity for influence even within committees. The Congress on the inside seemed no longer to fit the country on the outside.

For some time direct primaries had been the principal method for selecting Democratic and Republican nominees for Congress. But until the late 1950s, the primaries remained the province of the state parties or local party leaders. Any Democrat could enter a congressional primary in Cook County, Illinois, or Queens, New York, or Plaquemines Parish, Louisiana, but only the candidate slated by the local party organization had any chance of winning.

That began to change rapidly as the country moved through the 1960s. The bosses were losing control of their legions. The multitude of interests in new congressional districts made it impossible for any candidate to speak for everyone, and attractive candidates were emerging outside the party organizations to challenge the bosses of the old order. Deeply contentious issues—civil rights, Vietnam, abortion—sent new and unaccommodatable fissure lines through the traditional party organizations.

And a new breed of congressional candidate began to emerge, candidates whom no one had sent.[8] To understand the appearance of these new candidates and the timing of their emergence in congressional politics, we must recall the searing effect that the 1960s and 1970s had on American politics. It was a time when every institution of authority—churches, schools, corporations, the military, and government everywhere—became suspect. Deference to authority of any kind was no longer in vogue; questioning of authority was. Those who challenged the traditional order of things, for whatever reason, found a responsive audience. No scheme, however wild-eyed, was too cockamamie if it promised change, "empowerment," greater personal freedom, or a hotfoot to stodginess.

The challenge first emerged in the civil rights movement. Its leaders sought to turn the powerful instrument of the federal government to their purposes, to use it as a counterweight to racist state and local governments in the South. It was agents of the federal government who confronted Governor Ross Barnett of Mississippi and Governor George Wallace of Alabama when they tried to keep black students from enrolling in their state universities. It was federal troops who stood on the side of racial justice in Little Rock and Oxford. It was the federal Supreme Court that outlawed school segregation. And it was the federal Congress that prohibited the poll tax, voter discrimination, and segregation in public accommodations. None of this was easy, for within the power structure in Washington—and within the old order in Congress especially— the opponents of the civil rights movement were powerful indeed. The proponents of civil rights deemed it essential to challenge the ways laws were made in order to get the laws they sought, to change the rules in order to change the outcomes.

But it was the war in Vietnam that drew the real boundary between the old politics and the new, the point at which trust in government ended and skepticism began. Opposition to the war mobilized a generation not merely to accomplish certain political goals, but also to alter fundamentally the way the country governed itself. The problem, the activists argued, was not just that the federal government was wrong but also that it was morally bankrupt. The emperor had no clothes. The old order was the enemy of the future.

The end of the war did not end the spirit of skepticism or the political activism that the war had generated. The momentum survived and sought new outlets. One of those was national politics; and in the late 1960s the cutting edge of this new political activism, honed in the antiwar and civil rights movements, took on a new enemy: the Democratic Party establishment. The outside strategy turned inward; having fought against the system, the reformers now sought to colonize it.

They flocked first to Eugene McCarthy and then to Robert Kennedy in their campaigns for the 1968 Democratic presidential nomination. When the old rules gave the nomination to Vice President Hubert Humphrey, despite his failure to contest a single primary, the activists made those old rules their next target. In the interim between 1968 and 1972, the Democratic Party nominating process was radically altered. This permitted the new activists to control the 1972 Democratic Convention and to nominate George McGovern, an obscure U.S. senator from South Dakota whose principal appeal was his opposition to the war.

Richard Nixon overwhelmed McGovern in the general election, carrying forty-nine states. But Nixon soon came a cropper in the Watergate scandal. Meanwhile, the Democratic insurgents were beginning to penetrate the political system at other levels. Many of them sought seats in Congress, challenging local Democratic establishments as they had the national hierarchy. Toby Moffett of Connecticut, a former "Nader's raider"; Tom Harkin of Iowa, a legal aid attorney; Gary Hart of Colorado, McGovern's campaign manager, and many like them showed up in Congress after the 1974 election and in a steady stream after the elections that followed.

This was a group unlike the traditionalists they were seeking to replace and, to a significant extent, unlike any previous generation of national politicians. They tended to be young and highly educated. Few of them had much previous experience in government. Almost none had come up through the party ranks. And they were driven not by party loyalty, of which they had little, but by ideology and issue concerns and no small amount of personal ambition. They saw themselves as leaders, not soldiers. They had no interest in merely doing what they were told.

When Watergate destroyed Nixon's presidency and Republican chances in the 1974 congressional elections, the new breed of congressional candidate had a field day. The last few relics of the old Democratic Party system could not keep these rebels from the primaries or beat them there. Wounded Republicans could offer little resistance in the general elections. And when the Ninety-fourth Congress convened in January 1975, seventy-five new Democrats took their seats—26 percent of the Democratic majority. The new Congress was the youngest since World War II, with an average member age under fifty and eighty-seven House members under the age of forty.

The arrival of the class of '74 completed the transition that had begun with the election of 1958 and been accelerated by the election of 1964. The membership of Congress had been almost completely remade in that time. Of the entire congressional membership in 1975, 81 percent of the Senate and 87 percent of the House had not served there before 1958. And they were not just a new generation in Congress. They were a different generation from any that had come before: different in backgrounds, different in reasons for getting into politics, and different in expectations for congressional careers.

The new generation in Congress was distinguished from its predecessors by how hard its members had to work to get there. Because nobody was sending them, they had to begin early and work strenuously to secure a nomination and win election. For many that meant the most arduous kind of day-to-day, door-to-door campaigning. It meant aggressive and relentless fund-raising. And it meant thoughtful development and articulation of positions on a wide range of issues. When parties had dominated the nominating process, candidates had not worried much about any of these matters. Parties had raised the money, run the campaigns, and determined the significant issues, if any. The fading of party control had left these concerns to candidates and made election to Congress significantly more difficult and more expensive than previously.

Those who made it to Congress never lost sight of the hard road they had traveled to get there. And that remembering had two powerful effects on their behavior. First, they had no interest in standing on the sidelines and merely watching Congress at work. They had toiled mightily to get there, and they expected to participate fully in legislative work. Only a fool would expend so much effort for a sinecure, and few of the aggressive activists who came to Congress after 1958 were fools. Second, having labored so hard to get there, nearly all of them intended to stay. The prize of a congressional seat was hard won; it would be hard surrendered as well. All of the advantages of being in Congress would be used to stay in Congress.

What began to occur after 1958 and became the norm after 1970 was a new definition of what it meant to be a member of Congress. When parties controlled the gateways to Congress, many members served at the pleasure of their local party leaders and defined their responsibilities as little more than keeping party leaders at home and in Washington happy. Members did not initiate, they did not rock the boat, they did not knock themselves out relating to their constituents, and they spent little energy on their own elections.

Contemporary members take a view of their role that is almost completely opposite the one that dominated in Congress for much of the twentieth century. They value their independence. They are policy entrepreneurs, seeking out issues that interest them or matter to their constituents and actively proposing legislation or conducting inquiries in those areas. They go back to their districts as often as possible and leave no stone unturned in the search for better ways to serve their constituents. They run for reelection constantly.

Contemporary members are more oriented to their own careers and less to Congress as an institution. They are in their districts as often as they can be and in Washington as little as they have to be. While in Washington, they put in very long, heavily scheduled days. Their offices are scattered over several huge buildings. Members no longer live in the same hotels—most do not live in hotels at all—and they rarely dine or socialize together. In fact, despite lengthening tenure in office, contemporary members barely know one another. They usually communicate with each other through the mail or through staff intermediaries. On busy days there is little time for the clubbiness of the cloakroom or for political talk over drinks at the end of the day. Life is a blur, a constant rush.

Members of the contemporary Congress are driven by the instinct to survive, which seems to require unrelenting effort to be all things to all people—at least all people who are constituents or supportive special interest groups. Political scientist Burdett Loomis argued that members of Congress have responded to this new set of incentives by forming their own individual "enterprises." Combining the resources of their personal office with those they can obtain from their committee, subcommittee, caucus, and party leadership positions, members build small businesses that seek to ensure their political survival and enlarge their personal influence on policymaking. "They have established an issue-oriented, publicity conscious style that differs dramatically from that produced within the seniority-dominated Congress of the 1950s," wrote Loomis. "This style encourages politicians to reach out to national constituencies from a succession of legislative positions that range from subcommittees to party leadership slots and informal caucus chairs. The central elements of the new style include expertise and the willingness to work hard, often at the expense of comity, collegiality, and compromise."[9]

As members grew more self-reliant in getting to Congress, in staying there, and in shaping legislative careers to fit their personal objectives, they became less devoted to their colleagues, their parties, and their institution. Personal staffs and office allowances increased, subcommittees proliferated and grew more independent, substantive caucuses multiplied, and the research and investigative support arms of Congress expanded. More members of Congress could engage more issues with more knowledge than ever before. And they did.

But the parts were at odds with the whole. The collective activity of Congress commanded little commitment from individual members except when it served their individual purposes. The modus operandi became "every man for himself," and Congress at work came to resemble a confederation of independent, self-interested entities. By the 1980s Congress as an institution had become an embarrassment, a political liability, to many members. They sought reelection by running against Congress, often by attacking the very institution in which they wanted to continue serving.

Democracy Congressional Style

It is no surprise that the new members who entered after 1958 found little to like in Congress's procedures and internal organization. To those who sought influence on policy and the ability to act independently, the seniority system that dominated Congress was an obstacle. In the early battles over civil rights, liberals could not get the results they wanted from the relevant committees because conservative Southerners such as Representative Howard Smith of Virginia and Senator James Eastland of Mississippi controlled those committees. Even when civil rights legislation made it to the floor, the filibuster rule in the Senate allowed Southerners to control the debate and the outcome.

Like politicians everywhere who lose power struggles, liberals sought to change the rules. In the House in 1959, they formed the Democratic Study Group (DSG) to serve as the point of the lance in their assault on the old order. As the number of new members grew, the DSG became increasingly important as a forum for discussing ways to reorganize the House. An early call to arms, a book titled *House Out of Order*, was published by one of the most respected of House liberals, Representative Richard Bolling of Missouri. Bolling wrote:

> The state of the House has been revealed—it is a shambles. The Speakership as an institution has become atrophied. Power is dissipated among senior Democratic committee chairmen whose views often do not accord with those of the party majority. . . . Instead of ensuring a more effective legislative team by distributing positions of power equitably among them, [the Democratic leadership] allows key posts to fall to extreme conservatives who use them to block party programs. Key posts are also permitted to go to incompetents who, no matter how well intentioned, do not serve their legislative cause well. On occasion even a Member both arrogant and erratic rises to a committee chairmanship where he gleefully thumbs his nose at President, Speaker, and his own party's majorities.[10]

In the Senate, too, change was in the air, though institutional rules never constrained individual senators as much as their House counterparts. Liberals in the Senate focused their assault first on Senate Rule 22, the filibuster rule. Through every Congress until they finally succeeded in 1975, liberals sought to reduce the number of votes needed to end debate and force a legislative vote. In 1959 in another thrust at tradition, liberals persuaded their new majority leader to adopt what came to be known as the "Johnson rule": All Democrats would get one major committee assignment before any Democrat got a second major assignment. This gave junior senators greater access to the most powerful committees than they had previously enjoyed.

Reform momentum percolated in both houses throughout the 1960s. Subcommittees expanded in number, and more members became subcommittee chairs. As liberals, especially the large blocs elected in 1958 and 1964, became more senior, they began to ascend in the party and committee hierarchy. The election of Presidents Kennedy and Johnson helped overcome or work around some of the institutional barriers that had long deterred congressional liberals. But when Richard Nixon won the presidency in 1968, and Congress became the liberal hope for the foreseeable future, the old order could no longer be tolerated. Change began to erupt in 1970 and would continue throughout that decade and dramatically alter the operations of the national legislature.

For example, throughout the history of the House, it had decided on floor amendments—often the critical votes in shaping legislation—without recording the votes of individual members. That practice essentially ended in 1971 when recorded votes on floor amendments became the norm. The House also implemented an electronic voting system and required for the first time that votes in committee be recorded and made public as well. From 1950 through 1969 the House averaged 126 recorded votes per year; from 1970 through 1989, the average was 515 per year.

Throughout the history of Congress, committees had often conducted their business in secret. That, too, changed in 1973 when Congress required that all committee meetings be open unless a majority of committee members voted to close them to the public. In the decade preceding the change, 39 percent of all committee meetings had been held in secret; in the decade after the change, almost none were.[11]

In 1973 and 1974 a "subcommittee bill of rights" curbed the power of committee chairs to dominate subcommittees and substantially broadened access to positions of influence in the House. The Democratic Caucus was reinvigorated and became a more effective instrument for party control of maverick committee chairs. A new congressional budget act that expanded participation in the budget process and the modification of the "closed rule" that had long protected Ways and Means Committee bills from floor amendment weakened the established power of two of Congress's dominant—and most conservative—committees.

The arrival of the impatient class of '74 accelerated the momentum of reform. "We were such a large class," said one member, Representative Henry A. Waxman, "and so determined to be independent and to make a difference. We wanted to make sure the seniority system wasn't absolute and . . . progressive legislation could move." "There was a robust feeling in the group," said Representative Floyd Fithian, another member of the class of '74. And Timothy Wirth of Colorado remembers that "it was a glory time. There was a tremendous sense of mutual mission."

Reform-minded Democrats already in the House saw the new class as manna from heaven. "My God, the reinforcements have arrived," noted Representative Bella Abzug. Recognizing the power in numbers, the new class invited all the incumbent committee chairs to address them in advance of the organizing caucus for the Ninety-fourth Congress. When most refused, the class voted to withhold its support from any chair who failed to appear. Then the barons complied, in a parade of appearances that was one of the strangest spectacles ever to occur on Capitol Hill.

Several—Edward Hebert of Armed Services, W. R. Poage of Agriculture, and Wright Patman of Banking—were unimpressive or patronizing during their appearances. With the new members voting in nearly unanimous opposition, the caucus removed all three from their chairs, an abrupt violation of the seniority system that would have been unimaginable a few years earlier. "That sent a thundershock through this institution," recalled Speaker Thomas S. Foley.[12] It was the clearest possible statement that a new day had arrived in Congress. It was the day the old order died.

The congressional reforms of the 1970s produced four important kinds of changes. First, they decentralized power within the institution.[13] The rigid seniority system was abrogated, and party and committee leaders became more accountable to rank-and-file members. Positions of influence, especially subcommittee chairs, were distributed more widely and more equitably.

Second, individual members gained access to a much greater array of resources. Personal and committee staffs steadily expanded. Congress's research support institutions multiplied and grew. Increased office allowances permitted computerization, multiple district offices, more frequent mailings to constituents, and more trips home. Members acquired the wherewithal to build the independent enterprises that many sought.

Third, the legislative process became more penetrable. Committees lost their hegemony over policy areas as the number of committees and subcommittees expanded, as jurisdictions began to overlap, and as liberalizations of the rules permitted the referral of a bill to multiple committees. Rules changes provided greater freedom for members to debate and amend bills when they came to the floor. In the critical area of national finance, the Congressional Budget Reform Act of 1974 added a whole new layer of committees and more opportunities for review by the full membership to the enactment of the annual budget.

Fourth, public view of the operations of Congress was greatly expanded. The old Congress did much of its business in secret. Committee meetings were often closed to the press and public. Votes on the floor were usually recorded only on final passage of a bill. Members bore no burden to disclose their personal finances. And no cameras or recording devices were permitted in either chamber. All of that changed in the 1970s, and Congress began operating almost entirely in the sunshine. Closed committee meetings became a rarity. Recorded floor votes became the norm. Members were required to make annual financial disclosure. And in 1979 the television cameras were turned on in the House chamber.[14] A member of Congress who had fallen asleep in 1970 and reawakened in 1980 would have hardly recognized the place.

Divided Government

Members were not just reforming Congress to alter the structure of power within it. They sought as well to alter the balance of power between Congress and the presidency.

After the 1954 elections, divided government—one party controlling the White House, the other ruling Congress—became a common condition in American politics. From 1901 through 1954 the same party had controlled the White House and both houses of Congress in forty-six of fifty-four years, or 85 percent of the time. From 1955 through 1996 that pattern obtained for only fourteen of forty-two years, or 33 percent of the time. During most of these years the Republicans controlled the presidency and the Democrats, Congress. Both parties adapted to this new pattern by enlarging and fortifying the influence of the branch in which they dominated.

What occurred after 1968 was an unprecedented effort by Congress to alter the balance of power between the two institutions. In the mid-1970s it passed the War Powers Act to limit the president's authority as commander in chief, the Impoundment Control Act to reduce presidential discretion over federal spending, and the Foreign Military Sales Act to limit presidential freedom to sell weapons abroad. Congress added dozens of legislative veto provisions to new laws, thereby requiring congressional acquiescence in what had previously been areas of executive discretion.[15] The Senate toughened its standards for confirmation of presidential appointees. Congress delved ever more deeply into the details of government administration, raising constant presidential complaints of "micromanagement." And for only the second time in American history, the House moved close to impeaching a president—a president who avoided formal impeachment only by a timely resignation.

About these developments, political scientists Benjamin Ginsberg and Martin Shefter wrote:

> As the Democratic and Republican parties have developed bastions in different institutions and sectors of government, the character of American politics has been transformed. Intense institutional struggles have increasingly come to supplant electoral competition as the central focus of politics in the United States. Conflicts over the budget and trade deficits, foreign and defense policy, and judicial power that have raged during the Reagan and Bush years can only be understood in the light of these struggles.[16]

These changes only exacerbated the problems that a divided government poses in a system of separate institutions and shared powers. Congress has always struggled to develop effective, internal sources of leadership. Success has been rare. In the first half of the twentieth century, and in brief flashes thereafter, bold initiatives by presidents have filled the leadership vacuum in Congress. Congressional party leaders in this century have always functioned more effectively as lieutenants for presidents of their party than as generals trying to lead their own armies.

When the same party controlled the White House and Congress, Congress was capable of vigorous, even coherent legislative activity. We need only review the legislative process at work when Teddy Roosevelt was president in the first decade of this century or Franklin Roosevelt in the fourth or Lyndon Johnson in the seventh to understand that dynamic.

But Congress has never shown much inherent capacity for leadership or coordinated program development without external guidance. When party control is split between the branches, not only is such guidance absent, but also the congressional majority finds itself pursuing its own disjointed initiatives, seeking to direct a government whose administration it does not control. This dynamic cannot work. And it often results—as recently with Nicaragua, abortion, and civil rights—in not one government policy but two.

Yet another costly consequence of divided government is that it generates constant bickering between the president and Congress. The president seeks political advantage by blaming Congress for the ills of the country. Members of the congressional majority attack the president in return. The steady accumulation of such attacks weakens and denigrates both institutions in the eyes of the country. It is hard to admire a president when members of Congress stand before television cameras every day to heap abuse on him. It is hard to admire Congress when the president travels the country bashing it for its failure to pass his program and for the peccadilloes of a few of its members.

The Fossilization of the Congressional Parties

When Carl Albert became Speaker of the House in 1971, he fully expected to play the kind of important leadership role his predecessors, Sam Rayburn and John McCormack, had. But it was not to be. The House was changing rapidly, and neither the congressional parties nor their leaders would ever be the same. After three perplexing terms in a job vastly different from the one for which he had prepared, Albert retired quietly to Oklahoma.

The changing times were reflected not only in the power struggles I have already described but also in the ideological characteristics of the parties. In both houses of Congress in the 1960s, both parties had conservative and liberal or—as the Republicans called them—moderate wings. John Stennis and Mendel Rivers cohabited with Phil Burton and Ted Kennedy in the Democratic Party, Ed Brooke and Ogden Reid with Barry Goldwater and Bill Dickinson in the Republican Party.

In fact, for much of the postwar period party labels were not a very accurate road map to the ideological fissure lines in Congress. Controversial votes often produced a split between the liberals in each party, on one side, and the so-called conservative coalition, on the other. The conservative coalition was composed primarily of Republicans and southern Democrats, and it was an important ideological bloc in Congress in the decades before 1980. Party voting—that is, votes in Congress on which a majority of Republicans were on one side and a majority of Democrats were on the other—reached an all-time low of 27 percent in the House and 35 percent in the Senate in 1970.[17]

But then the effects of the Voting Rights Act, of reapportionment and demographic change, began to be felt. The old southern barons of Congress began to retire, die, be deposed, or moderate their views as their constituencies changed. They were replaced by very conservative Republicans in some cases and by moderate Democrats in others. Reapportionment in the North weakened the upstate rural areas that had produced the bulk of the moderate Republicans. In places like the North Shore of Massachusetts and the "thumb" of the Michigan peninsula, districts that had long been safely Republican were suddenly represented by Democrats, often quite liberal Democrats.

The impact of this rearrangement was a gradual increase in ideological homogeneity within each of the congressional parties. By the late 1970s party voting was on the rise. The election of Ronald Reagan as president and the emergence of Thomas P. O'Neill Jr., Reagan's ideological opposite, as Speaker of the House vastly accelerated that trend. With the parties in Congress becoming more ideologically distinct and with Congress and president facing each other across a genuine ideological divide, party voting rose to unusually high levels in both houses: to 57 percent of all roll-call votes in the House and 46 percent in the Senate during Ronald Reagan's second term.

Under different conditions this trend might have helped compensate for other changes then taking place in the federal government. Democratic theorists have long regarded unified, ideologically coherent parties as indispensable instruments of collective action. Such parties can develop agendas, push programs, construct majority coalitions—in a word, they can get things done. But in the period from 1973 through 1992, as the congressional parties were becoming more ideologically distinct, the country was also experiencing an extended period of divided government in which the president's party was almost always in the congressional minority. Under those circumstances, increasing party unity in Congress undermined, rather than enhanced, collective action. Presidents had greater sustained difficulty than previously in finding support for their programs in Congress.

It is revealing to compare changes in party unity in Congress with variations in presidents' success rates in securing congressional approval for their programs. Party unity scores in Congress were 10 percent higher

overall in the 1980s than in the 1970s; but presidential victories on legislative votes declined from 67 percent in the 1970s to 60 percent in the
1980s. Since defeat in one house is all that is needed to deter a president's
program, the pattern is even more apparent when we look solely at the
House of Representatives. Average party unity scores in the House increased from 75 percent in the 1970s to 81 percent in the 1980s.
Presidential victories, however, declined from 66 percent of all votes on
which the president took a position in the 1970s to 45 percent in the
1980s.[18]

Instead of the coordinated implementation of programmatic objectives
we would expect of ideologically congruent legislative parties, the outcome in these two decades was inefficiency, discord, constant bickering,
and few bold policy initiatives. Legislative comity was in short supply.
Presidential vetoes became a larger part of the legislative process than
had ever occurred in American history. And the mutual finger-pointing
and name-calling between president and Congress invited and received—and deserved—a Bronx cheer from the American people.

CONGRESS IN ACTION

All of these changes in the elements of Congress—its members, committees, rules, parties, and relations with the president—have altered its behavior as an institution. And because the legislature is the heart of any
democracy, changes in congressional behavior have modified the entire
pattern of self-government in the United States.

Nobody wanted the kind of congressional activity I am about to describe. It had no advocates before occurring and has had few defenders
since. Yet these patterns have become the warp and woof of the legislature, accepted by members themselves—indeed, shaped to fit the career
incentives of individual members—and they will be difficult to alter. The
contemporary character of congressional action is likely to be with us for
a long time to come.

Legislative Politics as Media Symbolism

A stark realization soon confronts anyone who visits the office buildings
on Capitol Hill these days: Congress is a media encampment. Small
crowds gather under bright TV lights as members are interviewed outside committee rooms. TV trucks with their large concave antennas park
on the streets outside. Young staff members scurry through hallways carrying armloads of audio- and videocassettes. TV and radio studios proliferate in the basements. Interns spend hours mailing press releases to
district newspapers. Members line up at the beginning of each day for

their one-minute speeches and at the end for "special orders," the self-presentations that C-SPAN will carry to millions of cable viewers nationwide and into their own districts especially.

Making news is now a very important component of every member's daily routine. It is a principal way in which many members get what they want from their congressional careers: public prestige, internal influence, policy initiation, and—most important—reelection. If we look at a congressional career from inside the head of a member of Congress, it is not hard to understand the importance of the communications media. Nor is it hard to understand the priority that so many members place on trying to manipulate how they are covered and perceived by the media. So much depends on it.

The media are principally important as means for communicating with constituents. Even the smallest House districts now contain almost half a million people. And even the most tireless members are unable to meet personally with more than a small portion of those people in a given year. So members present themselves—some would say, sell themselves—to their constituents through newsletters, press releases published (usually verbatim) in local newspapers, interviews with journalists from the district, and aggressive efforts to appear on local television and radio programs.

The resources available to members of Congress for conducting this sort of self-presentation have expanded dramatically in the past few decades. In 1970, for example, 366 House offices listed no staff member principally responsible for press relations. By 1986 that number had declined to 112.[19] In 1992 it was 70. Both houses have constructed elaborate facilities to accommodate journalists and to permit members to make their own video- and audiotapes. Computers and fax machines generate a steady stream of self-promoting, self-congratulatory reports on members' accomplishments.

A steadily growing cadre of journalists has arrived to consume the stories that members are so happy to feed them. The number of reporters with congressional press credentials doubled between 1968 and 1978 and then doubled again between 1978 and 1988. Today the number exceeds four thousand.[20] Timothy Cook, a political scientist studying the impact of the press on Congress, noted that the relationship between reporters and members has become one of "mutual benefit and limitation. Reporters need the news and the insights House members can provide; members need coverage to further legislative strategies. In effect, making news has become integral to making laws or, as one press secretary commented, 'press work is an extension of policy.'"[21]

As this relationship has grown in importance, as members have become more attuned to how their actions play on the airwaves and in the newspapers, they have increasingly shaped their behavior to fit a set of incentives to which the media are central. And among those, the overarching incentive is survival: to sustain the career they worked so hard to attain. This melding of media attention and individual activity has several notable impacts on the way Congress now functions as an institution.

For one thing, the extent of media coverage and members' enhanced success at manipulating that coverage enables contemporary members to develop images that are distinct from Congress. Many constituents, especially those most likely to vote, have some perception of their incumbent that distinguishes him and her from the rank and file of congressional membership. Members often seek that image by criticizing colleagues and attacking Congress. Members themselves are the media manipulation centers on Capitol Hill; their criticism carries because no one is looking out for, or defending, the collective image of Congress.

When members engage issues, often the most important objective is to be on the right side, not the winning side: to take a position that will play well at home rather than to participate in the bargaining and self-sacrifice that coalition building usually requires. This kind of "position-taking," as David Mayhew of Yale noted two decades ago, is now a commonplace of legislative life. "The electoral requirement," Mayhew noted, "is not that [the incumbent] make pleasing things happen but that he make pleasing judgmental statements. The position itself is the political commodity."[22]

Indeed, members often feel that getting coverage for a position they take or a statement they make is more valuable than getting support for it. Building support requires making deals and compromising and spending long hours in Washington in painstaking and often frustrating negotiation. Even if successful, the credit will often go to someone else. And the opportunity costs in time away from constituent service and away from the district are high. There are members of the contemporary Congress who undertake these efforts in spite of the costs. But their number is not large, and even for some of them legislative policymaking is itself a consciously chosen media strategy.

As the media have become more significant players on Capitol Hill, public image and skill in dealing with journalists have become more important criteria in the selection of party leaders. By and large the congressional party leaders of this century would not fit anyone's definition of mediagenic. Sam Rayburn was small, bald, and often shy in his public appearances. John McCormack was described as a man who always looked like a deal going somewhere to be made. Tip O'Neill so well personified the stereotypical, cigar-smoking Irish pol that Republicans in the early 1980s ran negative congressional campaign ads featuring an actor who closely resembled O'Neill. The newer breed of congressional leaders—Dick Gephardt, Tony Coelho, Newt Gingrich, George Mitchell—

have appealed to the colleagues who elected them in no small part because of their ability to present themselves and their party to a national television audience.

Understandable though this appeal may be, it has changed the order of priorities in leadership selection. Outside media skills, rather than inside coalition-building skills, now prevail, especially in an era of divided government where congressional leaders are often viewed as their party's principal public critics of positions taken by the president. These contemporary leaders surely possess some of the negotiating skills that have long been important for party leaders. But trying to be simultaneously an inside coalition builder and an outside advocate is an extraordinarily difficult juggling act. It is hard to build coalitions, especially across party lines, when one is also required to take firm and clear positions in public. Ambiguity and flexibility are essential in the former but deadly in the latter. The overall effect of these new media imperatives has been a decline in party leadership capacity for legislative coalition building.

The expanding prominence of the pursuit of publicity also inspires an increased emphasis on symbolic and diversionary issues. Members spend large amounts of time on matters of relatively small consequence and small amounts of time on matters of large consequence. The reauthorization of a welfare program or the farm bill or the initiation of new educational initiatives will draw the attention of few members of Congress, whereas votes on abortion or aid to Nicaragua or the Panama Canal treaties will tie up one or the other or both legislative chambers for weeks on end. In the 1980s Ronald Reagan used the media repeatedly to define the Sandinista government in Nicaragua as a major threat to American national security. Congress and the president fought more than a dozen major battles in that decade on aid to Nicaragua. Yet the Sandinista government killed not a single American soldier. During the same decade acquired immune deficiency syndrome (AIDS) made its appearance in America and became an epidemic. It commanded little attention by the president, and discussions of it consumed little time in the Congress. Yet AIDS killed more than one hundred thousand Americans in the 1980s.

What accounts for this apparent misallocation of congressional attention? In large part, it is Congress responding to the symbolic imperatives of a media-driven legislative process. What is important is often dull; what is trivial is often controversial. The limelight follows controversy, and members seek the limelight.

In 1992, for example, the House came perilously close to giving the necessary two-thirds majority to a proposed congressional amendment to balance the budget. Many of those who intended to vote for this bill harbored grave doubts about its wisdom. But in an election year when anti-incumbent fever was running high, when the federal budget deficit approached $400 billion, and when the House itself was in Dutch for a check-writing scandal, a vote in favor of a balanced budget amendment seemed a safe and highly valuable symbolic position—whatever its consequences for future management of the federal economy.

Scandals are yet another kind of diversionary issue made more prominent in recent times by the media on Capitol Hill. Congress is a complex institution with 535 members, more than one hundred committees and subcommittees, dozens of caucuses, and thousands of staff members. It is hard to cover because activity occurs in so many places and often in arcane ways that are difficult to explain. Scandal, however, is a story that everyone can understand and, in Congress, a story about which almost everyone has an opinion. So when even a hint of scandal appears in Congress, reporters flock to the story. All other congressional news takes a back seat as the American people receive their nightly dose of the "latest scandal" on Capitol Hill.

Not surprisingly, this emphasis contributes to an image of Congress as a haven of corruption. Since there is little news about the real work of Congress—about the difficult task of building majorities in the absence of national consensus and with no political party in control of the government—there is little to counter the impression of Congress as a den of iniquity. The media do not contribute to misbehavior on Capitol Hill, but the character of the coverage they provide encourages the view that misbehavior is the norm.

Michael Robinson, a student of television's impact on politics, broadened description of this phenomenon into what he called the First Law of Videopolitics: "Television alters the behavior of institutions in direct proportion to the amount of coverage provided or allowed; the greater the coverage, the more conspicuous the changes."[23] Of course, it is not television alone but all media activity that has altered the character of Congress. What was once a semiprivate, intensely personal institution is no longer. Where once members accepted their years out of the limelight as essential to the collective effectiveness of Congress, now members flit in and out of Washington seeking positive media coverage above all else and finding little appeal in the hard inside work of legislating. Serious legislative work is too rarely a good career move. Because of the incentives and opportunities the media create, Congress today is composed of too many members who act like legislators and too few members who legislate.

Retail Coalition Building

The greatest cost of the postwar changes in Congress is the steadily increasing difficulty in building legislative coalitions. Alterations in the kinds of members coming to Congress, the weakening of the national parties, the loss of committee autonomy in both houses, and a prolonged period of divided government have all complicated the task of constructing majorities to enact legislation. The voters who come into brief agreement to support a president or a congressional majority do not stay in place after the election. And there is no working mechanism in contemporary American politics to glue these electoral coalitions together. Not surprisingly, the ad hoc nature of legislative coalitions in Congress reflects the fluid character of political coalitions in the electorate. Former Speaker Thomas P. O'Neill Jr. noted that "in spreading the power, we now have 152 subcommittees, each with its own staff, each one trying to make its chairman look good. And it's just hard as hell to put the pieces together and put legislation through. . . . The party discipline isn't there."[24]

As a result, legislative coalitions are usually temporary and fleeting, constructed not of blocs or factions but of hundreds of individual parts. This is the hardest kind of coalition building known to humans. And as we have seen with regularity in the past two decades, it often fails. Even when such coalition building succeeds, it does so at high cost to the substantive integrity and rationality of public policies.

More and more in recent years, congressional coalition building has moved out of the committee rooms and onto the floor of the House and Senate. Committees no longer contain and channelize conflict in Congress. The partitions are down, and conflict spills out everywhere. More issues overlap multiple committee jurisdictions than ever before. Access to floor debate and amendment, especially in the House, has been broadly expanded. Members represent ever more heterogeneous constituencies and are thus interested in a wider range of issues.

To a growing degree, coalition building in the modern Congress is amendment politics. It is often played out on the floor of Congress, where battles are more participatory, more public, and more bruising than they were behind the closed committee doors of the past. The forging of the agreements necessary to build coalitions is further complicated by the involvement of staff as the primary negotiators. More layers of bargaining simply take longer to resolve.

The shift to retail coalition building has had at least two worrisome consequences. One is its cost. Building coalitions piecemeal is not only more difficult than the alternatives but also more expensive. Members join a coalition when there is something in it for them or, more often, for their constituents. Members are most likely to support those programs that provide visible benefits for at least some of the people they represent or that shift the costs of new programs to other segments of the population or to other generations. When the Bush administration proposed a savings and loan (S&L) bailout plan in 1989 that imposed a fee on S&L

depositors, for example, it could not find a majority in Congress. The S&L industry had broad support on the Hill and hated the depositor's fee. The administration then proposed a new plan that financed the bailout with an estimated $150 billion in general tax revenues. Although there was no offsetting tax increase and the bailout would thus substantially increase the federal deficit, this version of the bailout passed.[25] Members joined the majority when the costs of the policy were shifted from their constituents (and the S&Ls, an important source of campaign contributions) to future generations.

A second consequence of the emergent pattern of retail coalition building is that it inevitably contributes to ambiguity and dispersed accountability in new laws. To avoid controversy or overcome opposition, proponents write legislative language that is inoffensive or that lends itself to a variety of interpretations. Often, responsibility for specific definitions or interpretations is delegated to executive agencies or left open to judicial interpretation.

To mitigate the conflict that threatens passage of legislation, members of Congress employ ambiguous language and postpone important decisions. But then the battles first fought in Congress must be fought again in the agencies and then later still in the courts. Closure is never accomplished. Policy battles rage on for years. Those affected by public policies must endure years of uncertainty about just what those policies are. And they respond, as we saw in Chapter 3, by spending large sums to defend their interests across the multiple battlegrounds that have now emerged in government.

Political Bypass Operations

Gridlock in Congress has yielded one other, very significant consequence. With growing frequency and ingenuity, government leaders have sought to insulate complex decisions from politics. The goal has been to narrow the scope of conflict by putting decisions outside the normal legislative channels.

One technique for doing this is what some have called "automatic government." Decisions are made once and then altered automatically, usually by formula and on some fixed timetable. Most of the welfare programs in the federal budget, for example, now take the form of mandatory entitlements. Means tests or other qualifying standards are established in the original legislation, and then the annual costs of the programs are determined not in the yearly appropriations process, where political pressures abide, but in a summing up of the funds owed to all of those who are entitled to them under the law.

Those who meet the qualifying low-income standards, for example, are entitled to receive food stamps. The number of recipients varies from year to year, dependent not on legislative appropriations decisions about the amount of money to be made available, but on the accumulated needs of all of those who qualify for the food stamp benefits to which they are entitled under the law. The demand, not the supply, determines the level of government effort.

"Indexing" of programs has accomplished the same objective of avoiding legislative fights over how much to spend on programs. From the time of enactment in 1935 until 1972, social security benefit levels were debated by every Congress. No matter what level was finally established, some members were attacked politically for opposing sufficient increases for the elderly. To avoid the conflict endemic to these biennial debates, Congress altered the mechanism for determining benefits by tying them to changes in the cost-of-living index (hence the term "indexing"). Now benefits change each year as determined by the cost-of-living formula without any need for political decisionmaking. Indexing is also used to determine benefit levels for such programs as Medicare, unemployment assistance, veterans' compensation, and most government pensions. About 33 percent of federal spending and nearly 90 percent of all federal government payments to individuals are indexed.[26]

When faced with especially thorny political issues, Congress in recent years has turned with greater frequency to extraconstitutional mecha nisms. The intense debate over the future of the social security system was turned over in 1981 to the bipartisan National Commission on Social Security Reform, whose key members later met in secret and at some distance from the political forces swirling around the issue. It made recommendations that Congress followed closely in enacting a social security rescue bill in 1983.

Later in the 1980s when Congress could not decide which military bases to shut down, it created yet another bipartisan panel to study the question. And Congress agreed when creating the panel that its recommendations would be voted on as a single package with no amendments permitted. The Pentagon had been trying to close down bases for a decade or more but had always encountered the insurmountable congressional opposition of members in whose districts or states those bases were located. There being no way to build majorities under those conditions, the only way to accomplish the objective was to end run the political process. The bipartisan commission approach helped do so.

The cataclysmic battle over the federal budget in 1990 was similarly resolved not in Congress's elaborate budgetary process but in a summit of legislators and presidential aides held in secret at Andrews Air Force

Base. The summit produced an agreement that attracted little affection, but it did produce an agreement. That, at least, was more than Congress had been able to do through normal channels.

All across the political landscape in the 1970s and 1980s, these political bypass operations took place. Some of them were action-forcing mechanisms, such as the War Powers Act, the Congressional Budget Reform Act, the Impoundment Control Act, and the Gramm-Rudman-Hollings Balanced Budget and Emergency Deficit Control Act of 1985, which was designed to force an outcome where Congress had no collective will to produce one. Some operations were efforts, through mandatory entitlements, permanent authorizations, and indexing, to reduce the frequency of controversial decisions. Other operations, such as the social security and base closing commissions just described, sought to remove intensely political choices from the political arena. But the ultimate purpose in each case was the same: to tame overwhelming political forces by shielding decisions from the full impact of those forces.

It seems odd that the new breed of members of Congress, survivors of tough electoral battles and deeply interested in policy and ideology, would surrender legislative discretion over such important policy questions. That they have done so—and have done so with increasing frequency—is a clear measure of Congress's contemporary incompetence to perform its principal function: to legislate in the national interest.

The consequences of this abdication are widely apparent and dire. Government authority flows from the most democratic branch, Congress, to the least, the courts and the bureaucracy. The status quo becomes even more difficult to change, even—as in the case of huge budget deficits—when it commands no support anywhere on the political spectrum. And the policy focus contracts even more inevitably to the nearest available horizon, away from the long term. The temporary fix is often the only feasible action for a Congress without leadership, without consensus, and without penalty for failure.

CONCLUSION

The past several decades have produced a radical transformation of Congress. There has been a decentralization of internal authority: to subcommittees in the House and to individual members in the Senate. The Senate has become a kind of federation of 100 sovereign entities. As party leadership structures have expanded, leadership capacity has diminished. Congress has no head and no central nervous system. It can neither determine nor follow a sense of direction. The parts get stronger as the whole gets weaker.

The modern Congress has become less and less capable of effective collection action. And collective action—the aggregation of conflicting interests, the construction of majority coalitions, the pursuit of national policy objectives—is the primary task of a legislature. Congress is like a crew shell with strong rowers and no coxswain. The rowers stroke powerfully, but they do not go anywhere. There is no one to call the cadence or handle the tiller—So much motion, so little real movement.

In 1995 the performance of Newt Gingrich, the first Republican House Speaker in four decades, caused some commentators to reassess the capacity for leadership in the modern Congress. Gingrich handpicked the committee chairs and held his Republican majority together on many votes. But the long-term prospects for a revival of strong party leadership are not very promising. Republican committee chairs, like the Democrats they succeeded, will soon become accustomed to power and resistant to challenges, even from their own party leader. Rank-and-file Republicans will soon confront the dominant demands of reelection as constituents, like so many pied pipers, lure members away from the thrall of party loyalty. All of Gingrich's talent and boldness will be sorely tested not only by the realities of modern congressional dynamics but also by the constraints of a broader political context that provides few external supports for domineering congressional leaders.

In some ways, of course, Congress is a highly competent institution. One test of an institution is the caliber of people it draws to service. The contemporary Congress has perhaps the most talented membership in its history. The members are bright and hardworking. They have ideas and great energy. And they are well staffed and well supported in their work in Congress. This, and probably this alone, accounts for the success of Congress in fending off envelopment by the executive branch—a fate that has befallen many democratic legislatures in the postwar world.[27] This situation, of course, produces a peculiar paradox: Congress gets less competent as its members get more competent. And in some ways it produces the worst of all possible outcomes: a Congress that cannot be bossed from the outside but also cannot be led from the inside.

This new Congress is also terrific at one form of responsiveness: direct constituent and district service. Contemporary senators and representatives have organized their own time, structured their staffs, and employed the technological marvels of the age to produce something akin to instantaneous and nearly perfect communication with the people they represent. No ward healer ever had a better feel for his people, better ways to serve them, or greater likelihood of securing their gratitude and support than does the modern member of Congress. These smart, energetic, ambitious members have built a spectacularly successful system for responding to the particularistic needs of their constituents.

In this very important sense, government has come to replace politics. Functions once performed by local political organizations are now performed directly by members of Congress. The middleman has become obsolete. No people in the history of the world ever had a legislature more sensitive and responsive to their individual needs than the American people in the last decade of the twentieth century. It is not surprising, indeed it is only rational, that Americans keep reelecting their own representatives even as they scorn their Congress. Members serve them well; Congress does not.

But there is a high price to pay for this kind of Congress, whatever protection and service it might provide to our individual needs. Virtually all of the post-1958 changes have made interest aggregation more difficult and legislative policymaking more complex. As Harvard political scientist Morris Fiorina noted, "Through a complex mixture of accident and intention we have constructed for ourselves a system that articulates interests superbly but aggregates them poorly."[28]

The problem is compounded by yet another prominent development of the time. At precisely the time Congress was becoming more responsive to and more permeable by particularistic interests, the number and sophistication of those interests were expanding rapidly. We explored the interest group explosion in Chapter 3. And we saw there that thousands of new interest groups formed and descended on Washington in the years following 1958.

In a system that was open to those interests, staffed by members who wanted their money for their own campaigns, this proliferation of groups could produce only system overload. And that is precisely what occurred. We need only stand outside the meeting room of a congressional committee marking up important tax or trade or agriculture or energy legislation to sense the impact of this change. The hallways are crowded with well-dressed, aggressive lobbyists hanging on every turn of phrase, every factor in every formula, trying to get the best deal they can for the interests they are so well paid to represent. To the extent that legislative policy gets made at all, it often happens here in "Gucci Gulch,"[29] not in the White House, not in meetings of national party leaders, not in some small office where congressional oligarchs gather, and certainly not in national elections.

But the most frequent product of this altered legislature is nothing at all. As more and more interests have poured in to clog a system that has become more hospitable to them, less legislating gets done. Because it is so hard to broker and forge agreement among so many conflicting interests, because the national interest becomes in this environment almost totally evanescent, members turn their attention elsewhere. They seek personal satisfaction and career security in constituency service, position taking, investigations, and publicity generation. Congress is busier but less productive. More bills are introduced, more hearings are held, more days are spent in session, but fewer laws are enacted. Members work harder, do more, and accomplish less—at least less national legislation—than ever before.

We should not be surprised, for this pattern fits members' individual incentive structures almost perfectly. In a Congress where the strongest instinct is for survival, legislating is nearly irrelevant for career maintenance. Few members ever win reelection for their success as legislators; few ever lose their seats for their failures as legislators. Congress has come to be populated by a style of legislator unlike any previous generation. They are less amenable to compromise, more driven by issues, less experienced in the ways of legislatures, and more independent than their predecessors. There is among them, as Alan Ehrenhalt noted, "no culture of self-sacrifice."[30] Their individual triumphs more than compensate, in their own minds, for their collective incompetence.

The contemporary Congress suffers the effects of a kind of political jujitsu. Members, to protect themselves from each other, have become stronger and more resourceful. But as the parts have become stronger, the whole has become muscle-bound and immobile. No rational person would have designed such a legislature. No democratic theory suggests a role for a legislature that is far better at obstruction than coalition building. No other democratic country has such a legislature.

The modern Congress is the product of changing demographics and external political forces and of well-intentioned but ultimately uncontrolled reforms. A series of small changes over several decades has added up to a cataclysm for the American people. They have produced a Congress that nobody wanted and a Congress that virtually everyone, even its own members, has come to hate.

THE SISYPHEAN
PRESIDENCY

March 5, 1933.　Day one, new president. The ceremonies are over. The echoes of a stirring inaugural address have faded. It is time to govern. What did the opportunities look like to Franklin D. Roosevelt on that day?

Although it was a time of great national crisis, most Americans did not expect the new president to fix their broken economy or provide widespread relief for the suffering it had caused. The federal government was then, as it had always been, a small enterprise. Its total spending in 1933 was only 8 percent of the nation's domestic product. Americans were not accustomed to receiving benefits from the federal government, and most of them paid no direct taxes to Washington. By the standards of our own time at least, the expectations that fell on the new Roosevelt administration were very modest.

But Roosevelt had opportunities to do something about the national crisis. The coalition that elected him—the New Deal coalition, it came to be called—survived the election. Its component groups had a stake in his success and would continue to support him in the months ahead. The Seventy-third Congress elected with him in 1932 was overwhelmingly Democratic, with majorities of 60–35 in the Senate and 310–117 in House. And it was a Congress capable of action, with potent party leaders and committee chairs who could deliver votes. Many of its members had been at the Chicago convention where Roosevelt had been nominated, they shared his views, and they knew that their political fates were tied closely to his. Many had ridden the new president's coattails to Washington and were happy to declare, without shame or reluctance, that they were "New Dealers."

Politics in Washington was not very complicated. Congress was manageable. There were few special interest groups with headquarters or representatives in the city. International issues rarely crossed the national agenda or distracted the president. The press corps was tiny, its posture was not especially adversarial, and its members were meager and tame; none thought Roosevelt's paralysis worthy of comment or illustration.

The White House staff and the executive branch were still quite small and flexible. Roosevelt had most of his important appointments completed at the beginning of his term, and he was able—without the impediment of ethics rules, a cantankerous Senate, or stringent personnel restrictions—to bring bright young people to Washington and fit their talents to the demanding tasks the nation faced.

"This nation asks for action and action now," Roosevelt said in his inaugural speech. And action there was. The president's proposal to rescue the country's closed banks passed the House and Senate on the day it was introduced and was signed by the president in the evening. That passage was followed in quick succession by an economy bill, a farm bill, the Civil Conservation Corps, the Tennessee Valley Authority, the Home Owners' Loan Act, the National Industrial Recovery Act, and many others—all within a few months of Roosevelt's inauguration. The force and meaning of his election victory were quickly translated with the support of his co-partisans in Congress into sweeping new legislation for the country.

January 21, 1993.   Day one, new president. On the side of Bill Clinton's desk in the Oval Office was a bust of Franklin Roosevelt, one of the newly installed president's heroes. Clinton had Roosevelt's old job and lived in the house where Roosevelt had lived for twelve years. But the job Clinton held, the nation he led, and the opportunities he confronted were dramatically changed.

Clinton was a minority president. In a three-way race, he received only 43 percent of the votes cast. Forty-five percent of the eligible adults did not vote at all. Clinton actively campaigned for more than a year. To win the Democratic nomination, he had to compete in thirty-seven primaries and fourteen caucuses. Throughout the campaign he was followed by a corps of reporters who watched and often commented on what he did and what he said. Some of the country's best investigators dug into every aspect of Clinton's past. Nothing was off limits: not his family, not his travels and socializing as a college student, not his marriage, not any aspect of his character or private life. So constant and bright was the light peeking into the corners of his life that his victory bore little evidence of broad or deep popular support.

The Congress that Clinton faced was a very different kind of legislature from the one with which Roosevelt had dealt. Clinton had gained a higher percentage of the vote than the House winner in only five congressional districts; virtually no one in Congress had come to town on his coattails. Most members had had little to do with his campaign or his nomination, and none had sought to closely tie their campaigns to his. The 103d Congress was a body composed of independent politicians, highly resistant to the clarion call of party or president.

Awaiting Clinton in Washington was an enormous press corps and journalistic industry. His every public step and public utterance would be recorded for broadcast somewhere. Reporters and columnists would mull over every action he took or failed to take. He would be the main subject of dozens of TV talk shows and the main brunt of every TV comedian's jokes. For the thousands of people who made their living writing or telling stories, the new president was new meat.

Clinton had a full agenda for action on January 21. But few people were in place to help him get it moving. Because of the elaborate formalities of the appointment process, it would take months for most of his appointees to get confirmed. The White House staff was much larger than Roosevelt's but more bureaucratic and less flexible. The relationship between the executive branch and the Congress was a tangle of Gordian knots, and the bridge of political party that had once helped connect the two institutions was badly deteriorated.

Clinton's agenda was cluttered with scores of issues that had never crossed the national consciousness when Roosevelt took office. Many of them were international issues that reflected America's postwar status as a world superpower. Some, such as family leave and gays in the armed forces, resulted from changes in American lifestyles. Others grew out of the scarcities of land, water, energy, health care, and other essentials that demanded government solutions.

Many of these issues waited for Bill Clinton because solutions had eluded his predecessors. In a Washington characterized by weak political parties, an atomized Congress, a constant proliferation of potent special interests, an intense glare of media publicity, and a steadily escalating set of expectations imposed on the federal government, the new president's opportunities were tightly circumscribed by the enormity and complexity of the tasks he faced and the insufficiency of the support he possessed and the resources he commanded. To the clear-eyed among Clinton's advisers, the situation he faced was not a pretty sight.

The American presidency was radically transformed in the years between Franklin Roosevelt's first inaugural and Bill Clinton's. It became an institution, not merely a person. It came to bear the burdens of a complex new array of governmental and political responsibilities. And the president became the focal point of national attention. How all that came about and what it means are the topics of this chapter.

THE MAKING OF THE POSTWAR PRESIDENCY

Anyone familiar with the presidency that emerged from World War II has difficulty imagining the premodern version of that institution. The contemporary presidency is so different from its ancestry that no simple process of evolution can explain its development. The role of the chief executive in late-twentieth-century American political life and the nature of the institution the president inhabits are radically transformed from the office so briefly defined in the Constitution and from the modes of leadership provided by those presidents who preceded Franklin Roosevelt.

Of most pre–New Deal presidents little was expected. The government they led was tiny, its resources scarce, its obligations limited. Most of the important functions of government—schooling, commercial regulation, support of an infrastructure, enforcement of the law—were state and local responsibilities. Washington was a long way off, and the decisions made there were peripheral to the lives of most Americans. And most of the decisions were made by the Congress with little leadership or intervention from presidents. Foreign affairs were just that: foreign affairs. America's role in the world remained largely as George Washington had stated it in his farewell address, an avoidance of entangling alliances. Surrounded by large oceans and impotent neighbors, America had small need to worry about its national security or to undertake the centralization of authority that threats to national security often require of a country.

A federal government with limited responsibilities could endure presidents of limited talent. And that, in fact, is what often occurred. Many of the nineteenth- and early-twentieth-century presidents were mediocrities, thrust from obscurity as compromises between warring party factions, available to serve because they had little better to do, or filling the vacuum created by the disinclination of the most talented politicians of their time to seek the presidency. So, for example, in the age of Daniel Webster, Henry Clay, and John Calhoun, the likes of Martin Van Buren, William Henry Harrison, John Tyler, Zachary Taylor, and Millard Fillmore resided in the White House.

In fact, except for an occasional war, the pre–World War II presidency offered few opportunities for great national leadership or eminence. For most of our first century and a half, the presidency was filled by ordinary politicians without much to do. Their leadership abilities mattered little, for presidents were little expected to lead. Just a few years before becoming president himself, Woodrow Wilson wrote, "The president . . . is not expected to lead Congress, but only to assent to or dissent from the laws it seeks to enact and to put those which receive his signature or are passed over his veto into execution."[1] During his administration, Wilson rarely spent more than a few hours a day on the business of the presidency, and most Americans did not realize the magnitude of the stroke that disabled him for his last eighteen months in office. Calvin Coolidge often noted with some pride that he spent eleven of every twenty-four hours sleeping and was often absent from Washington for weeks at a time on lengthy vacations. This behavior seemed to trouble the American people very little; he won reelection with a huge majority in 1924 and probably would have again in 1928 had he chosen to run.

Herbert Hoover was the first president to have a telephone on his desk; Franklin Roosevelt, the first to fly in an airplane. Even the boisterous Teddy Roosevelt could not keep himself very busy in his duties as president. Early each summer he and his family left for Oyster Bay on Long Island, where for several months, "You rowed, you played tennis, you wrestled, you hiked, you chopped firewood, you swam, you shot at a target, and it did not much matter that you were President of the United States as long as the politicians and the reporters left you reasonably alone."[2]

Most of the time, the premodern presidency was a placid and primitive operation. Presidents traveled very little, and it was widely regarded as inappropriate for a president to leave the country during his term. Foreign visitors were rare. The only two foreign heads of state to visit the White House *in the country's entire first century* were the king of Hawaii and the emperor of Brazil.[3] Congress itself was in session for only a few months each year, so even the small amount of work generated by the legislature was a passing distraction. The task of faithfully executing the laws likewise demanded little attention from the president. There were few laws of consequence to faithfully execute. Most of the administrative work was routine and conducted by a few small agencies and departments. Presidents were not directly engaged in the budget process until the third decade of the twentieth century. They made few appointments. The issuance of administrative rules and regulations and of executive orders proceeded at a very slow pace. Presidents often felt heavily burdened by their duties, but it was usually the burden of paperwork and petty details that wore them down, not of legislative bargaining, policy development, or crisis management.

The premodern presidency was also a far less visible office than its contemporary counterpart. More Americans see and hear a modern president in one televised presidential address than heard or saw all the premodern presidents in all of their public addresses combined. This is partly the result of the unprecedented reach of modern broadcast technology. But contemporary presidents also travel much more than their predecessors. They make many more speeches. They are covered by a large and robust press corps.

Until Woodrow Wilson's administration, all of the formal communication between the president and Congress was in writing; presidents delivered no addresses to Congress. Presidents, in fact, were not expected to speak out on much of anything. At Gettysburg Lincoln had second billing after Edward Everett, a leading orator of the time. When Lincoln's successor, Andrew Johnson, was impeached by the House, one of the charges against him was that he was "unmindful of the high duties of his office and the dignity and propriety thereof [and] did make and deliver with a loud voice certain intemperate, inflammatory and scandalous harangues."

Because presidents did not have much to do, they did not need much help. The *presidency* was the *president* himself and not much more. Most of the nineteenth- and early-twentieth-century presidents had a secretary, who was their only staff assistant. The secretary was often a relative whose principal responsibilities were to assist the president in drafting correspondence and preparing certain papers and reports. The early secretaries were paid out of the president's pocket. Later, small sums were appropriated for the secretary's salary. Even when the administrative staff of the president began to grow slightly at the beginning of the twentieth century, virtually all of the White House employees were engaged in clerical tasks. The concept of the White House aide as a political or policy adviser was largely unknown through the first 125 years of American experience.

The first half of the twentieth century did bring some early glimmerings of the post–World War II presidency. President William Howard Taft worried about the efficiency of the federal government and appointed the first of many twentieth-century commissions to study the matter. Its principal recommendation was that a national budget should be prepared by the president and recommended to Congress each year. At that time the president had no formal role or authority in the budget process, and most of the cabinet secretaries sent their budget proposals directly to Congress without any central coordination in the executive branch. The commission also recommended the creation of a small, professional budget office to help the president manage the national budget. Congress had little affection for this recommendation and did not immediately act on it. Only a decade later, after World War I had put a severe strain on national finances, did Congress pass the Budget and Accounting Act of 1921, which established a national budget and the Bureau of the Budget to superintend its preparation and implementation.

The president's staff did grow slowly during the early decades of the century. In 1929 Congress permitted the president to hire three secretaries instead of just one, and this enabled Herbert Hoover to divide the labor among his three top assistants. He was the first president, for example, to have a press secretary. Wilson had begun the pattern of hiring secretaries with some political experience. Wilson's top aide, Joseph Tumulty, had once served in the New Jersey legislature and had been a political adviser to Wilson when the latter served as governor of New Jersey. Harding and Coolidge followed suit, also appointing personal secretaries with political backgrounds. Hoover did as well.

On the eve of the New Deal, the presidency had begun to emerge as an institution larger than just the president himself. But it was still much closer in form and function to its nineteenth-century ancestry than to the extensive operation it would become just a decade or two later. Herbert Hoover was much more of an activist than most of his predecessors, and he had larger staff resources than any of them. But the federal government was still a small enterprise with very few interests overseas. Even after the stock market crash in 1929, Hoover felt circumscribed by the limited authority of his office and the legacy of caution in legislative leadership that he had inherited from his predecessors. "I felt deeply," he wrote, "that the independence of the legislative arm must be respected and strengthened. I had little taste for forcing Congressional action or engaging in battles of criticism."[4] Two years into the Great Depression, he maintained that he wanted "to solve great problems outside of Government action."[5]

It took the depths of a profound economic calamity and a willful disregard for precedent by Franklin Roosevelt to begin the refashioning of the modern American presidency. The onslaught of the first 100 days of Roosevelt's presidency and the early years of the New Deal had many effects. One of them was that the federal government got a lot bigger. It had taken almost a century and a half for the peacetime federal budget to get to $3 billion. It doubled in the first five years of the New Deal and tripled in nine. New agencies sprouted and expanded. Informal advisory organizations were everywhere. Washington went from a quiet backwater to the center of national activity. The trains at Union Station disgorged bright young people by the thousands who came to Washington to fix the country. They were entrepreneurial and creative. Activity was frenetic. And the president in whose name most of this activity occurred had very little control over it. Now that there was much more government to manage, the primitive state of government management capabilities was very much in evidence.

By Roosevelt's second term, it was widely obvious that better management of the federal government was essential and that the capabilities of the president to lead that undertaking had to be strengthened. Roosevelt appointed Louis Brownlow and two other public administration specialists to provide management guidance. The Brownlow Report, issued in 1937, is a watershed in the development of the modern presidency. It called for the creation of a new executive office in which the principal functions of presidential leadership would be centralized. And it recommended an expansion of staff to assist the president in managing those functions. In 1939 Congress went along with much of what Brownlow had recommended, creating the Executive Office of the President (EOP), moving the Bureau of the Budget from the Treasury Department into the new EOP, and providing the president with six new assistants to aid him in his work. Even though some significant development of the presidency had occurred in earlier decades, 1939 clearly was a turning point, the year in which the modern presidency was born.

SHAPING THE MODERN PRESIDENCY

What the New Deal had wrought, World War II made permanent. Big government was here to stay. So, too, was the institution of the presidency at the center of this vastly expanded array of federal activity. Having first looked to Franklin Roosevelt to lead the country out of the Depression, the nation then looked to him to lead the way to victory. As Roosevelt himself put it, "Dr. Win-the-War" was called on to take over for his partner "Dr. New Deal."[6]

In the aftermath of World War II, the modern presidency came to rest on four new and sturdy props: an expansive domestic policy agenda, the cold war, an available technology of mass communication, and a requirement to manage a vast federal government. Each of these contributed to the formation and institutionalization of a presidency that was radically different from the one Americans had known for the first 140 years of their history. The change was rapid, abrupt, and unplanned. It generated new opportunities for government in America. But it also produced a legacy of unsolved and nettlesome problems.

The Domestic Presidency

In the face of the Depression's terrifying threat to economic security, passivity in the presidency was simply no longer acceptable. Herbert Hoover learned that lesson the hard way. The philosophy of limited government could not withstand the realities of massive unemployment, mortgage foreclosures, and business failures. Americans needed hope, and that is what government offered them. If many New Deal policies were misguided, mismanaged, or harebrained, at least the federal government was doing something. "The country demands bold, persistent experimentation," Roosevelt said. "It is common sense to take a method and try it. If it fails, admit it frankly and try another. But above all try something."[7]

New Dealers were not the first Americans to believe in a more active federal government or in more vigorous presidential leadership. The strain of American liberalism flowing through the abolitionists, Populists, and Progressives had always sought a more activist federal government—and federal executive—to counterbalance the conservative policies prevailing in many states. Herbert Croly, a leading intellectual among the Progressives, had written, "Anything which undermines executive authority in this country seriously threatens our national integrity and balance."[8]

But the liberal idea of government as a social and economic counterweight had never taken deep root in a society where commercial interests were the most powerful political forces and rural life and rural values dominated. The crisis of the Depression provided the opportunity, long awaited by liberals, to enlarge and activate government in pursuit of social and economic ends. The New Deal was the beginning of the long liberal hour in American politics. Central to the emergence of a new liberal politics were two important and enduring notions: first, that an activist federal government was essential to serve the interests and protect the rights of all of the people and, second, that an energetic and potent presidency was necessary to shape and build political support for the liberal agenda.

After the war Harry Truman continued much of the thrust of the New Deal in domestic policy. The Employment Act of 1946 gave new legitimacy to the president's role as manager of the national economy and created the Council of Economic Advisers in the EOP to assist the president's efforts to formulate economic policies. Truman pushed as well for new federal policies in atomic energy regulation, hospital construction, civil rights, housing, and airport development. By the early 1950s it had become clear that management of the president's domestic agenda was a task of growing magnitude. Increasingly formalized procedures were established in the Bureau of the Budget for preparation of the annual "program of the president" and "central clearance" of all the program initiatives emerging from federal agencies and departments.

Pre–New Deal expectations had normally been that the president would play a very narrow role in initiating new public policies. There were exceptions, of course, but they were not fundamental alterations in the pattern. British observer James Bryce wrote in 1891 that "the expression of [the president's] wishes conveyed in a message has not necessarily any more effect on Congress than an article in a prominent party newspaper. . . . In fact, the suggestions which he makes, year after year, are usually neglected."[9] A prominent senator of the late nineteenth century, George F. Hoar, said, "The most eminent senators would have received as a personal affront a private message from the White House expressing a desire that they should adopt any course in the discharge of their legislative duties that they did not approve. If they visited the White House, it was to give, not to receive, advice."[10]

By the end of the 1940s, however, those traditional expectations had been turned upside down. Increasingly, the American political system looked to the president for such initiatives. Beginning with the Eightieth Congress in 1947, congressional committees initiated a pattern of "direct referrals," asking the administration for its views before proceeding with legislative action.[11] By 1950 such requests were the norm.

Scholars of national politics watched to see if Dwight Eisenhower would return the presidency to the pre–New Deal status quo. It quickly became obvious that, a few rhetorical flourishes to the contrary notwithstanding, Eisenhower had no desire to diminish the presidency, nor would it have been easy to do so had that been his intent. The country expected Eisenhower to have programs to bring about economic prosperity. Congress sought his leadership on civil rights. Major new initiatives were undertaken during his administration to build a new national highway system, fund expanded opportunities in higher education, open the St. Lawrence Seaway, stabilize farm incomes, and expand the space program. Eisenhower formulated, and in 1956 the American people resoundingly endorsed, a moderate Republicanism that accepted the reality of a large federal government role in American life and the necessity of strong presidential guidance of that role.

Subsequent administrations demonstrated that there was no turning back—in the country and in the presidency—from the legacies of Franklin Roosevelt and his times. The 1960s brought another burst of government expansionism: civil rights regulation, environmental protection, welfare, health care, federal aid to education, economic development, consumer protection, and on and on through a whole host of policy undertakings. The conventional wisdom became that "presidents proposed, Congress disposed." But that was the postwar conventional wisdom only. From the founding of the republic through the end of the 1930s, most presidents proposed only rarely and reluctantly. There were few demands or expectations—in Congress or in the country—that they do so.

As the policy responsibilities of the federal government widened and the burden of expectations on the president for program initiatives expanded, the need grew for greater staff support in these tasks. That resulted in the creation of many new units within the EOP. These varied widely in character and duration. In 1970 Richard Nixon established the Domestic Council to oversee the development of domestic policies. Although its name has changed from time to time, each subsequent president has retained an office to superintend domestic policy development. Presidents have also set up networks of coordinating committees or councils in specific policy areas. Donald H. Rumsfeld, chief of staff for President Ford, noted the place of these in contemporary administrations:

The problems today don't fit the compartments. . . . It is therefore important that the White House serve the President by trying to bring the threads of a given problem toward him in a reasonably coherent way. The Domestic Council, the National Security Council, the Economic Policy Board, and the

Energy Resources Council—these are attempts to take those different domestic or foreign forums, departments, and agencies and their views and
bring them forward to the President in a way that is digestible and work-
able, so that he can make judgments in a timely fashion.[12]

Sometimes to give special energy and visibility to a new area of policy
initiative, presidents have appointed a "czar," or a point person, to direct
policy development. Sargent Shriver led the effort to formulate the Peace
Corps for President Kennedy and then to initiate the War on Poverty for
President Johnson. William Simon was energy czar for President Nixon.
William Bennett was drug czar for President Bush. And Kristine Gebbie
was AIDS czar for President Clinton.

The postwar emergence of the president's role in policy initiation
added new layers of structure and staff to the presidency. It also changed
the historical relationship between the president and the departments
and agencies. The departments were once relatively autonomous creators
and managers of a limited number of federal programs. The agriculture
secretary, for example, bore wide responsibility for farm policy because
the president had few resources for formulating such policy, for coordinating it with the activities of other agencies, or for closely overseeing the
work of the department. Today, much of the initiative for important new
policies has been internalized in the EOP, the work of the departments is
closely monitored and reviewed, and policy coordination is a high—if
sometimes imperfectly achieved—White House priority. Once a passive
and largely reactive participant in domestic policymaking, the postwar
White House has become the nerve center of the federal government.

The International Presidency

With World War II came the second prop of the modern presidency: the
end of American isolationism. Countries at risk are always under pressure to centralize authority. Protection of national security requires the capacity to mobilize and direct national resources against external threats.
The few significant, pre–World War II instances of centralized authority
in American history had all come during wartime: Lincoln's suspension
of certain civil liberties, for example, or the enlargement of the federal
government to fight World War I. World War II brought the greatest expansion of the federal government in American history, the most widely
applied conscription of citizens into the armed forces, a substantial increase in taxes, and widespread government restrictions on the purchase
and sale of consumer goods.

But World War II differed from previous American wars. The threat did
not go away when the war was over. With little pause for joy or comfort,

America moved almost immediately into what came to be known as the cold war. Here the threat was at least as menacing as the one posed by the Axis powers during the war: a large, furtive, mysterious, aggressive, and competent enemy perceived to be driven by an expansionist ideology and equipped with weapons of mass destruction from which America's geographic isolation offered little protection. It mattered little that some of the threat was rooted in ignorance, paranoia, and America's own provocations; the fear of communism was a driving force of American politics for more than four decades after World War II. And Americans looked to their president for protection in the face of that threat. The American people demanded that their presidents be tough and aggressive in "standing up to communism." The words of John Kennedy's inaugural address read now like a presidential anthem of the cold war: "Let every nation know, whether it wishes us well or ill, that we shall pay any price, bear any burden, meet any hardship, support any friend, oppose any foe, in order to assure the survival and the success of liberty." Of no cold war president was less expected.

The cold war presidency required a large standing armed force and vast networks of international and domestic intelligence activities. It mandated that presidents be international leaders, that they travel widely, and that they meet often at home and abroad with other world leaders. For the first time in American presidential campaigns, candidates trumpeted their foreign policy experience and boasted of their toughness in holding the line against foreign aggression. The Franklin Roosevelt of the 1930s was cautious about stirring up the isolationist impulses of the American people with talk of impending war. None of his successors would suffer such reluctance. America's role in the world changed dramatically after World War II, and the presidency changed with it. A better prepared and more vigilant nation required a more potent and better equipped national leader. Americans began to measure their presidents and presidential candidates by their foreign policy views and actions. Expectations were high, and presidents often had to expand and aggressively exercise their powers to meet those expectations.

President Truman persuaded Congress to pass the National Security Act of 1947, which combined the military services under a single cabinet secretary in the Department of Defense. The act also created the Joint Chiefs of Staff as a body of military advisers for the president and established the Central Intelligence Agency, whose director reported to the president, and the National Security Council in the EOP to provide the president with better opportunities to coordinate and direct national security policy. In that same year America began to provide foreign aid to devastated nations of Europe that seemed to be threatened by communist takeover. In 1948 the Marshall Plan gave birth to what became a broad postwar foreign aid program. America turned its back on George Washington's warning about "entangling alliances" and built alliances all over the globe: the North Atlantic Treaty Organization, the Central Treaty Organization, the Southeast Asia Treaty Organization, the Organization of American States. The United States led the way in forming the United Nations and provided the bulk of its budget. All of this occurred in less than a decade, but it was a decade in which new world realities demolished forever the isolationist tendencies that had dominated all of American history before that time.

Equally notable in impact on the presidency was the growth of the military and intelligence establishment. The president's constitutional authority as commander in chief took on broad new meaning when there were millions of troops to command. World War II brought the last formal declaration of war, but the years after World War II brought wars and "interventions" that were almost constant: Korea, Lebanon, Cuba, Vietnam, the Dominican Republic, Cambodia, Iran, Grenada, Nicaragua, Panama, the Persian Gulf, Somalia. American armed forces remained on post around the globe after World War II, American ships sailed every sea, and American spy planes and satellites surveilled every country. At the head of this enormous, ongoing operation was the president of the United States. A new, informal title was attached to the presidency after World War II: "Leader of the Free World." With it came new responsibilities, new powers, and a host of new expectations.

The burdens of the cold war added a dimension to the presidency that, save for fleeting glimpses, had not previously existed. Presidents became diplomats and negotiators. The practice of summitry that began at Potsdam and Yalta became a recurring feature of the postwar presidency. Presidents were expected to be shapers and manipulators of a world order and later of a new world order. Presidents called on their commander-in-chief powers to deploy American troops wherever diplomacy failed, threats arose, or friendly regimes needed propping up. Congress was powerless to do much more than complain about these deployments even after it passed the War Powers Act to limit presidential discretion.

The cold war heightened the president's visibility. Americans paid attention to a president who was keeper of their security. With a nuclear threat always hanging over the country, the federal government was no longer irrelevant or peripheral to any American's interests—nor could anyone easily disregard the person in the White House with the primary responsibility for keeping that threat at bay. More than anything else in American history, the cold war altered the relationship between the people and the president.

The Public Presidency

As presidential responsibilities grew, presidents sought new ways to engage the political community. New expectations to lead required new forms of leadership. Presidential habits and conventions came tumbling down after World War II as the modern presidents centralized in the White House the tasks of leadership that in earlier years had often been performed elsewhere in the political system.

With but few exceptions, the pre–World War II presidents had relied on their political parties to lead and shape public opinion and on the congressional leadership to form legislative coalitions. It was also quite normal in the days before World War II for presidents to enter office with governing coalitions in place—coalitions forged in electoral combat and sustained by party loyalty, patronage, and presidential coattails. After the war political parties deteriorated, Congress decentralized, and elections ceased to be very effective producers of governing coalitions. If presidents were to lead in the steeply changed postwar environment, they would have to take the reins themselves. That is precisely what they sought to do.

They did this by developing strategies for what political scientists came to call "going public."[13] Instead of relying on party and congressional leaders to bear the burden of shaping public opinion and building legislative majorities, presidents became actively involved in these tasks. There had been occasional foreshadowings of this approach in earlier times. Woodrow Wilson's cross-country tour to seek support for the League of Nations treaty and Franklin Roosevelt's Fireside Chats are prominent examples. But these were exceptions to the prewar norm. Even Franklin Roosevelt, whose administration marks a real turning point in the efforts of presidents to relate directly to the American people, warned that "the public psychology . . . cannot be tuned for long periods of time to a constant repetition of the highest note in the scale."[14]

Abetting, perhaps even encouraging, this change in presidential leadership strategies were some important postwar changes in the opportunities available to the modern presidents. When George Gallup decided in 1935 to ask the American people whether they approved or disapproved of the job the president was doing, Franklin Roosevelt took note of the value of the new science of public opinion polling as a potential instrument for presidents. For the first time, presidents might have a reliable and consistent way to answer the question that bedevils all public officials: "How am I doing?" The White House began to poll intensively after Roosevelt's Fireside Chats and to shape the tone and words of his message to elicit a desired response.[15]

Eisenhower's campaign managers used polling in the 1952 election to determine which issues most concerned Americans. When they learned that many Americans, especially independent voters, were troubled by the way the Korean War was dragging on, Eisenhower began to talk about that in his speeches. The response he received inspired an even stronger message: If elected, he would personally go to Korea. These lessons about the value of opinion polling were quickly absorbed by the other postwar presidents, and by the 1970s the presence of public opinion pollsters on the White House staff had become normal. Some of them, such as Pat Caddell (Carter), Richard Wirthlin (Reagan), and Stanley Greenberg (Clinton), became important advisers whose guidance often shaped presidential strategy and behavior.

FIGURE 5.1
Household Use of Selected Media, 1950–1994

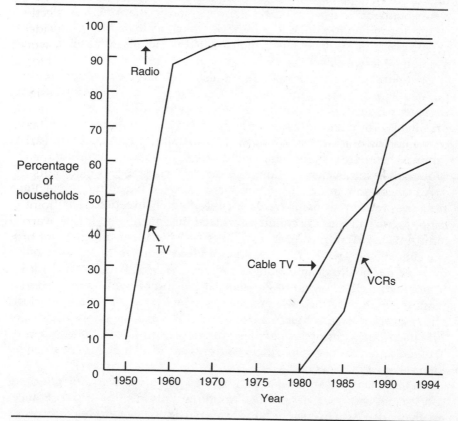

SOURCE: Adapted by the author from data in Harold W. Stanley and Richard G. Niemi, *Vital Statistics on American Politics*, 5th ed. (Washington, D.C.: CQ Press 1995), p. 47.

Emerging simultaneously were other important technologies that greatly enlarged presidential opportunities for going public. First radio became commonplace in American homes, then television. As Figure 5.1 indicates, these new technologies quickly permeated American households.

Television appeared first as a clunky, studio-bound, limited choice, black-and-white medium, exciting primarily for its novelty. The technology developed quickly, however, and by the late 1970s satellites, hand-held minicameras, color, computerization, and cable meant that communications between the president and virtually all Americans had become instant and constant. Within hours of the explosion of the *Challenger* space shuttle in 1986, Ronald Reagan broadcast live to the nation with a message of reassurance. When a coup against the Soviet government occurred while George Bush was on vacation in 1991, he first spoke by telephone to Boris Yeltsin in Moscow and then went out on the lawn in Kennebunkport and reported his conversation to the American people. While attending an economic summit in Tokyo in 1993, Bill Clinton was able to transmit a live, televised message to the victims of massive flooding in the Midwest back home.

Contemporary Americans take these technological wonders for granted. But they represent a remarkable change in the opportunities for presidential leadership. Most Americans before 1920 never heard the president's voice and saw him only in an occasional photograph or line drawing. The president was a distant figure, almost mythological, like a Japanese emperor, before the technology of mass communications brought him into American homes as a nearly constant companion.

Advancements in transportation technology added to the opportunities. The prewar presidents rarely left Washington, except for lengthy vacations. Trips around the country occurred infrequently and trips abroad almost never. Woodrow Wilson was the first president to travel outside the United States while in office. Franklin Roosevelt left the country only once during his first eight years as president. Harry Truman stuck close to home as well. He went to Potsdam at the end of the war for postwar planning with the Allied leaders, and he traveled once to Guam to meet with General Douglas MacArthur. Those were Truman's only trips outside the country during his nearly eight years as president. Roosevelt and Truman were very much like their predecessors in all this: American presidents stayed in America.

An important reason for that pattern was that travel was difficult, time consuming, and often dangerous. Woodrow Wilson's first trip to France for the Paris Peace Conference, for example, lasted eleven weeks. Storms were so heavy on the return trip that much of Wilson's naval escort turned back, and the president's own warship nearly went aground off the New England coast. But when jet engines were attached to airplanes after World War II, new opportunities emerged. With a sleek Air Force One at his disposal, a president could start the day at the White House, give a speech to a labor union convention in Detroit at lunch, visit a defense plant in St. Louis in the afternoon, attend a political fund-raising dinner in Atlanta, and be back in the White House at bedtime. In summer 1993, for example, Bill Clinton jetted to Tokyo for the G-7 economic conference. The trip lasted six days and included stops in Hawaii, Japan, Korea, and several American cities. Contemporary presidential trips are aggressively "advanced" so that every stop and every event are planned to maximize the political benefits of the president's appearance. Every contemporary president's staff now includes an advance office with responsibility for arranging the president's appearances outside the White House.

The mobility of modern presidents is a dramatic change from the immobility—and often the invisibility—of presidents in the past. When the logistical barriers to presidential travel dropped, the political opportunities rose. And as Tables 5.1 and 5.2 demonstrate, presidents hit the road. The postwar presidents did not simply poll more or travel more than their predecessors. They also spoke more often and appeared more often in public. From the presidency of Thomas Jefferson through that of William Howard Taft, no president ever appeared personally before Congress. When Wilson broke the pattern in 1913, he said, "I am very glad indeed to have this opportunity to address the two houses directly and to verify for myself the impression that the President of the United States is a person, not a mere department of government hailing Congress from some isolated island of jealous power, sending messages, not speaking naturally with his own voice—that he is a human being trying to cooperate with other human beings in a common service."[16] His words then seem emblematic of the efforts of presidents now to reach out to the American people, to specific constituencies, and to members of Congress—to appeal to them directly to support the president's objectives and programs. The postwar presidents, whatever their party, whatever their personalities, whatever their ideologies, were all peripatetic, vocal activists. They took to heart Theodore Roosevelt's description of the presidency as a "bully pulpit."

This was a new dimension of presidential leadership. Theodore Roosevelt, like the other prewar presidents, used the bully pulpit infrequently. Franklin Roosevelt, though he traveled and appeared in public and gave speeches more often than all of his predecessors, does not compare on any of those measures with his successors. One study found that "comparing 1945 to 1975, public speeches by America's chief executives increased almost 500%. . . . Jimmy Carter averaged one speech a day during each of his four years in the White House."[17] Although the strategy of "going public" had some slender roots and precedents in the presidents who preceded World War II, it is very clearly a postwar development.

TABLE 5.1
Appearances by Presidents
Outside the United States, 1945–1994

President	Average Number of Days of Foreign Travel Per Year	Average Number of Foreign Appearances Per Year
Truman I	3	2
Truman II	0	0
Eisenhower I	1	2
Eisenhower II	13	29
Kennedy	9	26
Johnson	6	11
Nixon I	9	27
Nixon II	9	14
Ford	14	29
Carter	13	17
Reagan I	9	21
Reagan II	12	13
Bush	24	29
Clinton (through 1994)	31	26

NOTE: Roman numeral after president's name refers to first or second term.

SOURCE: Adapted by the author from Lyn Ragsdale, *Vital Statistics on the Presidency: Washington to Clinton* (Washington, D.C.: Congressional Quarterly, 1996), p. 170.

The emergence of this new dimension placed new burdens on the presidency and contributed to its institutional growth and development. It was quickly apparent that a president who gave frequent speeches would not be able to write most of the words he spoke. Franklin Roosevelt was the first president to rely heavily on speechwriters. Several of his aides and many of his friends contributed to his speeches. Truman followed a similar pattern. By the Eisenhower administration, the speechwriting function had developed a staff locus. Specific staff members were assigned nearly full-time responsibility for speech drafting, and routines emerged for staff review of the president's speeches. In subsequent administrations even more formalization and routinization occurred.

Contemporary presidents now write virtually none of the words they speak. Even so-called spontaneous remarks in the White House Rose Garden and at gatherings of legislators or interest group leaders are carefully scripted. House Speaker Tip O'Neill once lost his temper with Ronald Reagan, for example, over the latter's practice of reading from notecards when meeting privately with legislative leaders.[18] People who wonder why presidents no longer speak with the eloquence of a Lincoln or a Wilson need only look to the character of the modern presidency. Lincoln and Wilson gave public speeches rarely, once or twice a week at most. They had

TABLE 5.2
Domestic Appearances by Presidents
Outside Washington, D.C., 1945–1994

President	Monthly Average of Domestic Appearances	Yearly Average of Domestic Appearances
Truman I	0.7	9
Truman II	1.1	13
Eisenhower I	1.6	19
Eisenhower II	0.9	11
Kennedy	2.8	32
Johnson	3.9	49
Nixon I	3.5	42
Nixon II	1.9	21
Ford	6.3	83
Carter	3.6	43
Reagan I	5.4	65
Reagan II	2.7	33
Bush	5.3	64
Clinton (through 1994)	7.8	94

NOTE: Roman numeral after president's name refers to first or second term.
SOURCE: Adapted by the author from Lyn Ragsdale, *Vital Statistics on the Presidency: Washington to Clinton* (Washington, D.C.: Congressional Quarterly, 1996), pp. 175–176.

few other duties and minimal staff support. They wrote their own speeches because they had little choice and because they had few speeches to write.

The effort of the postwar presidents to go public is also reflected in their wooing of interest group and opinion leaders. Although presidents have always sought to do this in one way or another, the process of connecting the president to specific constituencies has been structured and formalized in the enlarged postwar presidency. Herbert Hoover and Franklin Roosevelt had press secretaries, usually people with backgrounds in journalism who responded to reporters' requests for information. Contemporary presidents have press offices employing dozens of people. Some of them have journalism backgrounds, but many are trained in public relations or communications technology. Their work is pro-active, not merely responding to reporters but seeking to shape or "spin" the news and to create and sustain a positive image of the president.

The press office has become especially important to the modern presidents because the postwar period has been marked by a dramatic increase in the amount and intensity of journalistic coverage of the president. Even in Franklin Roosevelt's time, as national attention turned to Washington, the White House press corps was quite small, barely more than one hundred reporters in the early New Deal. Roosevelt held his press conferences in the Oval Office, with reporters arrayed around his desk. One study of the periodical literature found that Roosevelt averaged 110 stories a year during his entire presidency. That compares with 200 a year for Kennedy, 467 a year for Carter, and 503 a year for the first two years of the Reagan administration.[19]

By the 1990s Washington was a beehive of reporters—more than four thousand print and twenty-four hundred broadcast journalists by one count.[20] The competition for news grew increasingly ferocious, and the president became even more visible as not just a political leader but the country's leading celebrity. It is a rare day when stories about the president do not appear on the front pages of the national newspapers. Study after study has shown that newspaper and magazine coverage of the president has grown steadily in the postwar years.[21] This is not surpris-

FIGURE 5.2
Number of Washington Reporters, 1864–1994

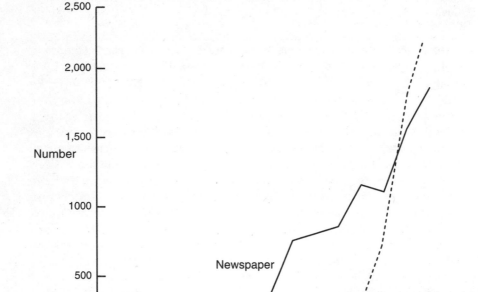

NOTE: Data indicate number of reporters registered with House and Senate press galleries.

SOURCE: Harold W. Stanley and Richard G. Niemi, *Vital Statistics on American Politics,* 5th ed. (Washington, D.C.: CQ Press, 1995), p. 52.

ing, given the dramatic growth in the number of Washington reporters indicated in Figure 5.2.

But the growth in presidential visibility has been most apparent on television. When the national television networks expanded their nightly news broadcasts to thirty minutes in the early 1960s, they also began to station their best reporters at the White House. Even if there was little presidential news on a particular day, there were powerful pressures to give airtime to the star correspondents at the White House. After the Kennedy assassination, no White House reporter ever wanted to be very far from the president. So presidents now travel, even in Washington, with large press entourages. After Richard Nixon converted the indoor White House swimming pool to a press room, reporters encamped day and night just a few feet from the president's office.

The emergence of the three major television networks after World War II changed the terrain of presidential news coverage and presidential communications more broadly. By 1963, 55 percent of the American people reported that they were getting most of their news from television rather than other sources; by 1988 the figure had grown to 65 percent.[22] The message was not lost on American presidents. Nor was the evidence showing that tens of millions of Americans were tuned to their television sets every night of the week. For modern presidents this led to two important conclusions. One was that the best possible way to shape and seek to lead public opinion was to ask the networks for airtime to speak directly to the American people. And this presidents did with increasing regularity. From 1949 through 1984 the presidents of the period in which television was dominated by the three national networks averaged more than five prime-time addresses per year, one every ten weeks for thirty-five years.[23]

The second lesson was that the news reported to Americans by the television networks would play a significant role in shaping perceptions and evaluations of presidential performance. It was therefore critical for the White House to be aggressive in seeking to shape the coverage the president received from journalists and from network television journalists especially. Eisenhower hired an actor named Robert Montgomery to help improve the president's appearance on television. That seemed a unique development at the time. But all of Eisenhower's successors have gone significantly beyond that strategy, hiring coaches and image makers and public relations specialists to help them put their best foot—and best face—forward.

Modern presidents have often been accused by reporters and editors of being manipulative, of trying to manage the news. That, of course, is precisely what they have sought to do. The news, particularly the television news, was critical to the efforts of the postwar presidents to go public in building support for their programs. As much as legislative or administrative success, the character of television news coverage has become a measure for the postwar presidents of "how they're doing." They hire staffs of talented image makers, and they deploy aggressive strategies of news management. And as journalist Sidney Blumenthal wrote, "At the end of the day, they become spectators, seeing their performance tested by the contents of the television news programs."[24]

The postwar presidents have felt compelled to go public because the changing political environment has left them little alternative. The deterioration of political parties, the atomization of congressional operations, and the recurrent inability of national elections to produce enduring coalitions have left contemporary presidents without any other effective prop or mechanism for leadership at precisely the point in history where leadership expectations have reached their peak. What is a president to do? He has made the best of a political situation full of constraints and impediments by seeking to build his own coalitions.

"The American president rule[s] by influence," Arthur Schlesinger Jr. wrote, and the postwar presidents fastened onto that hard reality.[25] However difficult to create and maintain, however complicated to translate into administrative effectiveness and legislative success, public support is nevertheless the only reliable source of influence for a modern president. And so presidents search for the right combination of ideas, words, images, and connections to pull together temporary coalitions to accomplish specific purposes. This is not what the Constitution contemplated, nor is it the path that most prewar American presidents traveled, but in the postwar political climate the search for public support has become the dominant element of presidential activity.

The Managerial Presidency

As the federal government expanded in size and range of functions, pressures grew for the president to manage more effectively what was becoming an enormous enterprise. These pressures were first perceived at the beginning of the century, and William Howard Taft appointed the first of many commissions to seek better ways to administer the nation's affairs. Slowly, the elements of a bureaucratic state began to appear: a civil service, a national budget, specialized management agencies, and an office of the chief executive.

In the postwar period, as the growth in government accelerated, management became a constant headache for presidents. The presidency had been invented in the prebureaucratic eighteenth century. The Framers of the Constitution had little experience in or conception of the problems of administering complex organizations. Twenty years after the ratification of the Constitution, the executive branch of the federal government they created still had fewer than two hundred employees in Washington. Even those agencies that were added to the government in the nineteenth century looked primarily to Congress for guidance on the functions they should perform and the manner in which they should operate. Congress appropriated their funds, approved their requests for personnel, and heavily influenced the choice of their leaders. Presidents had no direct role in the budget process and lacked any of the staff assistance necessary to play a consistent role in overseeing departmental activities. A sense of hierarchy was almost totally absent from nineteenth-century executive branch operations.

That changed slowly in the first half of the twentieth century. The president's role in the budget process was established formally in 1921. Presidential staffs grew slowly. Commissions appointed by Taft and later by Franklin Roosevelt focused attention on the need for better management of the federal government and enhancements of the ability of presidents to perform that task. Postwar pressures added even greater emphasis to government's administrative shortcomings.

In 1947 President Truman appointed the Commission on the Organization of the Executive Branch of the Government and called on former President Hoover to chair it. President Eisenhower sought to continue the momentum of administrative reform and appointed a second Hoover Commission in 1953. Their successors often felt a similar need to appoint a distinguished commission to seek ways to improve the efficiency of government operations: the Ash Council (Nixon), the Grace Commission (Reagan), the Gore government performance review (Clinton).

At the heart of each of these efforts was a simple but enduring dilemma. In seeking to operate democratically, government is different from virtually every other American organization. Most others—churches, universities, corporations, athletic teams—are structured hierarchies of authority designed to accomplish certain substantive objectives with maximum economy and efficiency. But the American political system was designed to emphasize values and procedures, especially openness, individual rights, representation, and limited concentrations of authority, which are frequently antidotes to efficiency. Efforts to make government more efficient often appear to be—and, indeed, often are—threats to certain democratic values and procedures. Efficiency and democracy are often at odds.

When it became apparent in the early decades of the twentieth century that the federal government was changing and could no longer operate as it had in the nineteenth, some thoughtful commentators called for an abridgment of the American tradition of separation of powers. They suggested consideration of a major overhaul of the Constitution to adopt something closer to the parliamentary model of government.[26] Such suggestions never attracted much support. What happened instead was a different pattern of reform, beginning in the early decades of the century and rapidly accelerating after World War II: the strengthening of the institution of the presidency, especially its resources for managing the executive branch, while a constitutional system of shared (and contested) powers was retained.

The White House staff itself grew in the postwar period. New agencies and offices, such as the Presidential Personnel Office and the Office of Information and Regulatory Affairs (OIRA), were opened in the executive branch to enlarge its managerial capabilities. In 1970 the Bureau of the Budget was transformed into the Office of Management and Budget (OMB), with expanded responsibilities for superintending the administration of the executive branch. In 1978 the old independent Civil Service Commission was replaced by the new Office of Personnel Management, which was in closer range of presidential control.

These changes resulted in the creation in the presidency of an independent set of functions and competencies that made it a new and powerful force in Washington. Presidents had greater control than ever before over who was appointed to executive and judicial offices because they now had staff support to manage the appointment process and protect it from external domination. Rules and regulations proposed by federal agencies were scrutinized more closely and controlled more tightly by a beefed up OIRA in the OMB. New management initiatives with names such as Program Planning Budgeting, Management by Objectives, and Zero-Based Budgeting steadily emerged from a White House with resources and incentives to pursue a more efficient, more economical, and better administered executive branch.

Some scholars called this beefed up executive office the "presidential branch." Table 5.3 indicates the postwar growth in its size. Nelson Polsby noted the postwar emergence of "a presidential branch separate and apart from the executive branch. It is the presidential branch that sits across the table from the executive branch at budgetary hearings, and that imperfectly attempts to co-ordinate both the executive and legislative branches in its own behalf."[27]

The effort to effect a managerial, rather than a constitutional, solution to the problems of big government rarely worked very well. Instead of bringing about a better integrated, better coordinated, more efficient, and economical executive branch subject to the discipline and leadership of a responsible chief executive, aggressive White House management efforts stimulated greater conflict with Congress for control of the executive branch. Congress paid ample lip-service to the tenets of good management but guarded its institutional prerogatives jealously. Congress was not prepared to strengthen the president's hand by weakening its own.

Where presidents sought to enhance their executive management functions, Congress often responded with a counterthrust. When Lyndon Johnson imposed Program Planning Budgeting throughout the executive

TABLE 5.3
Average Size of White House Staffs, 1924–1994

President	Total Executive Staff Average Number of Full-Time Employees for Term	White House Staff Average Number of Full-Time Employees for Term
Coolidge	137	37
Hoover	123	37
Roosevelt I	103	47
Roosevelt II	371	50
Roosevelt III	121,318	51
Truman I	78,389	188
Truman II	1,269	256
Eisenhower I	1,229	295
Eisenhower II	2,357	498
Kennedy	2,058	422
Johnson	3,839	304
Nixon I	5,227	478
Nixon II	5,277	563
Ford	1,905	583
Carter	1,758	412
Reagan I	1,624	375
Reagan II	1,568	365
Bush	1,759	378
Clinton[a]	1,574	387

NOTE: Roman numeral after president's name refers to first, second, or third term.

[a]Data for Clinton cover 1993–1994 only.

SOURCE: Prepared by author from data in Gary King and Lyn Ragsdale, *The Elusive Executive: Discovering Statistical Patterns in the Presidency* (Washington, D.C.: CQ Press, 1988), p. 205; and Harold W. Stanley and Richard G. Niemi, *Vital Statistics on American Politics*, 5th ed. (Washington, D.C.: CQ Press, 1995), pp. 247–249.

branch in 1967, many of the congressional appropriations subcommittees paid no attention and stuck to their tradition of line-item budget reviews. Richard Nixon's aggressive use of impoundments to direct the expenditures of federal agencies led to congressional enactment of the Impoundment Control Act, which imposed congressional review on such presidential actions. The establishment of the Office of Management and Budget in the executive branch was soon followed by the creation of the Congressional Budget Office in the legislative branch. When presidents expanded their personnel offices to improve their capacity for making good presidential appointments, the Senate became more aggressive in its exercise of the confirmation power, subjecting those appointments to stiffer scrutiny.

Wherever presidents sought to manage the executive agencies more closely, Congress countered with more insistent oversight and new statutory procedures (e.g., to mandate review of weapons sales, foreign aid, and transfers of funds). Congress imposed scores of legislative veto restrictions on the executive branch, until the Supreme Court found them unconstitutional in 1983. And proliferating, well-staffed congressional subcommittees poked ever more assertively into what had previously been regarded as executive territory, raising complaints from the White House that Congress was micromanaging the executive branch.[28]

These postwar presidential efforts to improve the management of the executive branch engendered great frustration and even more pressure for White House management capabilities to expand. By seeking to strengthen the presidency without altering the constitutional relationship between the executive and legislative branches, postwar reformers inspired steadily escalating institutional tension between the two branches, the principal object of which was control of the federal agencies and departments. As the range of government programs broadened, as federal agencies had more money to spend, and as the electoral benefits of influencing that spending became more manifest, the intensity of the conflict grew.

Many members of Congress understood the value of efficient management of complex organizations. But they also knew that obtaining sewage treatment grants and avoiding military base closures in their districts were damned helpful at election time. So their interest in the quality of executive branch management was subordinate to their political self-interest. The harder presidents struggled to cope with the management needs of an expanding federal government, the greater was the resistance they encountered from Congress. The larger the Executive Office of the President grew in its management capabilities, the more it needed to grow in order to overcome the steadily rising frustration of its efforts. This situation contributed to the swelling size of the presidency much more than to any expansion in its institutional competence.

CONCLUSION: THE CHARACTER OF THE MODERN PRESIDENCY

What emerged from the pressures and activity of the postwar decades was a presidency dramatically and categorically different from the one Americans had known before Franklin Roosevelt inhabited it. The presidency was an institution of growing structural complexity. Most of the people on Herbert Hoover's small staff saw the president every day. A majority of the people on a modern president's staff never have a personal meeting with him and see him only at staged events such as helicopter departures from the south lawn of the White House. Where once the bulk of the presidential staff had occupied the West Wing of the White House, today it spills over into the old and new executive office buildings and other facilities in Washington. Some members of a modern president's staff rarely enter the White House.

The postwar presidents have lacked the advantage of durable governing coalitions. Their elections do not produce such coalitions, the political parties do not provide them, and congressional leaders cannot create them. Hence a principal imperative of the modern presidency is retail coalition building. This requires relentless negotiations with legislators and interest group leaders, with different combinations of these for each issue. And this coalition building demands that presidents spend much of their time pursuing public support for their programs.

Presidents of old could linger at the edge of public consciousness, remote figures whose voices were never heard and whose images were rarely viewed. They spoke infrequently in public, and the government they led had little direct impact on the lives of most Americans. Modern presidents live in the eye of an intensely visible national celebrity system. And often they suffer from that. We follow their every move and every word. Their families have no privacy; their travels are logistical nightmares; pictures of their intestines are blown up on the front page of every newspaper when they are ill. When a modern president misspeaks, his words are replayed again and again on news broadcasts. When a modern president stumbles on the steps of a helicopter, he becomes the brunt of skits and jokes on late night television. Modern presidents are celebrities but not heroes. They are easier to laugh at than to love, more often a source of reverie than reverence.

As the American people have turned to the federal government for an expanding array of goods and services, so have they focused on the president as the principal provider of these commodities. And presidents—and candidates for the presidency—have learned that promises of government benefits are valuable ways to win electoral support. This symbiosis has produced a steady spiral of escalating promises and expectations. The more the people expect, the more presidents promise; the more the latter promise, the more the former expect. In the early postwar period when the national economy was ablaze and federal revenues were multiplying rapidly, presidents led the way as the federal government dished out hundreds of new programs. The perception of the president as provider became a fixture of the postwar period.

But presidents could never provide enough, could never meet the demand of a population that came to regard government benefits as a great individual bargain. The direct costs never seemed to equal the direct value. And, of course, the people were right, for today's benefits were often funded with tomorrow's dollars. By deferring payment, presidents could promise more, and the people could expect more.

For all this beneficence, however, and for all the ingenuity in pursuit of popular approval, the postwar presidents have rarely been a popular lot. We have no reliable instruments for comparing the popularity of the postwar presidents with their predecessors; survey research is an invention of recent vintage. But we have powerful indicators that the normal pattern for the postwar presidents has been a decline in their job approval rating over the course of their time in office. Figure 5.3 demonstrates the trend.

The postwar presidents have typically lost support as their terms wore on. The majority of them, in fact, have lost so much support that they were forced from office—by resigning, declining to seek reelection, or los-

FIGURE 5.3
Presidential Approval, Gallup Poll, 1938–1995

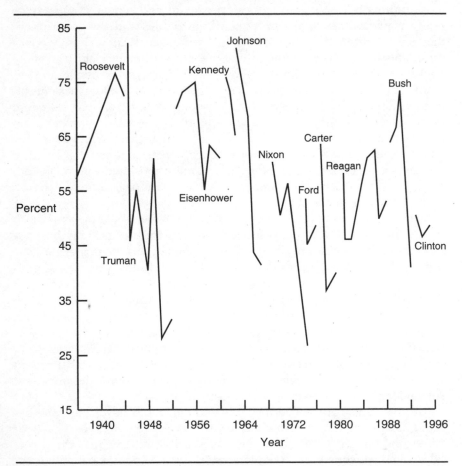

SOURCE: Harold W. Stanley and Richard G. Niemi, *Vital Statistics on American Politics*, 5th ed. (Washington, D.C.: CQ Press, 1995), p. 261.

ing to electoral challengers. Of the nine postwar presidents from Truman through Bush, only Eisenhower and Reagan left office with popular regard in relatively good shape. Truman and Johnson chose not to seek reelection, which would have been difficult to achieve. Nixon resigned. Ford, Carter, and Bush were all defeated when they ran as incumbents.

In many ways the postwar presidency devours its incumbents. It forces them to spend years in pursuit of the office, often in degrading and debilitating campaign activities. It imposes extraordinary expectations and enormous burdens on them. It exposes them to incessant and often mean-spirited public scrutiny. It provides them with more resources than their predecessors ever had but nowhere near enough to accomplish the formidable responsibilities they confront. And then, more often than not, it drives them from office.

Riding on a swelling crest of expanding expectations and duties, the postwar presidency became an institution larger and more complex than its prewar permutations and barely recognizable from its constitutional description. As the postwar decades passed, presidents promised more and delivered less, while Americans expected more and received less. The great hope of progressives and liberals at the beginning and middle of the century, the presidency frustrates and disappoints virtually everyone at century's end.

The unusual postwar pattern of divided government left lasting scars everywhere on the body politic, but they are most visible and painful on the presidency. When politicians became accustomed to thinking of the presidency as the Republican institution and Congress as the Democratic institution, each group of partisans sought to strengthen and fortify the branch it most often controlled. Republicans impounded funds more frequently, reorganized more aggressively, centralized regulation and appointments and budget control more effectively, and vetoed legislation more willingly because these were the instruments of power they most often controlled. Democrats expanded congressional committees and staffs, invented a new congressional budget process, and enacted statutory constraints on the president in the areas of arms export, war making, impoundments, and foreign commitments. Democrats investigated more widely, micromanaged more frequently, and—while the courts permitted—hung legislative vetoes all over the statute books. They came within a well-timed resignation of impeaching a president. Democrats also strengthened Congress's ability to oppose the president because they had majorities in both houses most of the time. The postwar period was marked by intense, ongoing institutional belligerency in which both parties had a high stake and to which both contributed. The machinery of government was in a constant state of remodeling, as both Republicans and Democrats sought to gain structurally an advantage that they could not gain electorally.

As the presidency grew in size and scope of activity, Congress grew apace. But rather than bringing about a collective increase in government competence, the muscling up of the two branches was separately guided and driven. They sought greater strength and effectiveness not so much for collective ends as for the specific purpose of thwarting the other. The result has been a kind of political jujitsu, with the legislature and the executive employing an ingenious array of new holds to immobilize each other. The contemporary term for this form of combat is "gridlock."

The problem created by this pattern of interbranch warfare is especially severe because the outcomes of each battle are written in law. The thrusts and counterthrusts are formal and permanent. The hundreds of legal strings that tie each branch down sum to a set of heavy and severely encumbering tethers. For the presidency this tethering has produced a familiar dilemma: The more that presidents are expected to do, the harder the doing becomes. Growing expectations have been accompanied at every turn by growing constraints.

The severity of the problem is exacerbated in the later postwar period by the emergence, on the one hand, of a host of politically devilish substantive issues and the disappearance, on the other, of the fiscal resources to cope with them. Wherever presidents looked—energy, welfare reform, health care, social security, deficit reduction—there were pressing issues that lacked politically appealing solutions. Charles L. Schultze, a leading economic adviser to Presidents Johnson and Carter, wrote in 1977:

> Until perhaps fifteen or twenty years ago, most federal activities in the domestic sphere were confined to a few broad areas: providing cash income under social security programs for which eligibility was fairly easily determined; investing in the infrastructure in a few areas of the economy, principally highways, water resources, and high rise public housing; regulating selected industries allegedly to control monopoly or prevent certain abuses; and operating various housekeeping activities such as the Post Office, national parks, the merchant seaman's hospitals, and the air navigation system. But in the short space of twenty years the very nature of federal activity has changed radically. Addressed to much more intricate and difficult objectives, the newer programs are different; and the older ones have taken on more ambitious goals."[29]

In some cases presidents found a peculiar phenomenon: Consensus on the need for a solution and even on the substance of that solution, but no political constituency to support their actions in those directions. Large majorities believed in the need for welfare reform, but there were few constituents for it and few votes in it. Large majorities believed in better planning for future energy needs, but, as Jimmy Carter quickly learned, there was little political reward in venturing down that road. Almost everyone believed by the mid-1980s that budget deficits had grown too large, but constituents for deficit reduction vanished when presidents proposed specific tax increases or program cuts to accomplish that.[30]

Most troublesome of all to the postwar presidents has been the difficulty of managing successfully their international responsibilities. The reality of America's status as a superpower in the postwar period created the simultaneous illusion of the president as the leader of the world. In fact, as every postwar president learned, presidents have no more real power to lead the world than they do to lead the United States. Lyndon Johnson's homely characterization put it most poignantly: "The only real power I've got is nuclear and I can't use that."

Postwar presidents found that they were often held accountable for events abroad that they had little real ability to shape. The new international responsibilities of the presidency enlarged expectations but offered few opportunities to deliver the goods. Presidents were victimized politically by oil boycotts, international commodity price increases, foreign trade policies, and acts of terrorism that were as difficult to predict as to prevent. Even moments of international activism often turned sour. The presidents associated with the wars in Korea and Vietnam were driven from office. A few Iranian radicals gravely diminished Jimmy Carter's political support. "Peacekeeping" efforts in Lebanon and Somalia became albatrosses for Ronald Reagan and Bill Clinton. The international realm in which postwar presidents operate has rarely been very hospitable to their leadership efforts. The ingenuity of American diplomacy and the technological sophistication of American weapons, though alluring to all presidents, have been comforting to few. Many of them left office muttering to themselves that maybe George Washington had had the right idea.

Now, as the century ends, new changes may be in store for the presidency. Two of the elements that contributed significantly to postwar alterations in that institution have come to an end. One of those is the first age of television, the era dominated by the three large networks. From television's emergence through the mid-1980s, most Americans who watched TV watched one of the three networks most of the time. Virtually all Americans who relied on television for news relied on the news staffs of one of the three networks. When presidents wanted to communicate directly with the American people, they needed only to request prime time from the networks to gain an audience of tens of millions.

But the hegemony of the networks is in accelerating decline. They command a shrinking share of the audience. Fewer Americans rely on network news as their primary link to national politics. The networks are less compliant to presidential requests for evening airtime, and fewer people watch even when the networks do provide time. Although 98 percent of American households had televisions by 1993, only 71 percent of those were tuned to one of the three networks in prime time.[31] When Bill

Clinton made a prime-time address to the nation seeking support of his deficit reduction package on the eve of the congressional vote in August 1993, only 21 percent of American adults watched until the end.[32] As Figure 5.4 demonstrates, the audience for televised presidential addresses has been declining steadily in recent years.

There is a large potential impact of this movement from television dominated by three national networks to television that offers viewers a wide array of choices. Presidents have begun to find it more difficult to communicate directly with huge audiences. They have also found that even when their staffs are successful at attracting favorable news cover-

FIGURE 5.4
Percentage of Households with a Television
Viewing Presidential Speeches, 1969–1992

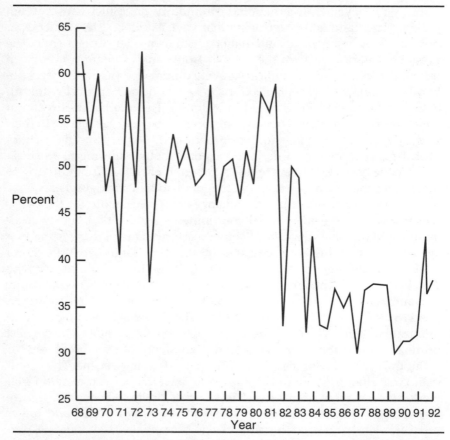

SOURCE: Nielsen Media Research, reported in Samuel Kernell, *Going Public* (Washington, D.C.: CQ Press, 1993), p. 114.

age or putting the right spin on presidential words, fewer people are watching. And presidents have come to realize that as the number of news outlets grows, competition among them intensifies, with the frequent consequence that unflattering stories about presidents are given more prominence than used to be the case.

All of this is bad news for present and future presidents. Just as Jay Leno cannot be Johnny Carson and Dan Rather cannot be Walter Cronkhite, neither can Bill Clinton nor his successors be John Kennedy. If the first age of television greatly abetted the emergence of the postwar presidency, its passing contributes to that institution's fossilization.

The end of the cold war is the other change that marks a turning point for the presidency. It is hard to imagine how the postwar presidency could have emerged as it did without the cold war to ensure a base of popular support for the institution, if not always for its inhabitants. In a time of great danger, Americans were almost always willing to give presidents the benefit of the doubt in matters of foreign policy. Even in an adventure so misguided and costly as the war in Vietnam, American opinion was slow to turn. Nothing so contributed to the reluctance of Americans to oppose the war as their unwillingness to abandon their commander in chief.[33]

In addition, the cold war was the justification for a lot of government and a lot of economic growth. A rapacious appetite for new and better weapons supercharged the federal budget and pumped trillions of dollars through the private economy into American paychecks. Although such confessions were rarely conscious, many Americans understood that because of the cold war they had never had it so good. Presidents benefited from that realization and from opportunities for prominence that came from foreign travels, summit meetings, confrontations with the enemy, and all the mystical paraphernalia of militarism and secrecy in which the cold war embedded presidential public images.

The end of the cold war kicks that prop out from under the modern presidency. In a less dangerous world, the president is simply a less important figure. Presidents receive a smaller benefit of the doubt when the risks of miscalculation or incompetence are not quite so grave. Popular attention to American involvement in Somalia or Bosnia is diminished without the subtext of superpower confrontation. The presidential stage is not so well lit, the presidential voice not so well amplified when thoughts of life and death are not so closely connected to presidential action. The presidency is a less important institution in the collective American psyche. The postwar president has always been more prominent than powerful. But the illusion persisted that presidents were possessed of large resources and were capable of greatness. Now even the illusion has faded.

Much of the undoing of modern presidents is their own doing. They have promised—sometimes grossly and disingenuously—more than they could deliver. When they fell short of expectations, the shortfall was often from expectations that presidents themselves had created and inflated. But there are other culprits as well. An altered electoral system discourages good candidates from running for president and often disfigures those who do; it usually fails to produce coherent and enduring governing coalitions. The modern political parties are thin shells that rarely help a president command or hold the support of co-partisans in Congress. Postwar legislative-executive relations have become a tangle of rules and laws that brake and constrain every effort at executive leadership. In efforts to escape these bonds, to be effective in spite of them, presidents have built large and complex White House staffs that often thwart the very purposes they were intended to accomplish.

The problem is clearly systemic. It is not, as some have argued, that we just need better presidents to make the system work well. Perhaps there were in America more competent people than those we elected to the postwar presidency. But if so, the postwar political system failed to attract them as candidates or choose them as presidents. In fact, our postwar presidents represent a range of backgrounds, experiences, and personality types that belies the argument that we just need better people as presidents to make the presidency work. We have had Easterners and Westerners, Northerners and Southerners. We have had some postwar presidents who came from state government and some who came from Congress. One was a great general of the army. Some were extroverts, some introverts. Some focused on the big picture, others on the details. Some were graduates of the best colleges and universities in the world; others were not. The one thing that all of them had in common was that they inhabited a presidency that rarely allowed them to lead the nation and the government in the way they wanted, that their authority rarely equaled their responsibility, that the expectations they faced always exceeded the actions they could muster.

In a democracy of a quarter billion people, it is a matter of large consequence when leadership institutions fail to provide the capacity to lead. Yet that has been the frequent condition of postwar American politics. The American presidency changed radically in the years after Franklin Roosevelt assumed it. The American people sought and supported more vigorous presidential leadership. The escalation of government responsibilities demanded it.

In bits and pieces, in fits and starts, the presidency changed. No one designed this change, though some thoughtful groups of reformers offered up interesting road maps and models. Instead the construction of the postwar presidency and the political and governmental systems that contained it was a process of accumulation, reaction, and even inadvertence.

The presidency served, in turn, as the primary hope of liberals and then of conservatives. But it disappointed them both. Its power never matched its promise. For all the sound and fury modern presidents produced, they rarely lived up to their billing. Americans craved better leadership but failed to design a politics or a government in which it could emerge.

COURTS UNCHAINED

In the years since World War II, federal courts have ordered a complete remodeling of the Alabama mental health system, required the U.S. Forest Service to stop clear-cutting timber, required equalization of school district expenditures on teachers' salaries, declared some state prisons unfit and ordered them closed, established elaborate food handling procedures and standards for plumbing and lighting in some public institutions, stopped the construction of roads on environmental grounds, specified the requirements for fire fighters' jobs, and required federal agencies to restore funding for programs. But there is more, much more. Federal courts in the postwar period have actively intervened in policy disputes at every government level and in virtually every substantive area. Little of the public life of the United States has been left untouched by the hyperkinetic energies and boundless interests of American courts.

American courts make public policy. In some ways, of course, they have always played a role in policymaking. Once or twice in each generation major court decisions—*Gibbons* v. *Ogden*, *Dred Scott*, *Plessy*, *Schechter*—redirected or retarded policy momentum. But today the federal courts make policy more often, in more detail, over more areas, and more exclusively than ever before. The business of government has been deeply altered by the single-minded and single-handed decisions of American judges.

This change is not merely evolutionary; it is dramatic and profound. Doctrines and rules that guided the courts for centuries have been abandoned. Boundaries beyond which courts long refused to trespass have been obliterated. In the years after World War II, an activist judiciary moved the courts to the center of American public life. There, for more than four decades, while ordering deep and lasting changes in American society, they have blurred beyond recognition the line between the legal and the political.

The twentieth century began with a lengthy period of judicial activism. From roughly 1890 to the late 1930s, the Supreme Court reformulated the meaning of the due process clauses of the Fifth and Fourteenth Amendments and assumed the power to review the substance of legisla-

tion, especially legislation intended to regulate business. Wielding the ax
of "substantive due process," the Court became a bulwark of the old
against the new, chopping down state and federal laws that outlawed
manufacturing monopolies, imposed an income tax, established maximum hours, minimum wages and safe conditions in the workplace, and
invalidated numerous policy initiatives of the New Deal. From 1900
through 1939 the Supreme Court invalidated 43 federal and 390 state laws
(compared to 20 federal and 145 state laws overturned in the preceding
four decades).[1]

The Court's decisions in this period were characteristically proscrip-
tive: denying expansions of state and federal power, protecting the sanc-
tity of contracts and employers' domains, shielding state autonomy.
Although the Court was often active in policymaking, its activism had a
strongly negative tint. It saw itself as a protector of the Constitution
against the intrusions of progressive social and economic legislation.
Faced with growing public pressure for policy change during this period,
the Supreme Court used the Constitution as a brake, not an accelerator.

A second period of twentieth-century judicial activism began toward
the end of the decade following World War II. But this period bore a very
different strain of activism than had the earlier one. The thrust of Court
decisions in the early decades of this century was to restrain government;
the thrust in recent decades has been to expand it. In a number of policy
areas, even a bolder characterization is justified. The courts have sought
not merely to support legislative expansions of government rights and responsibilities. Where such legislative action has been absent or muted, the
courts have leapt in on their own: setting standards, issuing detailed
rules, establishing goals—generally performing a broad array of what
had once been conceived of solely as legislative or administrative responsibilities. Where court participation in policymaking had once been
confined to the rather narrow task of judicial review, courts now play a
central role in defining the public policy agenda, identifying policy options, selecting among them, and overseeing their implementation. It is a
role without precedent for American courts. Courts have gone on the of-
fense, and in so doing, they have profoundly reshaped the operations of
postwar American government.

THE LAW EXPLOSION

America has always been a country with an affection for the law and legalism. "Scarcely any political question arises in the United States," wrote
Alexis de Tocqueville in the 1830s, "which is not resolved, sooner, or later,
into a judicial question."[2] Lawyers dominated the constitutional debates
and filled the early Congresses. Courts guarded their independence from

the start and quickly assumed a role as the arbiters of the Constitution's meaning—a role that later gave rise to the shopworn verity that "the Constitution means what the judges say it means."

But for all of American history before World War II, courts were small in number and, with only occasional exceptions, small in their impact on public policy. Most of the law practiced in the United States was practiced by sole practitioners handling the routine affairs of people buying property, making contracts, and dying. Few citizens—and few lawyers—regarded the law as a significant instrument of policy change. Even those rare attorneys who went to court to alter public policy, most notably those who sought expanded legal protection for civil rights and civil liberties, often found the courts deaf to their pleas, uninterested in challenging the prevailing sentiments in legislatures and public opinion. Courts rarely regarded themselves as policymaking bodies; lawyers rarely succeeded in convincing them otherwise.

All this changed after World War II. The role of law, and then the rule of law, swelled precipitously. The number of attorneys grew much faster than previously. So, too, did the variety of their work. Government expenditures on the legal system escalated dramatically. There were more courts and more judges. Court cases proliferated and evolved in character. Every feature on the physiognomy of the American legal system grew to new and unimagined proportions. The details tell the story.

One Million Lawyers

Folksinger Tom Paxton sang a song in which he foresaw:

> Lawyers around every bend in the road, lawyers in every tree.
> Lawyers in restaurants, lawyers in clubs.
> Lawyers behind every door,
> Behind windows and potted plants, shade trees, and shrubs.
> Lawyers on Pogo sticks, lawyers in politics.
> In ten years we're going to have one million lawyers.
> How much can a poor nation stand?

We will soon find out. On the eve of World War II, in a country of 132 million people, there were fewer than 180,000 lawyers, about 1 for every 733 people. Nearly two-thirds of them practiced alone, mostly as typical small-town attorneys. The ratio had not changed very much in fifty years. In 1890 there was 1 attorney for every 739 people.

But after World War II a set of forces coalesced to bring about a huge and rapid increase in the number of Americans practicing law. The GI Bill opened up the possibility of college and a career in the professions to people who in earlier times had only dreamed such things. When more people went to college, the number of colleges and universities grew. With more college graduates to feed law schools, their size and number grew. In 1940 there were 178 American law schools, with an average enrollment of about 173 law students. By 1980 there were 228 law schools, with an average enrollment of 565 law students.

Legal education, like the rest of postwar society, reflected the profound changes in women's lives. In 1940 there were 690 women attending law schools accredited by the American Bar Association (ABA). By 1980 there more than 42,000 women in ABA-approved law schools, and the number of female students had grown by almost 10,000 more in 1990. Overall, the number of law students of both sexes more than quadrupled between 1940 and 1990. By 1990 American law schools were producing more than 35,000 new lawyers a year. The total number of American lawyers had swelled from 180,000 in 1940 to nearly 800,000 in 1988, slightly more than 1 lawyer for every 300 Americans (see Figure 6.1). At current growth rates, as Tom Paxton feared, there will be more than 1 million American lawyers when the twenty-first century dawns.

To put this trend in some perspective, it is worth noting the comparison with other developed countries. In 1990 there were 281 American lawyers for every 100,000 people. Germany in the same year had 111 attorneys per 100,000 population; England, 82; and Japan, 11.[3]

Why does America have so many lawyers and what accounts for the dramatic growth in the legal profession after World War II? The answer has several facets. Because government now plays a much larger role in American society, it makes and implements more laws and thus requires many more lawyers to do its work. As government practices more law, other social and economic interests must practice more law in their dealings with government. The net effect is to increase the need for lawyers. There has certainly been pressure of this sort in the past fifty years. Nowhere is it more evident than in Washington, D.C., where one of every nineteen residents was an attorney in 1988.[4]

The number of lawyers has also grown because of changes in the legal marketplace. For years the organized legal profession succeeded in controlling the supply of lawyers. It required formal legal education and raised the standards for law schools. Bar exams were initiated and made increasingly difficult. Women and racial minorities were systematically excluded from law schools and thus from legal practice. For those who did practice, there were restrictions on advertising and other forms of demand creation.

In the period after World War II, most of these restrictions on the supply of lawyers vanished. Law schools grew in number and expanded. Women and minorities were no longer excluded, interstate mobility became easier, and the courts struck down restrictions on price cutting, advertising, and other unapproved legal practices.[5] At the same time, a

FIGURE 6.1
Number of Lawyers Practicing
in the United States, 1900–1988

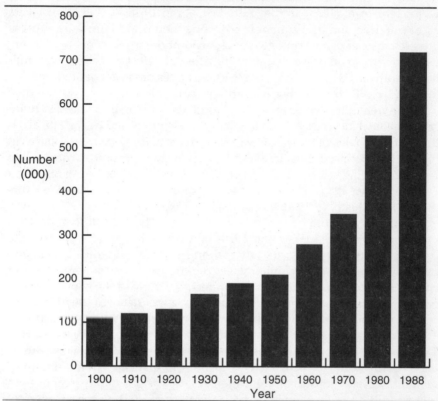

SOURCE: U.S. Department of Commerce, Bureau of the Census, *Historical Statistics of the United States: Colonial Times to 1970* (Washington, D.C.: GPO, 1975); U.S. Department of Commerce, Bureau of the Census, *Statistical Abstract of the United States, 1992* (Washington, D.C.: GPO, 1992); Richard L. Abel, *American Lawyers* (New York: Oxford University Press, 1989), pp. 278–279.

powerful demand for legal services was building. Some of this demand was directly stimulated by lawyers themselves. Their bar associations undertook studies that identified previously unrecognized "legal needs." Lawyers lobbied for legal aid for poor people, public defenders, more judges and courts, legal clinics, and group legal plans. They lobbied against no-fault insurance and divorce, tort reform, and other measures that would diminish the demand for legal services. After the courts removed the traditional proscription on legal advertising, more and more lawyers sought to stimulate business through the traditional techniques and media of product sales.

Some of these demand-creation techniques were dramatically success-ful. Legal clinics are private organizations that try to offer lower-cost legal services by practicing in volume and obtaining economies of scale. There were eight legal clinics in the United States in 1974. By 1980 there were eight hundred and by 1984, more than one thousand.[6] Group legal plans offer legal services to employees of a corporation or members of a union, usually with small or no charge to the client. In 1984 an estimated 7 mil-lion employees belonged to group legal services plans negotiated by their unions. By 1987 the number had grown to 17 million.[7]

Many were attracted to law school after World War II by the steady in-crease in legal incomes. A good lawyer could get rich, and by the late 1960s the best graduates of the best law schools were earning starting salaries in big cities that placed them in the top few percent of income earners in the country. Starting salaries at the largest law firms often exceeded $80,000 a year by the late 1980s. The average salary of the most experienced lawyers in private industry in 1990 was over $120,000 a year.[8]

But others were drawn to the law for reasons that had little to do with money. Events in the 1960s and 1970s contributed to an alteration in the perceptions of lawyers, especially among college students. Those who had watched attorneys challenge segregationist laws, defend indigent clients, argue for expansions in civil liberties, and lead the consumer and environmental movements were attracted by the idealism they hoped to satisfy in undertaking a legal career. Their models were a mixture of Thurgood Marshall, Ralph Nader, Sarah Weddington, and Perry Mason. These future lawyers sought not so much to be rich as to make a differ-ence, to do right, to fix what was broken in a society that sometimes seemed rife with injustice. Public interest law was one of the great growth sectors in the legal profession, and its growth feasted on the idealism of the baby boom generation.

For all of these reasons, the legions of American lawyers swelled. And as the legal profession grew in size, it changed in character. Before World War II, and especially before the New Deal, very little of the law clustered around government or corporations. Nine attorneys in ten were em-ployed in private practice, and nearly seven in ten worked alone. Even where law firms existed, few employed more than five attorneys. Most corporations had no legal department at all. Law school faculties were tiny by today's standards. Lawyers were a rarity on government payrolls.

The change in the past half century is remarkable. As the number of lawyers has escalated, the percentage in sole practice has shrunk to less than 33. Law firms have grown in number and size. The largest now em-ploy more than three hundred attorneys each. But equally dramatic is the number of attorneys practicing in government or working for businesses. Corporate law departments now employ about 10 percent of all lawyers.

Another 13 percent of all attorneys work for governments.[9] The number of lawyers employed by business has more than tripled since the end of World War II. And a vast number of attorneys employed by business—nearly 50 percent by one reliable account—work for the Fortune 500 largest corporations and the Fortune 50 largest financial services companies. Some of the largest companies employ more attorneys than even the largest private law firms.

The legal landscape of 1940 was populated largely by independent generalists who had limited resources and served the mundane legal needs of small communities. The legal landscape of the 1990s is very different, indeed. It is populated by large legal armies—in government agencies, law firms, and corporate offices; each has enormous resources and specialized talents and is prepared to do battle on national issues of great complexity and often of very great importance.

The Caseload Deluge

It is no surprise that this growth in the number of American lawyers has coincided with a caseload glut in American courts. In every court at every level, there are more cases being heard and decided in this decade than ever before. This is not merely a reflection of the growth of the American population; the number of legal cases has grown at a much more rapid rate since World War II than population. Table 6.1 reveals the steep pattern of growth, especially since 1960.

Most of the law practiced in this country is in the state and local courts. Counting the number of cases in those courts is no simple matter because of disjointed and inconsistent patterns of record keeping. The State Justice Institute reports, however, that the number of cases filed in state courts grew from 85 million in 1984 to over 100 million in 1990.[10]

In the federal courts, where record keeping is much more reliable, the number of lawsuits filed annually is smaller but growing rapidly. In the federal district courts, an average of 42,188 civil cases was filed each year during the 1940s; in the 1980s the average was 229,667 per year. The pattern of growth was even more rapid in the federal courts of appeals: On average 958 civil cases were filed each year in the 1940s compared to an average of 16,531 per year in the 1980s. Even in the U.S. Supreme Court, the most stable of American judicial institutions, the number of cases filed grew from an average of 1,223 per year in the 1940s to 5,259 per year in the 1980s.

In the period from 1940 to 1990, in which the population of the United States did not quite double, the number of federal civil and criminal cases filed increased by 367 percent in the district courts and almost 1200 percent in the courts of appeals. It is hard to determine whether the number

140

TABLE 6.1
U.S. Court Cases Filed, 1940–1990

Year	Supreme Court Cases Filed	Courts of Appeals Total Cases Filed	District Courts Private Civil Cases Filed	District Courts Total Civil Cases	District Courts Total Criminal Cases	District Courts Total Cases
1940	977	3,446		34,734	33,401	68,135
1945	1,316	2,730	758	53,236	39,429	92,665
1950	1,181	2,830	1,114	45,085	37,720	82,805
1955	1,644	3,695	1,363	49,056	37,123	86,179
1960	1,940	3,899	1,534	51,063	29,828	80,891
1965	2,774	6,766	2,677	62,670	33,334	96,004
1970	4,212	11,662	4,834	82,665	39,959	122,624
1975	4,761	16,658	6,252	115,098	43,282	158,380
1980	5,144	23,200	8,942	167,871	28,921	196,792
1985	5,158	33,360	15,743	273,670	38,500	312,170
1990	6,316	40,898	20,369	217,879	48,000	265,879

SOURCE: U.S. Department of Commerce, Bureau of the Census, *Historical Statistics of the United States: Colonial Times to 1970* (Washington, D.C.: Government Printing Office, 1975); U.S. Department of Commerce, Bureau of the Census, *Statistical Abstract of the United States, 1992* (Washington, D.C.: GPO, 1992); Harold W. Stanley and Richard G. Niemi, *Vital Statistics on American Politics*, 3d ed. (Washington, D.C.: Congressional Quarterly, 1992); Richard A. Posner, *The Federal Courts: Crisis and Reform* (Cambridge, Mass.: Harvard University Press, 1985), pp. 351–352.

of cases grew because the number of lawyers grew or vice versa. Probably, it was some of each. The dynamic of change in the postwar American legal system has been highly volatile and has caused an explosion in all of its elements: more lawyers, more cases, and more judges and courts. The explosion was fueled as well by elements outside the court system.

Ironically, because most Americans would assume otherwise, crime accounts for little of the explosive increase in the federal caseload. The crime rate grew significantly after World War II, especially as the baby boomers moved into their crime-prone years in the 1960s. But the judicial impact of that increase is most notable in the state and local courts. In the federal courts the number of criminal prosecutions hovered around 35,000 for most of the three decades following 1960.[11] Crime is not the answer; we have to look elsewhere to explain the growth in federal caseloads.

A larger, better educated, wealthier population is part of the explanation. More Americans had more money, entered more contracts, conducted more business, divorced more often, and engaged in a wide variety of behavior that brought them to court with greater frequency. As personal incomes grew, legal services became affordable to more Americans. Even those without much money could often qualify for publicly funded legal services, especially as those became more readily available after World War II. This availability was the result, in part, of court decisions declaring that everyone was entitled to an attorney if charged with a crime and of new federal programs that sought to provide legal assistance to needy citizens: the Neighborhood Legal Service Centers established under the Economic Opportunity Act of 1964, the Legal Services Program created in 1966, and the Legal Services Corporation Act of 1974.

Courts did not discourage this surge in lawsuits. Despite the remarkable rise in demand for services, courts did little to limit accessibility. As the cost of running the federal court system grew from $56 million in 1954 to $3 billion in 1994, little effort was made to shift the burden from taxpayers to litigants. The principal direct cost of court services is the filing fee that a litigant pays when commencing a case. But filing fees have barely grown at all since World War II. So the threshold of entry to the courts has not risen enough to deter many potential litigants.

At least two other significant factors have contributed to the growth in the caseload of the federal courts. One is a significant set of changes in the doctrines that courts employ to determine whether a case merits a hearing, whether it is "justiciable."

The other important cause is the work of Congress and the successive postwar presidents in enacting new legislation that created new rights and privileges and often actively encouraged citizens to commence cases in court to secure their rights or pursue their policy goals. Such legislation ranges from environmental protection to consumer protection to civil rights. But it is the last, more than any other area of legislation, that demonstrates most clearly the new role that courts have come to play in American public life and that helps explain the caseload explosion.

In 1960 only 200 civil rights cases were filed in all of the federal courts. Twenty years later 25,341 civil rights cases were filed.[12] Through legislation and judicial decision, Americans have obtained a broad array of new rights. They have gone to court with increasing frequency to protect those rights or to seek redress for their violation. Courts, by and large, have welcomed these entreaties, which in earlier times were not regarded as the business of government or worthy of the attention of judges. An obvious consequence, as federal judge and legal scholar Richard Posner noted, is that the American court system is "on the verge of being radically changed for the worse under the pressure of [this] rapid and unremitting growth in caseload."[13]

Bureaucratizing the Courts

Impelled by all these new pressures—some of them self-inflicted—the federal courts have grown. They have grown in number, in size, and in complexity. When the twentieth century began, the number of federal judges in all courts was 114 and the total number of federal judicial branch employees was 2,730. By 1945 little had changed. The number of federal judicial branch employees at the end of World War II was 2,706—fewer than it had been at the beginning of the century.

Then the cases began to flood in. To keep pace with the demand for judicial services, the court system expanded steadily in the years after World War II. By 1990 the number of circuit courts of appeal had grown to 13 and district courts to 90. The Territorial Court, the Court of Customs and Patent Appeals, the U.S. Claims Court, the Court of International Trade, the Tax Court, and the Court of Veterans Appeals had all been created. The number of judicial branch employees reached 10,000 in 1975 and 22,399 in 1990. Judicial branch employment for 1990 was nearly nine times what it had been at the end of World War II.

The number of judgeships grew as well. At the end of the war, the federal judiciary was a small fraternity of 262 people. The number of judges then grew to more than 500 in the early 1970s, to 657 by the end of that decade, and 875 by 1990. The pattern of growth in federal judgeships is traced in Figure 6.2.

Increasing the number of courts and adding more judges were not enough to keep up with the caseload burden, however. And so other court personnel were added as well. In the 1930s appellate justices in the federal system began the practice of hiring recent, talented law school graduates to serve as assistants for a year or two. These young people came to be known as law clerks, and each Supreme Court and appeals court judge had one. In the 1940s district court judges were also authorized to hire one law clerk a year. After World War II this practice began to expand. Members of the Supreme Court were authorized a second clerk in 1947. A second clerk was authorized for the district judges in 1965 and for the circuit court judges in 1970. The Supreme Court justices got a third clerk in 1970 and a fourth in 1978. In 1980 the circuit judges were authorized a third law clerk.[14]

In the same period the courts of appeals began to employ "staff attorneys" who performed work similar to that of law clerks but who were not permanently assigned to any judge. The federal courts also began to use "externs," law students who earned credit for assisting judges in their work. All of these new employees have added to the size and resources of the federal courts in the period since World War II. They have helped the courts, especially the appeals courts, keep pace with the dramatic growth in their caseloads.

FIGURE 6.2
Number of Federal Judges, All Courts, 1900–1990

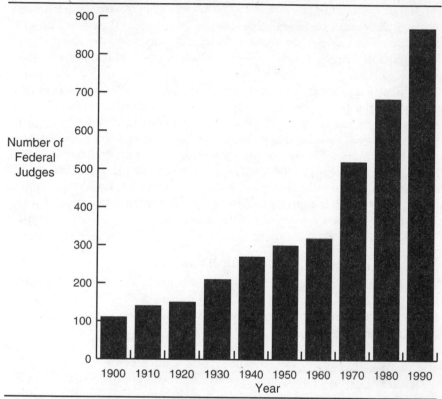

SOURCE: U.S. Federal Judicial Center.

But the addition of these employees has also changed the way in which the courts work. Before World War II, when judges were fewer and professional support was essentially nonexistent, judges did much of their own research and wrote most of their own opinions. They soaked, perforce, more deeply in the smaller number of cases they considered and thus brought more expertise and understanding to their decisions. A consistency of legal doctrine and opinion style often flowed from that direct confrontation with the substance of cases and the legacy of precedent. To the extent that judges made law, it was really *judges* who made law.

The proliferation of support professionals in the courts has altered the process by which decisions are reached and opinions are written. The role of the judge, according to Judge Richard Posner, has been transformed from "a draftsman to an editor."[15] Judges now do little of their own research, and many judges do little original writing. Much of the work of their courts has been delegated—delegated to very bright but very young people who have less political and practical experience than even the judges themselves. "What are these able, intelligent, mostly young people doing?" asked the late circuit judge Alvin Rubin. "Surely not running citations in *Shepard's* and shelving judge's law books. They are, in many situations, 'para-judges.' In some instances, it is to be feared, they are indeed invisible judges, for there are appellate judges whose literary style appears to change annually."[16]

The contemporary courts, then, are different from those that bore the judicial burden before World War II. There are more of these courts, and they are led by many more judges. They have thickened down as well as out, with more clerks and staff attorneys and other professional assistants. More judges handle more cases with less direct penetration. But that is not all. The judges themselves are different not just in number but in character. The kinds of people who now serve on the court do not much resemble their predecessors of earlier generations. And that change, too, is worthy of our consideration.

Selecting Judges

As the number of judgeships grew—and as judges took on a larger role in shaping public policy—the task of selecting federal judges became more important and more complicated. Franklin Roosevelt appointed an average of sixteen judges a year at all levels of the federal court system. Jimmy Carter, in contrast appointed an average of sixty-six a year and Ronald Reagan, forty-seven. In Roosevelt's time all of the district court appointments and many of the appointees to the circuit courts were, in fact, selected by senators from the states or regions in which those courts were located. The act of presidential appointment was little more than a formal ratification of a choice made by individual senators under the practice of the time known as "senatorial courtesy."

Senatorial courtesy still survives, but in truncated form. Although senators of the president's party still participate in judicial selection, they do so increasingly under procedures and guidelines established by the White House. Jimmy Carter was the first president to attempt systematically to centralize the judicial selection process by setting up commissions that reviewed candidates and sought to secure broader representation on the federal bench for female and minority judges. Ronald Reagan went even further, creating the nine-member President's Committee on Federal Judicial Selection, chaired by the counsel to the president and composed of White House and Justice Department officials who carefully scrutinized all potential judicial nominees to ensure their bona fides as ideological conservatives in the Reagan mold. Computerized searches were employed to examine the writings of every judicial candidate. Members of the committee often had lengthy individual interviews with potential nominees. Candidates' views on abortion and other matters were closely examined, and those who failed these "litmus tests" were turned away even when they had the strong endorsement of the relevant senator.

In Roosevelt's time the state and local political parties played a major role in judicial selection, often yielding up the candidates whom senators would then identify for the president's ratification. When the parties played this kind of strong hand, a great many federal judges came from the ranks of practicing politicians or politically active lawyers and prosecutors. More recently as party organizations have dissipated and centralization has enlarged the White House role, prior judicial experience and ideology have replaced political experience as the dominant criteria in judicial selection. It has come to matter less and less whether a candidate for a federal judgeship ever before ran for office or even practiced much law in a courtroom. It has come to matter more and more whether a candidate has previously worked as a judge and whether his or her prior judicial opinions reveal the "correct" ideological views. We are seeing simultaneously a professionalization of the federal judiciary and a greater emphasis in judicial selection on substantive ideology.

At the federal district court level most notably, there has been a significant increase in the number of appointees with prior judicial experience. Slightly more than 33 percent of Lyndon Johnson's and Richard Nixon's district court appointees had judicial backgrounds. For President Carter, however, the percentage was 54.5. And both Presidents Reagan and Bush hovered around 50 percent.[17]

The importance of ideology can be detected more anecdotally, though it is widely recognized by close observers of recent judicial selection practices. A case in point is Dennis G. Jacobs, President Bush's last judicial appointment in New York. Jacobs was nominated and confirmed in 1992 to a seat on the Second Circuit Court of Appeals, one of the nation's most important courts because its jurisdiction includes New York, Connecticut, and Vermont. Previous members of this court have gone on to serve with distinction on the Supreme Court, and at least two previous members, Learned Hand and Henry Friendly, are among the best known and most highly regarded federal judges to have been appointed to the Supreme Court. In that historical context, Dennis Jacobs's appointment is an odd fit.

Jacobs graduated from law school in 1973 and then spent his entire legal career prior to his appointment with a large corporate law firm in New York. He never held or apparently ever sought public office. He had no record of participation in politics or public affairs. He produced no significant body of writing on the law or any other matter. He was never a prosecutor, he did not participate in a single civil rights case, nor did he litigate on any significant constitutional issue—the major business of the court to which he was appointed. His work focused solely on a narrow area of insurance law, and it earned him a large income: about $1 million a year prior to his federal appointment.

Judge Jacobs's sole qualification for so important a judicial appointment seems to have been his membership in the Federalist Society, identified by its statement of purpose as "a group of conservatives and libertarians interested in the current state of the legal order."[18] For much of the Reagan and Bush years, the Federalist Society served as a place where legal conservatives could demonstrate their ideological purity on issues of concern to the Republican administrations in Washington. The route that Dennis Jacobs followed to a federal judgeship typifies the new selection process of the late postwar period. It could not be more different from the judicial appointment process that prevailed before World War II.

Nowhere is the change in appointment criteria more apparent than in the membership of the U.S. Supreme Court. Political experience is out; ideological purity, judicial experience, and representational diversity are in. One hundred eight individuals served on the U.S. Supreme Court from the beginning of the republic to the end of 1995. Most of the eighty-seven justices appointed before 1950 had come from the hurly-burly of politics. Seven had served in the Continental Congress, sixteen in the House of Representatives, fourteen in the Senate, twenty-seven in the Cabinet, five as state governors, and one as president of the United States. Many others had held other state and local offices or served as prosecutors at the state or federal level.

That pattern was almost completely truncated after 1950. The last justice to have served in the House of Representatives was Fred Vinson, who died in 1953. The last senator to have served on the Court was Hugo Black, who retired in 1971. The last member of a president's cabinet to have served on the Court was Tom Clark, who retired in 1966. And the last justice to have been a state governor was Earl Warren of California, who retired in 1969. Therefore, not since 1971 has there been a member of the Supreme Court who was ever a member of Congress, a governor of a state, or a cabinet secretary. It is enlightening to compare the Supreme Court that handed down the *Brown* decision of 1954 with the Supreme Court in place at the end of Bill Clinton's third year in office.[19] (See Table 6.2.) Note that none of those on the Court in 1954 had ever before been a judge, but five had held elected office, and the other four had all held appointed positions in the federal executive branch. The 1995 court, by contrast, had only one member who had ever been elected to public office (a state legislator) and only three who had been appointed to executive branch positions. Eight of the latter Court's members, however, were judges at the time of their appointments.

TABLE 6.2
Backgrounds of Supreme Court Justices, 1954 and 1995

Justice	Background
1954 term	
Hugo Black	U.S. senator
Harold H. Burton	State legislator; mayor of Cleveland; U.S. senator
Tom Clark	U.S. attorney general
William O. Douglas	Chairman, Securities and Exchange Commission
Felix Frankfurter	Professor, Harvard Law School; assistant U.S. attorney; labor "troubleshooter" for Woodrow Wilson
Robert Jackson	Counsel, Internal Revenue Service; special counsel, Securities and Exchange Commission; assistant attorney general; solicitor general; U.S. attorney general
Sherman Minton	U.S. senator
Stanley Reed	State legislator; counsel to the Federal Farm Board; general counsel, Reconstruction Finance Corporation; U.S. solicitor general
Earl Warren	Governor, California; 1948 Republican candidate for vice president; state attorney general and prosecutor
1995 term	
Stephen Breyer	Federal judge, U.S. Court of Appeals; congressional staff member
Ruth Bader Ginsburg	Federal judge, U.S. Court of Appeals
Anthony Kennedy	Federal judge, U.S. Court of Appeals
Sandra Day O'Connor	State legislator; state judge
William Rehnquist	Assistant U.S. attorney general
Antonin Scalia	Chair, Administrative Conference of the United States; staff, Office of Legal Counsel, U.S. Justice Department; federal judge, U.S. Court of Appeals
David Souter	Attorney general of New Hampshire; federal judge, U.S. Court of Appeals
John P. Stevens	Federal judge, U.S. Court of Appeals
Clarence Thomas	Assistant secretary, U.S. Department of Education; chair, Equal Employment Opportunity Commission, federal judge, U.S. Court of Appeals

SOURCE: Congressional Quarterly, *Guide to the U.S. Supreme Court* (Washington, D.C.: Congressional Quarterly, 1979); *Congressional Quarterly Weekly Reports.*

Judges' backgrounds are not the sole determinant of their behavior on the bench, and caution is appropriate in this kind of analysis, but the change that has occurred in the last few decades is stark and noteworthy. The old path of judicial selection in which appointees were often drawn from the realm of hands-on, practical politics exists no longer. Judges now travel to the federal courts, and especially to the highest court in the land, on the path of judicial experience, often in the vehicle of ideological correctness. For potential judges, the important question is not what they have been or how they have performed, but what they believe and how firmly and aggressively they believe it. For potential Supreme Court justices, it also helps to be wearing a judicial robe.

Every Supreme Court has had some devoted ideologues; no Court has been composed solely of politicians. But the trend of recent decades has been toward the former and away from the latter. And that directly reverses the pattern that had prevailed for all of the decades before World War II. It is a profound change in the way the federal courts, and the Supreme Court especially, are composed. As the work of the courts grows steadily more diverse and complex, the on-deck circle for future judges grows smaller and smaller.

THE NEW LEGALISM

In the century and a half that followed the ratification of the Constitution, the courts served as the federal government's primary brake. With few exceptions, their role—self-defined but widely accepted—was to say "no" when a state government or one of the other federal branches acted beyond its authority. The courts said no when the state of Maryland sought to tax the national bank, when President Lincoln suspended habeas corpus during the Civil War, when Congress sought to limit hours for child labor, and when Franklin Roosevelt emplaced the National Industrial Recovery Act as the keystone of the New Deal. Politicians of the moment sometimes viewed the courts as overly conservative, overly cautious impediments to progress. But it was widely understood that caution was an appropriate legal posture for federal courts and a necessary restraint on rambunctious majorities.

Courts were also conservative in the way they dispensed their services. Access to courts was limited by firmly held, traditional legal doctrines. Courts would hear only genuine cases in law and equity, with litigants who had standing to sue, on matters that clearly fell within the courts' jurisdiction, and where courts could provide genuine remedies. Standing, jurisdiction, and justiciability: These were the key concepts of court access, deeply branded on the minds of every first-year law student. Courts would not hear moot cases, cases that had already been settled elsewhere, or cases in which the parties no longer had a real stake or dispute. Neither would courts deal with "political questions" that ought to be settled by legislators, not judges. Federal courts would not hear cases involving state law that had not yet been resolved by the state courts.

These and other rules of justiciability circumscribed access to the courts and limited their utility as a forum for resolving public policy issues. The courts did occasionally redirect the course of public policy, but it took a special alignment of preconditions to get a landmark case to court, to get the judges to agree to hear it, and to get an opinion that swept beyond the particular interests of the direct parties. The common tendency was for courts to guard their autonomy by throwing procedural rules in the way of controversial cases. Chief Justice John Marshall set that precedent in *Marbury* v. *Madison* (1803) when he declared that the Court's original jurisdiction did not extend beyond the specific language of the Constitution. A later court held in *Massachusetts* v. *Mellon* (1923) that all the citizens of Massachusetts did not have standing to challenge provisions of the Federal Maternity Act. As recently as 1946, in *Colegrove* v. *Green*, the justices declared that the egregious malapportionment of Illinois congressional districts was a "political question" and was thus beyond the Court's jurisdiction. When the rules of justiciability provided a convenient way to avoid controversy, courts often used them to deny access to petitioners.

All that has changed in recent decades. The rules of justiciability have been steadily relaxed, and the range of issues on which courts now feel free to rule has been greatly expanded. However, these significant changes in legal doctrine result from no concentrated effort at legal reform. They were not the work of a bar association committee, congressional legislation, or any notable school of legal scholarship. There was no important book or seminal law review article calling for broad-scale changes in the rules of justiciability. The changes just happened, and they happened in different places at different times—disjointed, ad hoc, unconnected to any consensual goals of legal reform. Like so much that we have seen in this book, the legal system changed on its own. A new legalism emerged, but it had few thoughtful advocates, no conscious connections to the rest of the political system, and, eventually, no real support, even among its most successful practitioners.

Congress helped invent this new legalism, but the courts have been accomplices as well. Neither institution fully imagined the extended impact its tinkering would have. Together they threw open the doors to American courts, and in response a broad range of American social and economic interests left Congress and the agencies behind and began to take their business to court.

Who could blame them? The courts offered attractive possibilities for action—and sometimes for desired delay—that Congress and the agencies could not match. Like wise consumers, political interests shopped around for the venue that promised them the most satisfactory outcome. It was the rational thing to do.

Court Doctrines Reinvented

Much of the inspiration for the new postwar legalism came from the Supreme Court over which Earl Warren presided from 1953 through 1968. The Warren Court was dominated by a liberal, activist majority that held together for more than a decade. Warren himself and Justices Hugo Black, William O. Douglas, and William Brennan were at its heart. They were later joined in number and spirit by Arthur Goldberg, Abe Fortas, and Thurgood Marshall. The Warren Court paid less feasance to legal doctrines of justiciability than had any of its predecessors, hearing cases on issues that for decades had failed to pass that test. On school desegregation, the rights of criminals, freedom of expression and religion, and apportionment, the Warren Court shoved old justiciability questions aside to get at substantive issues that compelled the attention and legal passions of its members.

The assertiveness and broadened horizons of the Warren Court encouraged other courts and later Supreme Courts to sweep widely in their own activities. But these factors also encouraged Congress to delegate more policy questions to the courts. Many members of Congress, sympathetic to the liberal bent of the Warren Court but trapped in a seniority-encrusted legislature, found growing comfort in the transfer of policy questions from the legislative or executive branch to the courts. In 1983, for example, Chief Judge Charles Clark of the U.S. Circuit Court of Appeals for the Fifth Circuit identified over three hundred subjects on which Congress had invested jurisdiction in the federal courts.[20]

In addition, Congress itself contributed to the liberalization of traditional justiciability restraints. Congress widened the realm in which courts could hear class action suits—those involving multiple parties whose collective interest or harm was large enough to justify a legal action even if none of their individual interests or harm were. Congress expanded the substantive and procedural rights of American citizens and charged the federal courts to secure the exercise of those rights. And Congress added to the remedies that courts could provide in cases involving rights. The granting of redress and relief became substantial elements of court business after World War II, in part because judges sought to focus more attention on those matters, but also because legislators wanted judges to do just that.

All of these developments sum to a profound change in the way the federal courts now operate. More litigants have standing to sue than ever before. Class action suits have become common elements of court dockets. The old rules of "mootness" and "ripeness" have been modified—some would say obliterated—to permit the courts to decide on cases before they have been exhaustively litigated elsewhere and after petitioners may have found a remedy or lost the need for relief. And the "political question" restraint has virtually vanished. The courts now constantly trespass into the "political thicket" from which Felix Frankfurter shunted them away in 1946. Although the trend has not been perfectly even or consistent in its development, the direction is clear: Actions by government and private institutions that would have been regarded as out of bounds for the courts before World War II are now routinely accepted for adjudication.

And once courts take on these cases, there are a wider range of instruments available for resolving them. The traditional response of the federal courts when they found a government agency had exceeded or abused its authority was to find for the plaintiff and order the agency to devise a remedy. Even in *Brown* v. *Topeka Board of Education*, the landmark school desegregation case, the Supreme Court discharged its obligation to grant relief by ordering local school boards to end segregation "with all deliberate speed." No particular remedy was specified, no timetable imposed.

Contemporary courts are rarely satisfied with mere calls for action. Now, instead, they issue detailed decrees with rigid timetables and carefully defined courses of action that agencies must follow. In the case of *Wyatt* v. *Stickney* (1971), for example, Judge Frank M. Johnson imposed a highly detailed administrative structure and set of operating standards on the entire mental health system of the state of Alabama—standards that, when fully implemented, would cost the state an additional $60 million. To further ensure compliance with court decrees, the federal courts sometimes appoint special masters to take charge of entire government functions: a public school system, a state prison, or a state mental health program. Courts have forced the restructuring of governmental units, expanded the number of recipients entitled to public services, and imposed new agency operating procedures that required new appropriations and new taxes.

All of these changes have profoundly altered the molecular element of the legal system: the lawsuit. In a seminal law review article, Professor Abram Chayes compared the lawsuit form that had dominated for much of American history with the new style of lawsuit that emerged after World War II. Table 6.3 summarizes his comparison. In this new style, more citizens have more opportunity to enlist the aid of federal courts in more ways to accomplish more political and economic objectives.

In many ways courts, by their own design, by pressures placed on them by litigants, and by the deference or indifference of legislatures, have be-

TABLE 6.3
Abram Chayes's Comparison of Traditional and New-Style Lawsuits

Components	Traditional	Emerging New Style
Actor	Identifiable individual	Abstract collection of people or nonidentifiable person, possibly predecessor or defendant
Time of act	Immediate past	Distant past, continuing, or potentially in future
Nature of act	Specific	Nonspecific or a variety of acts
Unlawful by virtue of	Specific statute or clear court precedent	No clear statutory provision or judicial precedent
Harm	Palpably injurious	Intangible
Who hurt	Identifiable individual directly harmed by actor	Many persons, not necessarily identifiable and not necessarily directly affected by actor
Relief	Narrow, directly related to injury	Broad, not necessarily deducible from the nature of the harm
Will bind	Parties only	Nonparties, potentially millions
Court's involvement	Ceases on entry of judgment	Continues indefinitely

SOURCE: Jethro K. Lieberman, *The Litigious Society* (New York: Basic Books, 1981), p. 31, based on Abram Chayes, "The Role of the Judge in Public Law Litigation," 89 *Harvard Law Review* (1976): 1281–1283.

come the institutions in the American government most responsible for patching fissures and repairing breakdowns in the social order. "The idea of redress," wrote Jethro Lieberman, "acts like a gas in a vacuum; it rushes about filling in empty space."[21] And so it has, making courts the special target of opportunity for every interest in American society seeking a place at the table, a fairer shake, or a larger piece of the pie.

New Realms of Intervention

American courts have responded to this new and escalating set of demands by making more decisions on more issues than ever before. The list of policy areas into which courts have moved is long, but a few examples suffice to suggest their new reach. Environmental policy became a national preoccupation after Earth Day in 1970. Congress had enacted some conservation and clean water and clear air legislation in the 1960s and then generated significant new environmental legislation at the end of that decade: the National Environmental Policy Act, the creation of the Environmental Protection Agency, and bold new initiatives against air and water pollution. This was legislation in largely virgin territory. The new environmental laws were full of compromises and hedged bets because they generated hot disagreements between those who wanted stiff protections for the environment and those who wanted to continue to produce fossil fuels, manufacture inexpensive cars, and avoid the costs of installing antipollution devices such as smoke stack scrubbers. Much of this new environmental legislation was unclear in meaning and applicability. It would have to be cleaned up in implementation and in court.

The most notable example of this pattern was the attacks that environmental groups began to make on the environmental impact statements (EISs) required by the National Environmental Policy Act that Richard Nixon signed into law on January 1, 1970. Designed by legislators to raise the environmental consciousness of all federal agencies, the EIS became a valuable handle for environmental groups. So, too, did the Endangered Species Act of 1973, which put severe restrictions on any project that jeopardized the survival of any species. With the acquiescence of federal courts, environmentalists began to initiate lawsuits against a number of states and federal agencies challenging the adequacy of the environmental impact statements for new projects. Courts were asked to be arbiters on these questions, and most of the time they accepted the assignment.

This situation put federal judges in the position of deciding whether massive projects such as the Tellico Dam and the Seabrook nuclear power plant could move forward, whether changes were necessary to minimize their environmental impact, or whether they would be stopped in their tracks. Environmental litigators sprung up widely—the Natural Resources Defense Council, the Sierra Club, the Wilderness Society—using the courts to challenge corporate and governmental practices on environmental grounds. The focus of environmental policy making began to shift from a Congress increasingly knotted in political wrangling to the federal courts, where access was widening and judges were willing to issue decisions, even on the most complex technical issues. As Roderick Cameron, the executive director of the Environmental Defense Fund, noted on Earth Day in 1970, "The judiciary is the one social institution already structured to provide wise responses that may enable us to avert ecological disaster."

Prisoners' rights became another area of intensified court activity. This intensification resulted not from new legislation but from broadening court interpretations of the Fourteenth Amendment, the Habeas Corpus Act of 1867, and Section 1983 of the Civil Rights Act of 1871. In a series

of cases beginning with *Cooper* v. *Pate* in 1964, the Supreme Court opened
the door to prisoners who wanted to challenge their convictions in state
and federal courts and their treatment in prison. Their legal standing was
broadened, they were granted greater access to attorneys, and some restrictions were lifted on mail censorship, the practice of religion, and access to medical care. Prisoners responded by seeking even greater procedural and substantive protection from the courts. A flood of prisoners'
rights cases kept this issue on court dockets for years. And in so doing,
this reliance on litigation steadily shifted authority for determining criminal procedures and prison conditions from Congress and the state legislatures, from criminal justice and corrections agencies, to the federal
courts. In 1970 the federal courts invalidated the entire prison system of
Arkansas. By 1983 the prison systems of eight states had been found unconstitutional. And by 1986 thirty-seven states had prisons or corrections
officials operating under federal court orders, and nearly all states had at
least one prison facility engaged in litigation.[22]

Nowhere, however, is the expanding policymaking role of the courts
more evident than in civil rights. Not merely in determining the rights of
racial minorities, but also in securing legal, economic, and social protections for women, children, inhabitants of public institutions, recipients of
welfare services, public school students, the mentally ill, refugees, and
many other individual categories, the federal courts have become dominant determiners of the form and substance of the relationship between
government and individual in the United States.

In the period since World War II, no statute has had greater impact on
the work and influence of the courts than Title VII of the Civil Rights Act
of 1964, which banned discrimination in employment practices. The onslaught of cases resulting from this law has given the courts ample opportunity to redefine the rights of individuals in countless employment
and other settings. But it has been the courts themselves, not Congress,
that bear primary responsibility for the "rights revolution" that has occurred in the postwar period. Some of the burden assumed by the courts
has been in response to an endless flow of litigation based on the
Fourteenth Amendment. "No patent medicine was ever put to wider and
more varied use than the Fourteenth Amendment," Justice Douglas once
wrote in what could stand as a fitting description of the postwar period.
But the Court has found many other foundations for the emplacement
and strengthening of new rights: the Habeas Corpus Act of 1867, the Civil
Rights Act of 1871, the Fourth and Fifth Amendments to the Constitution,
and a number of postwar statutes whose provisions were interpreted
much more broadly than their authors had ever intended.

The new legalism of the postwar period is the product of several trends
converging. One is the widening of access to courts. Litigation became

particularly attractive as an alternative to legislation when the ability of Congress to resolve thorny political issues steadily eroded. A second trend has been the reconfiguration of the lawsuit from a narrowly focused disagreement between individual parties over highly specific questions to a conflict between competing social forces over major issues of public policy or individual rights. A third trend has been the evolution of a judge's role from referee in unique conflicts to guarantor of social justice. The result, as legal scholar Gary L. McDowell noted, has been a growing utilization of the judicial power

> not as a necessary means of resolving concrete disputes but as a necessary political power to oversee and, when necessary, transform society in light of abstract principles. The new jurisprudence holds that the "central function" of judicial power is the "determination of the individual's claim to 'just' treatment." The intellectual force of this procedural jurisprudence has been sufficient in lawsuits dealing with public questions to shift the emphasis from the character of the parties to the character of the claim; the issue has become more important than the litigants.[23]

Changes in doctrine, changes in demand, and changes in rules of procedure have all profoundly altered the role that courts play in shaping American public life. It is a change that emerged prominently after World War II and then mushroomed after 1960. The practice of civil law is now a major strand in American public policy making. Courts and lawyers are key players. Now the Constitution means—and the law means—what the judges say it does.

IMPLICATIONS OF JUDICIAL ASCENDANCY

Litigation is not evil. Neither, necessarily, is the practice of courts making public policy. Courts are human institutions, like legislatures and executives; they are capable of acting nobly or nuttily. But even the most acerbic critics of contemporary American courts would note that they have done much in recent decades to improve the quality of individual American lives and to enhance equity and justice.

Nor are judges always busybodies, aggressively intervening in public policy questions. Sometimes they are, but often judges have little choice but to act. The American tendency to judicialize everything has forced many issues onto court dockets that might well have been resolved elsewhere. The default or incompetence of other branches or levels of government may have thrust some decisions on the courts; outright violations of the Constitution impose others. The growing role that courts have played in public policy making has not always been intentional or self-determined.

Nevertheless, the new reign of judicial intervention in public policy is deeply troubling. Courts are peculiar institutions. They have their own agendas and operating styles and biases. They follow certain kinds of procedures and produce certain kinds of policy outcomes. These are often different from the procedures and policy outcomes we would get if policy choices were made by other institutions. In some important ways, American public policy is different—and the quality of the American democratic process is different—because of the enlarged role that courts have played in our public life since World War II.

For one thing, significant court decisions often fly in the face of public opinion. Some would argue the benefits of that function: Courts exist to protect individuals and minorities from the oppression of public opinion, from Tocqueville's "tyranny of the majority." And, no doubt, there are times when American politics needs the jolt of a court decision like *Brown* v. *Board* as a legal contribution to an evolving public dialogue on a controversial issue.

But a steady tendency by courts to issue decisions that contravene public consensus is corrosive over the long term. Persistent nonmajoritarian activity inevitably undermines public support for government action. It breeds dissatisfaction, which quickly festers into disaffection. The legitimacy of government itself may be cast in doubt.

Democracy is defined by procedures as well as ends. The *way* we decide contributes as much to the character of our government as *what* we decide. A robust democracy can tolerate an occasional procedural detour if it serves a popular or just purpose. But the institutionalization of routine policymaking processes that provide little voice for public opinion and issue decisions that often directly contravene the expressed public will have a draining effect on popular support for government itself.

Commentators on the Supreme Court have long treated the question of the Court's responsiveness to public opinion with aphorism rather than analysis. They quote ad nauseam the fictional Mr. Dooley's comment that "th' supreme coort follows th' iliction returns." No close observer of the postwar Court could possibly draw such a conclusion, however. It is based on two unverifiable assumptions: (1) that election returns offer clear indications of public opinion and (2) that the Court has been assiduous in aligning its decisions with those indications. Yet in 1954 the Supreme Court's landmark school desegregation decision followed a presidential election in which the party of the leading civil rights president of the first half of the century was rejected in favor of a new president who had no civil rights agenda and who had initially opposed the racial integration of the armed forces. In 1973 the Supreme Court struck down many state restrictions on abortions just two months after the landslide reelection of a president who opposed abortion and the repudiation of his opponent, who was an advocate of freedom of choice. Over this same period the federal courts increased protections for imprisoned and accused criminals, mandated school busing programs, imposed corporate and local affirmative action plans, stopped construction on major public works projects on environmental technicalities, banned prayer and other religious expressions from public schools, and weakened many local obscenity laws. Public opinion encouraged little of this activity and opposed most of it. The Supreme Court was not following the election returns or anything of the sort. In many of its most important postwar decisions, in fact, the Supreme Court treated public opinion as little more than a petitioner without standing. The Court did what it did, willy-nilly.

The court ascendancy in policymaking also raises troublesome questions about accountability and responsibility. Federal judges never stand for reelection. The Constitution permits their impeachment only for "bribery, high crimes, and other misdemeanors"; impeachment is not a recourse for judicial incompetence or policy usurpation. The only political accountability, then, is the election of presidents who will appoint no more judges like the ones who have distressed us. And fetching on the public clamor for greater judicial accountability, recent presidential candidates have aggressively made such promises.

But the practical—and political—reality is that judges rarely have to endure consequences for the pain their decisions impose. When a court finds an environmental impact statement unsuitable and delays the construction of a power plant or manufacturing facility, imposes new burdens on the process of arresting and incarcerating criminals, or forces a sweeping school busing plan on a reluctant city, affected citizens have no democratic channels through which to act on their opposition or anger. Instead, they resort to "direct action," to street demonstrations, and to violence. It is hardly surprising that the growing popularity of such noninstitutional forms of political expression and action has coincided with the growing involvement of courts in policymaking.

Nor do judges have to face up to the budgetary implications of their decisions. However right-minded courts may be in elevating the standards for equal opportunity in public employment, better treatment of the mentally ill, or desegregation in public schools, judicial decisions have budgetary consequences. Judges rarely suffer those consequences or their fallout. If the Framers of the Constitution were in consensus on nothing else, they were of one mind on the singular importance of placing the power to tax the people in the hands of the people. Hence, the Constitution requires that measures to raise revenue be initiated in the popularly elected house of Congress. Yet courts these days often impose standards of performance on governments that they cannot evade and that have the inevitable impact of increasing expenditures and thus raising taxes. Legislators and executives may pay a political price for such actions, but judges never do.

The expansion of the judicial role in policymaking also contributes to irresponsibility among elected officials. Knowing, as they now must, that many of their most controversial decisions will ultimately be reargued and redecided in court, public officials are relieved of much of the pressure to act responsibly. When they have reason to believe that legislative or executive decisions will not count—because courts will be the real decisionmakers—legislators can shape their own actions to suit their political self-interests or those of their constituents without regard to more general or national consequences. When Congress debated legislation to prohibit the burning of the American flag in 1989, few legislators believed that congressional action would be the final word on the issue. It was widely assumed that the Supreme Court would review the constitutionality of whatever Congress decided, just as the Court's review of the prosecution of a flag burner in Dallas had inspired initial congressional interest. Knowing that any legislative decision was merely a preface to the "real" decision in court, members of Congress felt free to engage in demagoguery and to give speeches on the floors of their chambers that were intended largely for home consumption. Concerns about constitutional issues or the nuances of the First Amendment were largely irrelevant. Court action was for real; congressional action was for show.

Dependence on courts to resolve public policy controversies is a problem in another way: Courts provide little basis or sustenance for collective action. And in democratic government, the most effective actions have always been collective ones. When the popular will is mobilized, when public officials act in accord with a popular consensus and contribute to its creation, policy falls on fertile ground. The enactment of the personal income tax, the creation of the social security program, the passage of the Voting Rights Act: All of these were policies that followed years of discussion, of false starts, of national debate, of painstaking construction of national consensus and majority coalitions. These laws may have been radical reconfigurations of public policy, imposing real sacrifice on sizable segments of the population. But the soil in which they were planted had been carefully tilled, and they quickly took root.

But when courts jump into a controversy and make a decision in advance of national consensus and without benefit of coalition building, the policies they impose rarely sit well. Implementation is often fitful and incomplete, in part because the implementers themselves have no stake in and no stomach for the policy they have been charged with carrying out. The Boston School Committee did everything in its power—and much that was beyond its power—to eviscerate the school desegregation decision imposed on the city by a federal judge in 1974. Few policy changes in our history have inspired more ingenuity—much of it aimed at evading the central premise—than the Supreme Court's legislative reapportionment decisions in the 1960s. Reliance on courts to make controversial policy decisions causes the democratic process to short-circuit and accelerates action in advance of the deliberate process of decision. Policies imposed on a democratic citizenry before public opinion is ripe for action are received like immature wine: with a bad taste.

A broader problem results with the persistence of judicial policymaking. The hegemony of courts diminishes the energy that goes into popular mobilization. As judges make more and more of a society's important decisions, elections and legislative debates become steadily less relevant. Why invest time in election campaigns or voting if the purpose is only to pick officials who make speeches, not policy? In a rational political system, citizens who care about policy choices direct their energies at those who have the real power to make such choices. To a growing extent in the American system, those people are judges. And, as we have seen in this chapter, resources have been piled into the effort to influence judicial decisions. The flip side of that development has been a diminished interest in popular mobilization through the traditional vehicles of political parties, large interest groups, and national popular movements.

As the process of policy change has become more retail in character, seekers of change have narrowed their political focus to the retailers, particularly the courts, congressional subcommittees, and operating bureaus in the executive branch. At the same time, and for similar reasons, seekers of change have steadily abandoned the policy wholesalers, especially the political parties and the big coalitional interest groups. The cost of this abandonment has been a deterioration of the capacity for popular mobilization, which has led to a diminished systemwide ability to construct proper foundations of popular support for new policy initiatives. Hence, broad policies are harder to change, and changes are harder to implement.

The principal case for judicial ascendancy is framed in negatives. Advocates argue that the changing role of the courts is desirable not because courts enhance the character of democracy or make better policy decisions than the traditional policymaking institutions, but because the other institutions have defaulted on their policymaking responsibilities. Courts have to decide; other institutions do not. At least courts can act; at least they can produce real change. This cautious support for judicial ascendancy assumes that courts have the capacity to make wise decisions on a wide range of policy questions and thus to produce real change. But a growing body of evidence challenges these assumptions and thus calls into question even the timid support that now exists in some quarters for the larger role that courts have assumed in policymaking.

As noted earlier, the size of the federal court system has grown significantly since World War II. There are more courts and more judges and more law clerks. The federal government spends substantially more to sustain the judicial branch. But caseloads have grown much faster than the court establishment both in number and complexity.

Congress and the bureaucracy have responded to the complexity of contemporary public life not only by expanding—according to some measures, much more rapidly than the courts—but also by steadily specializing. More and more the work of Congress and the federal executive branch is parceled out to subcommittees and bureaucratic subunits with staff and resources that allow them to build substantial expertise on the issues in their narrow jurisdictions. More and more—though sometimes at the cost of speed or consensus—legislative policymaking has fallen into the hands of specialists and experts.

This is not the case in the judicial branch. Judges are generalists. They have little control over the subjects of the cases that come before them. In the course of a year, a judge may be required to make decisions in dozens of different policy realms. The judicial docket is a smorgasbord, and judges have to try a little of everything. Even those judges who come to the bench with significant specialized knowledge in a particular field will be able to take advantage of their expertise in only a small portion of the cases they decide.

The postwar period has strained judicial competence. Not only are judges deciding more cases and more complex cases covering more substantive areas. There also is evidence of some decline in the collective and individual competence of the federal judiciary. Although comparison of the judges of one era with those of another is difficult, it is at least worth noting that many forces at work in how courts are staffed and function may well have diminished their competence.

When there were fewer judges, appointment to the federal bench was a rare distinction. It is less so now, and such appointments are therefore less appealing to good lawyers. Judicial salaries have grown in the postwar period, but not nearly so fast as the compensation of the best attorneys in private practice. Associate justices of the Supreme Court earned $159,000 in 1992; judges in the appeals and district courts earned less. At some large, big-city firms, senior associates made more than that; partners made substantially more. The average profit per partner in a survey of selected large law firms in 1991 was $304,125.[24] The suspicion grows among many scholars that the quality of judges recruited to the federal bench—with growing salary disparities, more patent ideological litmus tests, greater fear of abusive confirmation inquiries, stricter conflict-of-interest standards, heavier workloads, and less prestige—is in decline. Empirical evidence is imprecise on this question, but some scholars have noted the steady falloff in recent years in the ratings given judicial nominees by the American Bar Association's Standing Committee on the Federal Judiciary. Whereas 38 percent of Eisenhower and Kennedy appointees to the federal district and circuit courts received ABA ratings in the lowest "not qualified" and "qualified" categories, approximately 50 percent of all subsequent appointees have fallen into those lower two categories.[25]

Judicial turnover is another potential indication of declining judicial competence. The turnover rate for federal circuit and district courts judges was 30 percent higher in the period from 1944 to 1987 than in the period from 1900 to 1943.[26] The escalating rate of judicial resignations and retirements had many causes, but its principal effect was to diminish overall judicial experience levels and encourage the appointment of even more new judges, many of whose initial qualifications fell substantially short of those of the departees they were replacing.

The collective competence of the courts has also been threatened by the growing gap between the demands placed on courts and the resources available to respond to those demands. Judges have handled more cases in large part by relying more heavily on subsidiary personnel: law clerks, staff attorneys, and externs. Less research is actually done by the judges who make decisions. Fewer opinions are actually drafted by the judges who sign them. Judges have fallen more deeply into the role of managers of the decisionmaking and opinion-writing processes while growing more detached from the details of the cases they decide and the precedents they cite.

Another postwar trend that reflects on judges' competence as policymakers is the steady decline in consensus on the Supreme Court. In the early decades of the twentieth century, dissenting and concurring opinions were a rarity in Supreme Court cases, occurring in less than 10 percent of all cases. After the war dissents and concurrences became more common as Court consensus diminished. By the 1980s dissenting and concurring opinions accounted for approximately 60 percent of all Supreme Court opinions.[27] As the Court became more active in policymaking, its fissures multiplied and widened. As the importance of the Court's opinion grew larger, its ability to speak with one voice grew smaller.

The irony here is particularly keen. The judicial role in policymaking is expanding at precisely the same time that judicial competence is shrinking. As courts grow less worthy of our reliance, we rely on them more heavily. Individually and collectively, judges simply may not be up to the increased responsibilities they have assumed. The peril in these conflicting trends is clear.

Finally, we must confront the assumption that courts, whatever else their imperfections, deserve credit for producing real and positive changes in the quality of American life. Courts ended segregation in public schools and public accommodations. Courts facilitated the full acceptance of women in the workplace, in education, and in legal status. Courts legalized abortion, corrected legislative malapportionment, and accelerated efforts to clean the environment.

Or did they? Even here, in what are broadly assumed to be matters of demonstrable court influence and success, fundamental questions are being raised not so much about the costs of shifting authority to the courts as about the benefits. Are courts really competent to produce the kinds of sweeping changes their advocates suggest? The chorus of doubts grows louder.

A powerful recent book by political scientist Gerald N. Rosenberg raised profound empirical skepticism, for example, about the claims that courts brought about many of the major social and economic changes of the postwar era. It is a complex work, worthy of careful scrutiny. Rosenberg noted that the Supreme Court's decision in *Brown* did not end school desegregation in the South. A decade after Brown 98.8 percent of black schoolchildren in the South continued to attend all-black schools.[28] Real change occurred, he argued, only when Congress acted through the Civil Rights Act, the Voting Rights Act, and federal aid to education to put the teeth of federal enforcement powers behind the words of *Brown*.

Nor, Rosenberg argued, did the legalization of abortion begin with *Roe v. Wade*, the Supreme Court's landmark abortion decision in 1973. He systematically demonstrated that liberalization of state abortion laws was well under way before *Roe* and that, in fact, the most rapid increases in legal abortions occurred before, not after, the *Roe* decision.[29] The findings are similar in women's rights and reapportionment and environmental action. Courts either make decisions that have little broad support and little real impact, or their decisions come after a social movement is well under way and thus simply contribute to a momentum for change that they did not initiate.

Rosenberg's conclusion is notable for its strong empirical base and its lack of hyperbole: "U.S. courts can almost never be effective producers of significant social reform. At best, they can second the social reform acts of the other branches of government. Problems that are unsolvable in the political context can rarely be solved in courts. . . . Turning to courts to produce significant social reform substitutes the myth of America for its reality. It credits courts and judicial decisions with a power that they do not have."[30]

All of this suggests one other reason to be wary of the growing reliance on courts to make difficult policy choices. Their ability to do so effectively may well be illusory. At a minimum it is more constrained than most commentators have recognized or admitted. Judges are not sorcerers. They cannot make consensus appear when none has formed, nor can they make resistance vanish simply by wishing it away. When courts practice policy-making, they are political, not magical, institutions. They are called on more often than ever before by a frustrated polity to resolve its conflicts. They often respond to the call. But their responses produce higher costs and fewer benefits than the conventional wisdom has cared to confess.

CONCLUSION

A political society that relies on courts to make its most difficult decisions may experience the temporary illusion that some efficiency has been achieved, some gridlock broken. But the longer-term consequences are a clogging of the essential channels of democracy, a loss of public interest in or support for government decisions, and ultimately a failure of accomplishment.

The new legalism of the postwar period has deeply altered the operations of the judicial process and the role of the courts. Groups in American society, particularly the dispossessed and the politically underrepresented, sought this expanded court role as a way to better protect their own rights and benefits. Judges went along, encouraging the change. As the venue of policymaking shifted, the system adapted. More and more groups went to court to get policy changed. Legislators began to delegate more authority to courts, especially when unable to disentangle legislative politics sufficiently to decide complex questions themselves.

But few of those who participated in this pattern of court hegemony sought to justify it as an improvement in the practice of democratic self-government. The change inspired few positive assessments; it inspired even fewer clarion calls to "let the judges dominate." It was a watershed in practice without foundation or justification in democratic theory. The growing policy role of the courts was undesigned, unintended, and largely unapproved. But it happened in the postwar period. And it had consequences that reverberate, largely unhappily, throughout all of American society.

THE STALEMATE SYSTEM

American politics changed profoundly in the half century after World War II, but few of the changes improved the country's capacity for self-government. On the eve of a new century, Americans distrust their government and hate their own politics. Political leaders can rarely lead. Elections fail to resolve conflicts or set directions. Representative mechanisms proliferate, but representative institutions lose their grip on policymaking. As government's impact grows, more and more of its most important public choices are made by judges and bureaucrats. Ours is an age of immobilism in which thousands of social and economic forces are locked in escalating political stalemate.

That American government is in disarray is a fact that has escaped no one's notice; political leaders themselves have been saying so for years. But most of the diagnoses suggest that current problems are the result of bad political choices in the recent past, of overzealousness on the Right or the Left. The conservative critique lays fault on the shoulders of the social engineers of the New Deal and the Great Society. America pays the price now, they argue, for too much overselling of government capacity and competence, for decades of "tax-and-spend liberalism," for soft-headedness and woolly thinking about human nature.[1] The liberal critique faults the paranoia of the cold war call to arms, a national indifference to human needs and human suffering, and the failed financial legerdemain of Reaganomics.[2]

But the search for good guys and bad guys is misleading. It is the central argument of this book that American government and politics have gone off track not because of the bad choices of the people in charge but precisely because no one has been in charge. The major ailments of our public life are diseases of structure and process, not the excesses of ideology or partisanship. Our government does not work well. It cannot perform with any consistency or reliability the simple functions of democracy.

Fault for the breakdown lies not with liberals and conservatives or with Republicans or Democrats seizing power and implementing bad policies. We are all guilty parties—all of us who have sought to play the parts off against the whole for material and political gain, all of us who damned the system while seeking to manipulate it for our own advantage. In the years after World War II, with phenomenal sophistication and unrelenting energy, Americans—no matter what their political bent, no matter what their ideological hopes, no matter what their policy goals—sought to enlarge their advantage by altering the portion of the political system within their grasp. The consequence of the accumulation of so many people and groups doing that over so wide an expanse of political terrain for so many years is a political system that is simply no longer coherent.

The problems that have occurred in post–World War II American politics and government were not the result of the bad guys winning and the good guys losing. These problems did not reflect the impact of some evil force that overtook American politics. The American people often found much to admire—and much they wished to maintain in individual changes and reforms. In almost every case, these changes were the work of well-intentioned activists, do-gooders, good government people—reformers who tried, in the light of their own vision, to make government better.

And in some ways, they succeeded. In some important ways, government is better. It is more open. Participation is easier and cheaper and therefore broader. Government has taken on responsibilities that seem to be required of modern governments in industrial societies and has tackled the kind of intractable problems that only government has the scale of resources necessary to address. And it has had some large successes: polio vaccine and other kinds of disease control, substantial progress in breaking down the legal underpinnings of segregation and discrimination, partnership with an economy that generated millions and millions of new jobs for baby boomers after World War II, and the defense of American security in a dangerous world.

But for every problem solved, dozens of others linger unresolved. For every channel of politics opened wide, dozens of others remain closed or clogged. For every successful act of leadership, there are dozens of failures. Whatever occasional substantive successes these postwar changes might have helped accomplish, their systemic effects have been almost entirely negative for democratic self-government. With few exceptions, these changes have:

- Made it harder to bring the collective will of the American people to bear on the actions of their representatives.
- Made it harder to forge an effective definition or vision of the national interest.
- Made it harder to form enduring governing coalitions.

- Weakened the capacity for political leadership throughout the governing system.
- Deterred many of the most talented and creative Americans from seeking leadership positions in government.
- Diminished the interest and enthusiasm of the American people and dramatically altered the manner and intensity of political participation.
- Shifted policymaking authority 'from the most democratic elements of the political system to the least democratic.
- Consequently made it more difficult than at any time since the Civil War for the institutions of our federal government to address and resolve the most difficult problems facing the country.

GETTING INTO THIS MESS

In the preceding chapters, I traced the filaments of change that have so altered the politics and government of postwar America. A brief recapitulation here will help pull this explanation together.

American society changed in rapid and profound ways after World War II. The population doubled, its growth fueled especially by the postwar baby boom. Groups formerly at the margins of politics and the economy—black and Hispanic Americans, women, homosexuals, young people—became significant economic and political forces for the first time. Education levels soared. Americans gained access to unprecedented disposable income.

Over the course of the twentieth century, the economy evolved from agriculture in the early decades, to manufacturing in midcentury, to growing reliance on service industries by century's end. Americans followed the evolution from farm to city and then to suburb. At the century's beginning nearly 40 percent of the American people lived on farms. By century's end more than 50 percent will live in suburbs. The movement to the suburbs occurred almost entirely after World War II, spurred by the ready availability of automobiles and new housing, the massive program of road building, the search for good schools, and the simple need of a burgeoning population to expand somewhere.

While the American population was evolving, its government was growing and moving steadily into more and more aspects of American life. The New Deal had opened the door for bigger government, but just barely. It was World War II, with its massive penetration of American society, that really paved the way for the big government to which Americans in the second half of the century quickly became acclimated.

Government both generated and responded to social and economic changes. The GI Bill opened the possibility of higher education and home ownership to more Americans than ever before. The Federal Highway Act laid pavement across the countryside and accelerated the move to suburbia. The cold war lingered through four postwar decades, justifying massive military spending and tying the jobs of millions of workers to defense contracts. Prosperity enabled new federal expenditures on public schools, the arts and humanities, medical insurance for the elderly and indigent, space exploration, and aid to foreign countries. The federal government took on unprecedented roles in the pursuit of social justice, the regulation of industry and commerce, and the protection of the environment.

All of this action cost money. The federal budget grew from less than $10 billion just before World War II, to $100 billion in 1962, to $1 trillion in 1987. More Americans paid taxes in larger amounts. With more money to be had in federal contracts and benefits and more money to be lost in federal taxes and regulations, the stakes of politics increased enormously after World War II. When the stakes changed, so, too, did the intensity levels. Politics in postwar America mattered like never before.

Two different dynamics drove the changes. First, modern technology overtook traditional politics and rendered much of it obsolete. Television, jet travel, computers, advances in telecommunications, and sophisticated opinion polling created new ways for public officials to interact with voters, to measure and manipulate public attitudes. The need for candidates to harness these new technologies created an entirely new breed of political magnate, the independent campaign consultant. The costs of employing these technologies and retaining the consultants who managed them made campaigns formidably expensive. Political fund-raising became more pervasive and aggressive. By century's end the dynamics of fund-raising dominated most campaigns for national office. A new electoral reward system replaced the old. Where once government jobs had been the prize for votes delivered and victories won, now policy benefits were exchanged for campaign contributions.

Second, traditional politics also fell victim to internal forces of reform. As the actions of government came to affect more people in more ways, demands grew for broader participation in candidate selection. The proliferation of direct primaries and caucuses, the end of the unit rule, and party-mandated constraints on convention delegation composition shrunk the authority of the political bosses. They quickly went the way of the dinosaurs.

Party conventions had dominated the presidential nominating process from the mid-nineteenth century to the mid-twentieth. Party potentates from around the country gathered to pick a candidate who could win the election and hold the party together. By the 1970s party conventions had become little more than sideshows in the nominating process. Every major party nomination after 1960 was a fait accompli by the time the convention opened. The bosses were going or gone. A new breed of delegate—younger, more diverse, often new to politics, passionate about issues—came to the fore. Interest in holding parties together, even interest in winning elections, increasingly took a back seat to choosing candidates with the "right" positions on the dominant issues of the day. Not uncommonly, delegates to these postwar nominating conventions were attending their first convention. As delegates and their causes came and went, parties lost their prime position as coherent, continuing, meaningful entities in American politics. They served as little more than convenient battlegrounds for contemporary interests seeking access to political power for narrow purpose. Political parties that had once been lifelong homes for voters became hotels—places to stay briefly on business. Suddenly many of the stakeholders in American politics were transients.

Politics became more rootless—and more intense. When the desire for ideological correctness supersedes the goals of winning or party maintenance, as it did increasingly in postwar American politics, process loses all meaning. Rules and procedures become little more than leverage points for gaining political advantage. Competing interests fight over the shape of political processes, but not to ensure the creation of systems that serve a broad vision of the public interest or that generate talented leaders and abet their efforts. These interests seek instead to shape processes to self-serving goals, to gain procedural advantage that can then be converted to political advantage in the creation of public policy.

This decentralized, ad hoc capture and reformulation of the elements of the process were the dominant dynamics of change in postwar American politics. There were more interests and interest groups than the nation had previously seen. They all wanted a hook in the system, a piece of the action. Jack Walker, the keenest student of this aspect of the new politics, emphasized the change it wrought:

> The increase in the level of political mobilization in the American system during the past 35 years resulted from fundamental social changes, such as the growth of a large, new, educated middle class, from the emergence of many new institutions prepared to subsidize political organizations, and from the steady expansion of the power and responsibility of the federal government. Increases in the number of specialized membership and non-membership organizations involved in policy formulation and advocacy have led to a dramatic increase in the range of interests being represented and the number of issues.[3]

Groups sought advantage and impact wherever they could find either. If the primary access to political power came through the courts, groups sought changes in legal procedure that enlarged their influence. Environmental groups, for example, sought for years to get courts to broaden the definition of allowable class actions so that polluters could be sued by large numbers of people pooling resources and acting together. When the courts did finally open this door, class action suits came rushing in. If the most promising access point was the presidential selection process, aggressive activists sought to alter the nominating rules to enhance the possibility of nominating a candidate who would advance their interests. Antiwar protesters in the late 1960s and 1970s found just such opportunities in the Democratic Party. They captured the party through primaries and caucuses, kicked out the boss of bosses, and reshaped party rules to suit their own objectives.

All across the landscape of government and politics, leverage- and access-seeking interests muscled up the institutions they controlled, challenged old practices and traditions, altered rules, and reshaped procedures. Although some of these new interests adopted the rhetoric and self-righteousness of the old good government reformers, they bore little of the objectivity to which these interests pretended. In almost every case, their goal was not to serve the national interest, not to forge a better democracy, not to adapt government to the profound demographic, social, and economic changes going on around it. Their goal instead was to control the policymaking process to advance or protect their own interests.

Aggressive self-interest of this sort was hardly a postwar innovation. Self-interested individuals and groups have always been a feature of American politics. Aggressiveness and cleverness are not new either. What was different in the postwar period was the huge multiplication in the number of interests seeking influence, the extraordinary instruments available to help them, and the intensity of their actions because of the stakes of the outcome. The most important difference was the weakness of the center, its inability to hold or even to resist when the onslaught began.

The political dynamics of postwar America put the parts at war with the whole. It was a slaughter. There never had been much of a center in American politics. The dominant political parties maintained some control over politics and government because the federal government was pretty small potatoes and party hegemony was rarely challenged. When potent economic interests occasionally intersected with government, the parties were penetrable enough to accommodate these interests. The big trusts of the late nineteenth century, for example, were able to establish colonies within the parties and the legislatures when in need of favors and protections from government. The trusts had little need to set up their own mechanisms to influence policy decisions. Most of the significant challenges to the major parties came from minor parties. These "third parties" were generally dispatched with ease by the major parties and then absorbed by them. Interests were few enough and weak enough that the party system could survive, fundamentally intact, for almost a century and a half.

After World War II, however, the party system passed quickly into obsolescence. It was simply overwhelmed by too many interests with too many resources. The biggest surprise was not that the old party system passed away but that it vanished so quickly. It was more fragile than most journalists and scholars—and certainly most party leaders—had been willing to admit. A group of young right-wing radicals shoved aside the eastern establishment and captured the Republican Party in 1964. Four years later a small band of college kids rallied around an obscure midwestern senator, forcing a powerful incumbent president into early retirement and initiating a reform effort that in four years turned the Democratic Party upside down.

In Congress, too, the old order fell hard and quickly. No close observer in the late 1950s could have predicted or imagined how dramatically that institution would change in the following fifteen years. Almost everything that had been written about the "folkways" and "norms" of Congress in the 1950s was dead wrong by the early 1970s. Younger and junior members had been kept at arm's length from any real legislative influence for decades. But when their numbers and anger swelled in the late 1960s, they pulled off a succession of reforms that replaced the old power structure with one much more amenable to their interests. In Congress, as in the parties, the center could not survive a significant challenge, and it dissipated quickly.

When the dust began to settle on all these changes, one pattern was starkly clear. In the conflict between the parts and the whole, wherever it was fought, the parts won hands down. Access points multiplied geometrically. Influence thinned and spread broadly across a wide spectrum of interests and actors. Power was carved into smaller and smaller pieces. Decentralization and disintegration were the dominant modes of change in postwar politics and government.

Efforts to counter the flow were almost always doomed. Every attempt to concentrate political power met an equal and opposite reaction. When corporations seeking political influence began to form potent trade associations, their opponents formed similar organizations to meet the challenge. When presidents impounded appropriated funds to alter priorities and hold down federal spending, Congress passed an impoundment control act. When environmental groups hired attorneys to take alleged polluters to court, the sued companies beefed up their own legal departments. When business groups such as the Chamber of Commerce invented new techniques of grassroots lobbying, labor and consumer groups soon adopted the same tactics and techniques.

The quest for political advantage unfolded everywhere in postwar public life, but it rarely yielded deep or lasting success. What it yielded instead were disaffected citizens and frustrated political leaders. The number of interests and activists grew steadily. So, too, did their energy and commitment and expenditure of funds. Politics filled more space and took more time. Elections lasted years instead of months. The enactment of the annual budget, like spilled paint, seeped into every nook and cranny of government. Legislative struggles consumed dozens of committees and subcommittees, hundreds of journalists, thousands of lobbyists, and millions of dollars, but produced fewer new laws—so much activity, so little movement.

Events of the late twentieth century overwhelmed America's eighteenth-century Constitution. The cautious democrats who wrote that Constitution designed an ingenious set of impediments to concentrations of power. For more than a century and a half, America lived with those impediments, often relying on the political process to provide the concentrations of power necessary for change. After World War II, however, the jig was up. Government was larger and more important than before. Demands for government action spiraled. But the political system fell into deep disarray, Congress decentralized, and the presidency accrued little new authority. What the Constitution constrained, politics could no longer overcome. Without means to concentrate power for effective political action, the federal government seemed to wallow in a deep and lingering stalemate, producing what Walter Dean Burnham described as a "crisis of legitimacy":

> When a hugely increased load of demand and output is processed through such a power centrifuge . . . the traditional partisan channels connecting rulers and ruled, across the great fault lines at the center known as "separation of powers," decay. As they wither, the fragmented pluralism this constitutional structure encourages keeps growing. Political executives, legislators, and judges have every incentive to go into business for themselves and for their clients, and they do. This becomes increasingly obvious to the public, especially to the unorganized "great middle" sectors, as more and more groups organize and get their pieces of the public pie. In consequence, a generalized crisis of legitimacy develops while the surplus declines. The "cultural contradictions of capitalism"—its persistent tendency to corrode general-interest bonds and to emphasize short-run personal gain—become the core of an explicitly political problem.[4]

In the postwar decades Americans broadly remodeled their politics and government. They did not intend to do so—surely not on so sweeping a scale. The agents of change were everywhere, but they were myopic. They wanted only to alter the segment of the government or the political process that affected them. They wanted only the changes necessary to increase their leverage, to strengthen the institution they controlled, to enlarge their own access. They were thinking about self-interest and political gain, not about broad, systemic change. But a little reform here, a little reform there, and eventually everything is different.

The attack on the old order was incomplete, oblique, and ill-explained. As the process of change unfolded, few stakeholders were created in the new government that emerged. In fact, the response to that new government was dismay far more often than joy. Even those who exulted in the narrow political reforms they achieved often lamented the broader outcomes to which they contributed. Nobody wanted to claim this new government; almost everyone was against it. It was incoherent and extraordinarily difficult to operate.

THE POSTWAR LEGACY

We all respond to the incentives and constraints the world imposes on us. Institutions do as well. The profound alteration of American public life since World War II has changed the incentives and constraints that shape political behavior and government action. We govern ourselves differently—profoundly differently—because of these changes. In four important ways especially, the consequences of these postwar changes now plague our efforts to govern ourselves well.

A Gravely Diminished Capacity for Collective Action

The American system of government is unable to concentrate power. The forces of fragmentation are stronger than ever; the counterforces are weaker. The capacity for interest articulation has grown; the capacity for interest aggregation has shrunk. The whole is held hostage by the parts.

The only truly effective action in a democracy is collective action. Real progress occurs, clear directions are set, and persistent problems are solved only when the purposes we hold in common supersede the purposes we hold separately. Collective action has never been easy under the American Constitution; now it is the rarest of political occurrences. Elections, even landslides, rarely produce calls to action or programmatic goals around which Americans coalesce. We can only occasionally elect a congressional majority and a president of the same party. Congress itself has come to resemble a federation of independent sovereigns, safely distanced from the lash of leadership or the pull of party. Even when the confluence of exceptional political energy and good fortune allows the president and Congress to produce a law of consequence—on the environment or civil rights or energy, for example—it will be subject to years of subsequent judicial and administrative mining and sapping.

Legislating on complex matters has become so painfully difficult that we now mark as major legislative successes the enactment of new laws that have little real effect on most Americans. Plant closing notification, motor voter, family leave, the Brady Bill—all great legislative battles of recent years—will leave little mark on the character or quality of American life. We regard each as a legislative landmark because there is so little else to acclaim. In a desert even a small bush stands out.

The diminished capacity for collective action hurts in two deeply felt ways. First, it prevents us from confronting and resolving genuine problems or from responding to real and significant demands for political action. Situations fester. The national budget deficit grew by $2.2 trillion in the 1980s. No political leader sought or defended that accumulation of deficits; everyone was against it. Yet no consensus emerged on how to shrink the annual deficit; no enduring coalition formed to accomplish that. Similarly, reform of the American health care system has been a persistent political demand for almost three decades. Not until 1994 did it even come close to significant legislative attention. But then health care reform, too, suffered the common fate of major policy initiatives—not defeat in a clear-cut vote but slow death in procedural wrangles and the cross fire of special interests.

Second, the incapacity for collective action permits and encourages policy inertia. We go on doing what we have been doing because we cannot generate the energy for change. The status quo takes on a life of its own. So as the world changed dramatically, we maintained a pattern of foreign aid distribution that looked much as it did in the midst of the cold war. A space program that no national politician has successfully justified to the American people continues to consume more than $10 billion in tax dollars every year. We began to subsidize honey production in the 1940s to ensure a sufficient bee population. The subsidy survived beyond any necessity for it—almost half a century.

Some would explain the diminished capacity for collective action as the consequence of disagreements about the form that national health care should take or how the budget deficit should be reduced or how to change the foreign aid program. In fact, however, the causes of that incapacity are far more political than substantive. The problem is less that Americans lacked consensus on the details of a health care program or deficit reduction package than that government leaders and institutions were unable to act collectively to overcome disagreements about the details. Wherever consensus occurs in American life—in labor negotiations, in corporate policy making, in state and local government—it is a manufactured product. Governing coalitions, like the champions who used to adorn the Wheaties box, are made, not born.

It is a common crutch of contemporary commentators to say that politics is stuck in gridlock because there is so little consensus among the American people. This position assumes that in the periods in our past when we have moved boldly—to fight a depression, to win a war, to build the infrastructure for industrialization—we were blessed by a popular consensus. This was not so. We proceeded, often roughly and fitfully, to follow policy directions carved out by political leaders fortunate enough to have more tools—or fewer counterforces—than do leaders at the end of the twentieth century.

To say that government could not act because consensus was absent is to point the causal arrows in the wrong direction. As anyone who has ever been a parent well knows, consensus is not a naturally occurring phenomenon in the social or political universe. It is a product of successful politics, not a precondition of it. The failure of contemporary politics is not caused by an absence of consensus so much as by an endemic inability to mobilize consensus.

Sometimes, in fact, when something approaching consensus does occur, contemporary politics has a remarkable capacity for dissipating it. The debate over national health care in 1993 and especially in 1994 is an example of that dynamic. Every legitimate public opinion poll in early 1993 indicated that a significant majority of Americans believed in the need for a program of national health insurance. But after months of tortuous wending through an endless policymaking process suffused in lobbying and advertising that seemed to specialize in oversimplification, misinformation, and even disinformation, we ended up not only with no national health care program but also with heightened public disgust at the failure of government to act on the consensus that had existed at the outset of the process. In a remarkable irony, the public seemed to wonder if it really wanted a national health care program operated by a government too incompetent even to enact one in the first place.

Procedural Democracy Run Amok

Can a democracy be too democratic? For some, the answer is no. The more power the people have, the better. Multiple procedural access points, no secrecy, the broadest possible participation in deliberation, regular and frequent election of a wide range of leaders, firm constraints on political and legislative party leaders: All of these, in the view of some, are critical ingredients in "genuine" democracy.

Indeed, we do not have to dig very deeply into the political history of the postwar period to uncover examples of reformers seeking to "broaden popular participation," "strengthen democratic procedures," or "empower the people" by proposing the kinds of changes described in the previous paragraph. The effort to make the federal government more open, more participatory, more accountable—in all of this, more democratic—has been one of the most prominent and enduring of all the patterns of postwar politics.

Congressional committees held many of their meetings in secret before and immediately after World War II; now they rarely do. The floor votes of most members of Congress were unrecorded for most of our history; now they are nearly all recorded, and all occur under the watchful eye of the C-SPAN television cameras. A handful of congressional committees and their chairs dominated legislative decision making in the early decades of the twentieth century. Now there are hundreds of committees and subcommittees and a vast multiplication of the access points to the legislative process. Contemporary leaders in all branches of government must make annual public reports of all of their personal finances and assets. Because legislative requirements and judicial and administrative practices have greatly expanded the opportunities for reopening policy discussions after laws are made, closure has become one of the rarest events in contemporary policymaking. Everywhere on the political landscape, we have experienced an outbreak of procedural democracy, of openness, of ingenious new methods of holding public officials up to scrutiny and accountability.

Accelerating the trend to openness and public visibility has been the simultaneous expansion in media coverage of national politics and government. The news business has exploded in postwar America, especially in the areas of television news and investigative journalism. Everything that happens in Washington, and much that happens elsewhere, is now the public's business. The bright lights are always on, whether in the rooms of committees marking up bills, on the floor of the House or Senate, at the president's every engagement, or in the front yards of public officials accused of impropriety.

It is easy to understand the political momentum that inspired these changes and the "motherhood" arguments that sustain them. These changes have, in fact, opened some doors to participation, raised ethical standards, and heightened the visibility of the government at work. But the costs of all this—and they are large costs—have gone largely unnoticed and unremarked, except by those left to govern under all of these new procedural exigencies.

In postwar America we have substituted individual accountability for collective accountability. We pay much more attention to what individual political actors do than to what political parties and political institutions do. That helps explain the most peculiar of all postwar phenomena: the habit of constantly reelecting incumbent members of Congress despite broad public disenchantment with the institution of Congress. We do not let our public officials get away with a thing, while we let our institutions murder our dreams.

The simple fact is that governing is much harder in the bright glare of publicity, especially a publicity tinged with contempt and skepticism for the motives of those who govern. As previously noted, effective collective action requires the construction of governing coalitions. In the changed postwar political environment, where parties are feeble and elections rarely produce either mandates or coherent majorities, coalition building is a retail activity based on multiple agreements arranged between individuals and small blocs of legislators. That kind of coalition building is difficult under the best of circumstances; it is difficult in the extreme when the bargaining and discussion must occur in public. As political scientist Nelson Polsby noted:

> One characteristic of the emerging style of political intermediation is that it is done in the sunshine. . . . One difficulty with such an arrangement is that when politicians must announce themselves and their preferences on national television, they may get locked into position before they come to understand one another's point of view. Deliberation and negotiation, in which mutual accommodation and mutual learning are encouraged, are hard to arrange without causing one or more public figures embarrassment.[5]

The impetus for democracy and openness has also unfolded in new and increasingly elaborate procedural layers in the policymaking process. Public comment periods required by the Administrative Procedure Act of 1946, environmental impact statements subject to legal challenge, the obsession with oversight in a Congress overgrown with too many committees, the breakdown of the political questions doctrine and the subsequent policy preoccupation of the courts: Everywhere anyone looked in postwar America new steps and obstacles were added to the policymaking process. "When we wonder why we have an energy problem, or why economic growth fails to meet our hopes," the *Wall Street Journal* recently suggested, "we ought to notice that we are being bled to death by berserk proceduralism."[6]

The postwar period has also been marked by escalating efforts to root out corruption in government. Although well intentioned and sometimes useful, these new ethical rules have also added to the difficulty of governing. We have responded to every scandal by enacting new legislation or more cautious interpretation of existing rules to try to make government scandal-proof. Public reporting on personal finances, divestiture of potentially conflicting assets, detailed restrictions on use of government property and interactions with private sector representatives, rigid restrictions on outside earned income, limitations on postemployment activities: Each of these new rules—and they are virtually all creations of the postwar period—was enacted for some specific purpose, usually to plug a recently identified hole in the ethical dike. Whether they have given us the kind of squeaky clean government their proponents promised is debatable. That they have made it more difficult to govern is not.

The weight of all the new "thou shalt nots" falls heavily on the process and quality of government staffing, particularly when combined with the painfully slow growth in top-level government salaries in the postwar period. It takes longer than ever before to staff new presidential administrations. A year had passed in both the Bush and Clinton administrations before half the appointed positions were filled by a Senate-confirmed appointee of the new president. Presidential personnel aides report their constant difficulty in recruiting highly talented individuals, especially for subcabinet positions; they routinely turn down such offers. Even those who come into government soon bristle under its extraordinary demands and petty restrictions; they often leave quickly. More than one-third are gone within a year and a half of their appointment. Turnover levels are higher than ever among federal judges as well and have been especially high in recent Congresses.

In our efforts to make government more democratic, we have made governing more difficult. This has produced a paradox of very bad timing. In a period in our history when bargaining has become more essential to public policy making, it has become more difficult and more constrained by a contemptuous, skeptical publicity and a daft proceduralism. We wanted more democracy, and we got it. But we did not get better government as a result.

Reduced Incentives for Electoral Participation

For much of the pre–World War II history of American politics, the key to success in government was success in politics. Winning elections was the most reliable way to get control of the instruments of power and thus to alter public policy. Hence, the trick was to mobilize a portion of the electorate sizable enough to win elections. Thomas Jefferson accomplished that in 1800, and his success led to the first real transfer of power in the new American republic. Almost three decades later Andrew Jackson mobilized a new coalition of voters, and government changed direction again. When the party system of the first half of the nineteenth century could not contain the swelling conflict over slavery, new parties emerged, bringing new coalitions to power. And in the face of the crisis wrought by the Great Depression, Franklin Roosevelt forged a new majority, which came to be called the New Deal coalition. It wrested control of government from the long-dominant Republicans and changed the course of American public policy.

One of the important political theorists of the mid-twentieth century, E. E. Schattschneider, drew our attention to this historical dynamic of governmental change—the mobilization of new voters: "The outcome of every conflict is determined by the extent to which the audience becomes involved in it. That is, the outcome of all conflict is determined by the scope of its contagion. The number of people involved in any conflict determines what happens: every change in the number of participants, every increase or reduction in the number of participants affects the result."[7]

But the postwar period has produced a counterdynamic. Even though government and the political process have become more penetrable to interest groups and activists in the ways described earlier, the postwar changes have simultaneously diminished incentives for popular participation through elections. This is a striking contradiction. Government has become, at once, more open and less popular.

More Americans are permitted to vote than ever before. Registration is easier than it has been at any time in this century. Information about government is more readily accessible than even the boldest imagination would have predicted a generation ago. There are more candidates for national office and thus more options for voters. Campaigns are more prominent and longer lasting. Voters are better educated. By what possible rational calculation could all of this add up to diminished popular participation? And yet it does because the new openness of American politics has not made participation in elections more attractive to most Americans. The new instruments of mass communication are better at magnifying the awkwardness of democratic decisionmaking and the flaws of politicians than at mobilizing support. The complexity of issues has grown faster than the capacity of even better educated voters to comprehend them. Longer campaigns produce boredom and disgust in doses at least as large as information and inspiration.

Barely 50 percent of eligible adults now take the time to vote in presidential general elections; fewer than 20 percent typically participate in the primaries and caucuses that determine party nominations. In midterm congressional elections, participation levels hover around 35 percent. When a new president is elected, even in what is called a landslide victory, he rarely has the votes of much more than 25 percent of American adults. In securing the Democratic nomination in 1992, Bill Clinton won the votes of only 52 percent of the primary voters in his own party.

The gap between those who govern and those who are governed has never been greater. Few Americans feel much real investment in their government. Most did not vote for their representative in Congress or their president. Most do not feel themselves part of some grand governing coalition. Most, in fact, feel disconnected from their leaders and their government. The opening up of the political process has not tightened the bonds between the electorate and the elected.

Modern government is an insiders' game. The complexity of issues and the intricacies of policymaking are beyond the comprehension of most Americans. Elections are simply too blunt an instrument to bring about much change in a system with so many access points and such resistance to concentrations of power. When Americans tell pollsters that they do not vote because it does not matter who gets elected, they are reporting their own perceptions accurately. If voting does not seem to accomplish much, why vote?

The insiders exacerbate this perception by relying on weapons of political combat that discourage popular mobilization. Mobilizing support through elections is too difficult, too uncertain, too expensive. To those who have political influence, mobilization is anathema. They seek instead to contain policy battles within the confines of their influence. As political reporter E. J. Dionne recently noted:

> Over time . . . fewer and fewer questions got settled through the electoral process. Instead, political battles were fought out through court decisions, congressional investigations, and revelations in the media. The result has been a less democratic politics in which voters feel increasingly powerless. In the meantime, the sheer volume of money that flooded through the electoral process made it an increasingly technocratic pursuit. Democratic politics is supposed to be about making public arguments and persuading fellow citizens. Instead, it has become an elaborate insider industry in which those skilled at fund-raising, polling, media relations, and advertising have the upper hand.[8]

An American people who have not been active participants in selecting their leaders, who do not view themselves as stakeholders in a current presidential administration or congressional majority, are highly vulnerable to disenchantment. The president is not their president; Congress is not their Congress. They can criticize the government—they can even hate the government—because they see it as an alien power from which they are isolated and in the success of which they have no stake. In a democracy such widespread popular indifference is a natural recipe for immobilism and drift.

Swelling Costs of Governing

In the business of coalition building, retail is more expensive than wholesale. When governing coalitions are not routinely generated by elections and cannot easily be produced or sustained by the tethers of party, there is little recourse but to purchase the votes necessary to construct majorities for individual pieces of legislation. The sum of all those purchases, accumulated over hundreds of legislative votes each years has added substantially to the dollar cost of governing in the postwar period.

Majorities are often constructed one region, one state or city delegation, even one member at a time. The proponents of a bill begin with those who support the bill on principle or for the inherent benefits it brings to their constituents. Then proponents start the search, often across party lines, for others who can be enticed to support the bill by the addition of some benefit for their region or district, by the elimination of some cost that falls on their constituents, or by the promise of benefits in other legislation or administrative action. The pot is sweetened, in the argot of congressional insiders, by addition to and subtraction from the substance of legislation to enlarge its political support.

For example, the Bush administration in its early months in office proposed a rescue plan for the savings and loan industry that would have financed some of the costs by imposing a fee on S&L depositors. The S&L industry was able to parlay its broad influence among members of Congress into outright rejection of that proposal. The administration withdrew and regrouped; it then proposed a financing scheme without the fee on depositors and with most of the funding coming from general revenues. As political scientists Benjamin Ginsberg and Martin Shefter noted about this maneuver and the pattern of coalition building it epitomized, "The necessity of building majorities on a piecemeal basis also enables members of Congress to demand that, in exchange for their support, the interests for which they speak be relieved of the costs and burdens associated with new programs. This allows powerful interests to shift these burdens to others—often to the public treasury."[9]

One of the most common techniques of contemporary coalition building is piling up the pork. Proponents of legislation spread the benefits around so that they fall in many congressional districts. The Model Cities legislation originally proposed by Lyndon Johnson envisioned sizable demonstration grants to nine cities. By the time Congress was done with the legislation, Model Cities funding was thinned out over 150 cities—in 150 different congressional districts. Legislators also "earmark" funds for specific projects to guarantee local benefits and narrow the discretion of executive agencies in contracting and grant making. Sometimes legislators permit utterly nongermane expenditures in the form of "riders" to add support for their bills. Tactically included benefits may also take the form of revenue reductions or what economists call "tax subsidies."

The impact of this pattern of coalition building on the direct dollar costs of governing is obvious. There is also an indirect cost. Retail coalition building is rational only politically, not substantively. What is rational to get laws enacted under the postwar rules of the game is often utterly irrational in terms of the kinds of programs the process creates. Does it truly make sense to build a weapons system of parts manufactured in sixty different places, their locations determined solely by the need to attract the votes of their congressional representatives? Does it make sense to earmark millions of dollars for a university construction project of questionable value, without any peer review, simply because the university is located in the state of a member of an appropriations committee?

The answers are obvious. Federal programs are more complex, less connected to any clear national purpose, and more costly because of the deeply flawed dynamics of postwar policymaking. Nobody sought this outcome. Almost everyone laments it. But if you want to play under the new rules of the game, you've got to pay.

THE SEARCH FOR A BETTER WAY

The long history of this country helps us understand what has gone wrong with our politics and government. If there is a powerful enduring dynamic to political change, it is that over the course of American history demands have tended to get ahead of government capability and then capabilities have had to be changed to catch up with demands. For the most part this trend has happened successfully, usually as the consequence of some group of reformers identifying the problems, offering solutions, and then building the political coalitions necessary to get at least some of those solutions enacted. The revolutionary generation did it; so, too, in one measure or another did the Jeffersonians, the Jacksonians, the Progressives, and the New Dealers. They generated the political momentum necessary to realign government with a rapidly changing society.

The politics of the postwar period does not seem to fit the historical pattern. Demands have once again outstripped capability, but recent changes in government and politics seem to have diminished, rather than enlarged, our adaptive capability. As our institutions and processes evolve, our problems are exacerbated, not solved. Government is less and less able to perform its central, essential roles in resolving disputes, crystallizing collective goals, and setting national priorities. As government is paralyzed by its own incompetence, demands accumulate and disaffection builds. Expectations are unmet, problems fester, and the people get angry.

At the core of our contemporary difficulties is our continuing reliance on outmoded ways of governing ourselves. Our basic institutions and processes of government were created in the eighteenth century by a group of wise and thoughtful politicians who were very sensitive to the realities of their time. They were brilliant, and in some ways they were brave.

But we are a very different people, and we live in a very different country. We need a different kind of government for it to be effective. We have to stop believing our own myths and bicentennial press releases. Just as the Framers of the American Constitution could no longer live with the governments established in the seventeenth century, neither can we endure much longer with a government rooted in the eighteenth century. We have to change our government because our country is so changed.

This notion is heretical, of course. Americans are myopic about government. We have spent so much time in the postwar years holding our own government up as a model to the world that we have overlooked its increasingly prominent cracks and age spots. Like addicts and alcoholics, we have denied that our problems reach as deeply as they do. We try to define away the real problems as failures of leadership.

This excuse will not wash. The postwar period has given us every type and caliber of leadership we could possibly imagine or want. Republicans and Democrats, legislative insiders and big-state governors, brilliant rhetoricians and policy wonks, divided government and unified government: No matter what the leadership pattern, the quality of governance has deteriorated, and the connection between politics and government has withered. As political scientists John Chubb and Paul Peterson noted, "Established structures no longer can contain political tensions between Congress, the president, and the bureaucracy, and, riven by conflict, they often do not permit successful management of the nation's problems."[10]

No hero is coming to the rescue on a white charger. It's not that simple. The problem is systemic, not personal. We cannot solve it simply by finding the right leader or combination of leaders. "Reinventing" government with the latest management fads and new microprocesses is not the solution either. One can almost hear the deck chairs being rearranged on the Titanic.

We need, instead, to confront a harder reality: We have outgrown our own public institutions and processes. They are artifacts of the eighteenth century, and we are about to move into the twenty-first. We are not our parents and certainly not our ancestors. We put ourselves at great risk if we continue to try governing as they once did. We can recapture a meaningful capacity for self-government only by significant alteration of the way we do our public business.

The recent pattern of a little reform here, a little reform there cannot get us out of the morass in which we now find ourselves. The contemporary landscape is full of reform agendas and proposals. Many of them contain good ideas. But few of them penetrate to the real source of our current

state of perplexity and dismay. As journalist Robert Shogan recently
pointed out:

> The counterreformers are following in the footsteps of the reformers down a
> much traveled dead-end street. The new revisionists, like their predecessors,
> are concentrating on jiggering and rejiggering political machinery. Their pro-
> posals leave untouched the relationship between politics and government,
> which suffers from fundamental defects and which requires fundamental
> change.
>
> At the heart of the problem is what amounts to a gap between politics and
> government. The gap was not created by recent presidents, or by modern re-
> forms. Instead, . . . the gap is imbedded in our lives and sustained by our
> customs. Its origins are in the constitutional impediments to the healthy de-
> velopment of political parties and the abiding public suspicion of both par-
> ties and politics.
>
> The purpose of politics is to express the often conflicting concerns of the
> voters. The role of government is to resolve these concerns equitably. To put
> it in simplest terms, politics defines what people want; government decides
> what they get. For democracy to work, government must respond to poli-
> tics.[11]

Significant reform is a prospect that makes us swallow hard. Tinkering
will not do. It was tinkering that got us into this mess. We need bolder
changes to fix government machinery that is outmoded and ill-fitting.
The simple reality is that if we keep doing what we have been doing, we
will keep getting what we have been getting.

In admitting this, we confront a stubborn paradox: Nothing that would
make a difference is easy to do; nothing that is easy to do would make a
difference. Bold change is itself a potential victim of the political dynamic
described here. The potential change agents—our political leaders—are
either deeply invested in the status quo or imprisoned by it. Those most
capable of leading the way to significant change are little disposed to do
so. So it will not be easy to make the changes necessary to rescue
American politics from its current state of disrepair.

It is possible, I think, to significantly improve the American capacity for
self-government without a complete rejection of age-old institutional
forms. We can retain our existing institutions, but we need to alter their
interrelationships. We can retain much that is familiar in our politics, but
here, too, we must alter some elements of their timing and character. I
have some proposals for change. I suffer no pretense that they will be
easy, or perhaps even possible, to effect. They run too strongly against the
grain of self-interest and into the face of procedural inertia that now dominate American politics. I doubt that, even if enacted, these proposals
could fix all that is broken in American politics and government. Their
discussion here is heuristic, if not practical. It suggests, at least, the cen-

tral problems we have to confront and the scope of change necessary to solve them.

And what are the central problems we have to address? Although there are many candidates for the honor, three seem to emerge above all others.

1. *The inability to concentrate power for collective purpose.* Those who are supposed to lead cannot lead. Decisions made in one place are easily unmade in others. Closure is rarely accomplished.
2. *The disjunction between politics and government.* The electoral process has steadily evolved away from its primary functions of choosing talented leaders and giving them a set of directions to follow in office.
3. *The fragility and transience of coalitions in government.* Bargaining and negotiation, the keys to successful collective action, are constrained by rules that neutralize their effects. Coalitions are hard to construct and nearly impossible to sustain.

The proposals that follow directly address these three critical flaws. A government that can work effectively at the end of the twentieth century has to counteract these current flaws in a number of ways. Only an integrated pattern of significant change can begin to fix what is currently broken. Too often in the past, we have compounded, rather than solved, our problems with reforms that were disjointed, incoherent, and aimed principally at enlarging the political advantage of one group or special interest. The proposals offered here are not more of the same. They are unlikely to be enacted, of course, because there are few incentives or opportunities in our current politics for change that is not self-serving. And even if there were such incentives, the policymaking process that survives fifty years of societal change and political reform makes such bold reform almost impossible. But these proposals at least suggest the character and magnitude of what it would take to develop a twenty-first century capacity for effective democratic government in America.

The Relationship Between President and Congress

1. The House of Representatives should be enlarged to 500 members and the Senate to 125 members. In each house, 20 percent of the members should be appointed on the sole authority of the president.

These appointed members of Congress would serve at the pleasure of the president. They would have no state or district affiliation. Their only constituent would be the national interest as defined broadly by the president. They would have no responsibility for constituent service to any individual citizens or special interests; indeed, they would be barred from performing that kind of direct constituent service.

With these appointments, presidents would have an opportunity to put into Congress people with broad government and professional experience: former presidents, former secretaries of state, distinguished former civil servants or ambassadors, policy experts, former governors, business leaders, intellectuals. They would be people with strong sympathy for the president's program and a commitment not only to support it but also to help broaden support for it among the other, elected members of Congress. Those appointed members who could not support the president's program could be replaced by the president at any time.

Twenty percent of the membership is a number large enough to ensure the president a majority for his party most of the time and give him al-

FIGURE 7.1
Hypothetical Effects of Proposal 1 on Percent of Seats Held
by President's Party in House and Senate, 1969–1995

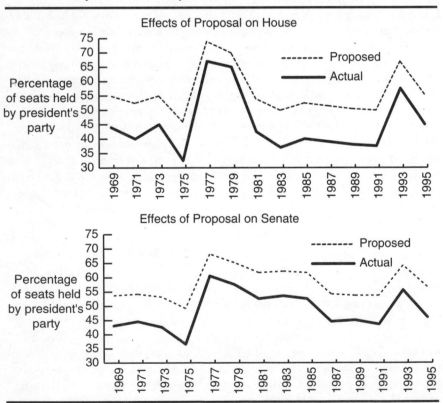

SOURCE: Author's calculations.

ways the core of a working majority in Congress, as Figure 7.1 indicates. But it is not so large a number as to overwhelm the elected representatives of the people, who would still enjoy a 4–1 numerical advantage. This proposal would effectively put an end to divided government.

One of the principal problems with contemporary politics is that the parts are at war with the whole—not just the geographical parts but also the special interest parts. It is every state and every district and every member of Congress and every agency in the bureaucracy and every special interest group for themselves. They come together from time to time for purposes of mutual self-interest, to protect from broader intervention the special jurisdictions they share. But they have few incentives and are subject to few forces that require them to adhere to some broader vision of the national interest. One of the notable trends in the changing structure and operation of postwar American politics and government is that it has become easier for the parts to win and harder for the whole to do so. It is important, therefore, to suggest ways that strengthen the whole against the parts. This is one such way.

2. The terms of members of both houses of Congress should be set at four years and aligned with the president's term.

The fears that inspired the Framers of the Constitution to keep terms short in the House and long in the Senate have never really panned out. The cost of two-year terms in the House greatly exceeds the benefits. And senators rarely feel themselves safely distanced from the next election. What we have under our current electoral system is virtually constant electioneering and fund-raising for members of the House. Even if they are not acutely concerned about what voters are thinking, they are acutely concerned about what potential funders, PACs, are thinking. With terms so short, every vote a legislator casts becomes a kind of minireferendum on her or his electability—or at least fundability. There is virtually no latitude for representatives to think in broad national terms. Every vote is so close to the next election that every voting calculus has to include a dominant factor of reelection impact.

Senators, usually with much larger and more diverse constituencies than House members, have to raise more money for reelection: $3.6 million on average for winners of Senate seats compared to $535,000 on average for winners of House seats in the 1991–1992 election cycle.[12] The benefits of longer terms as a defense of the people against what Federalist No. 63 called "their own temporary errors and delusions" no longer exist.[13] Hence, shorter terms for senators will cause no significant loss of deliberation or broad perspective in the legislative process.

Four-year terms aligned with the president's are an old idea—and a good one. They would have two great advantages over current practice.

First, they would provide more time—badly needed time in these days of complex coalition building—to debate and enact new programs and to finance them more responsibly. The momentum of new administrations dissipates quickly after their first year in the current political context. This change would alter the context and permit longer and deeper concentration on the president's program.

Second, with the entire government standing for election at the same time, and with leadership of that government concentrated in one party, there would be greatly improved opportunities for American voters to judge and direct their government. Members of the majority party, confronted with the new reality that they are all in this together, would face new and potent incentives to work together in developing a record of programmatic accomplishment that could win the favor of the voters.

The Operations of Congress

3. The Senate filibuster should be eliminated.

Although used infrequently, the filibuster is a very important strategic weapon. It permits a minority of the Senate to close off the legislative channels in that body by extending debate indefinitely. The cloture rule, the only device for ending a filibuster, requires sixty votes—a number often larger than the membership of the Senate's majority party.

The possibility of a filibuster requires the president and the leaders of majority coalitions to do much more negotiating with the minority than they should to ensure that they have the extraordinary majorities necessary to bring legislation to a vote. Lip-service has long been paid to the filibuster for its value in protecting the rights of minorities—preventing the "tyranny of the majority," in Tocqueville's elegant phrase. In reality, however, the filibuster is most often used or threatened by members seeking to protect the special interests or special privileges of their constituents or campaign contributors from sensible legislation that serves the national interest. The filibuster has principally become an instrument for subverting the rights of the majority and for diminishing the legislature's ability to perform is central task: to get its business done.

The continued existence of the filibuster is made all the more aggravating by the steadily growing malapportionment of the U.S. Senate. The heavy postwar population shift into a few large states has left them—the people of California, Florida, and Texas especially—grossly underrepresented in the Senate. A filibuster can be sustained by the senators of the eleven smallest states. In the 1990 census, those states had a combined population of 28 million, just 11 percent of the country's total population. Under Senate rules the representatives of that 11 percent of the population can prevent the representatives of the other 89 percent from even voting on important legislation.

What is really needed is an end to the gross malapportionment of the Senate and the imposition there of the "one man, one vote" principle that now applies to every other legislature in America. But the Framers of the Constitution of 1787 made that virtually impossible by the unamendable language of Article V that "no state, without its consent, shall be deprived of its equal suffrage in the Senate."

Although Senate votes rarely split along big-state/small-state lines, the broad variance in the size of Senate constituencies magnifies the risks and inequities in the continuing—and growing—use of the filibuster. If reapportionment of the Senate is not feasible, at least its worst effects should be mitigated. Unlimited Senate debate is an arcane historical practice. It is woefully out of place amid the complexities of contemporary government.

4. Congressional committees should regain the freedom to write legislation out of public view.

For all but the past quarter century of American experience, congressional committees usually held their markup sessions—the meetings at which they actually draft legislation—in private. The move toward open committee meetings was part of the vast reform wave that broke over Congress in the 1960s and 1970s. Although some of those reforms were highly desirable and long overdue, the elimination of committee secrecy has failed to accomplish the purposes of its proponents and has produced obnoxious unintended consequences.

The theory that drove the movement to open committee meetings was that committees play a critical role in shaping legislation and that the public ought to have the opportunity to see its representatives at work in their committee rooms as it does on the floor of each chamber. The theory was reasonable. In practice, however, the opening up of committee meetings, especially markup sessions, has not served the interests of the public nearly so much as it has elevated the advantage of the lobbyists for special interest groups.

When a congressional committee meets these days to mark up an important bill, lines form early in the morning at the committee's door. The higher the stakes are, the longer the lines are. But who is in these lines? Tourists passing through Washington? A random sample of the American people? Hardly. Listen to a description of the commotion surrounding the markup of the 1986 tax reform act:

> Lobbyists—or often their young, lower-paid assistants—lined up early each morning to get seats at the tax-writing markups. At Ways and Means, before the sessions were closed to the public, some eager committee watchers

would arrive as early as 5:30 am to get at the head of the queue and have a chance for a front-row seat. The line sometimes stretched the entire length of the hallway, a city block long, and then wrapped around the corner. There were so many people that it looked like the committee was giving something away—which, at times, it was.[14]

The cost of this new way of doing business is not simply that it has given wondrous new access and leverage to special interests. Because reporters are there as well, members of Congress have little opportunity to negotiate quietly with their colleagues to build legislative coalitions. It is show time, not work time, for many members, and often their primary concern is not in crafting sound, effective legislation but in saying and doing what will curry the right kind of favor with important interests. With lobbyists so close at hand and the glare of a watching press so prominent, it is simply very difficult to dislodge members, even briefly, from their personal and political concerns to focus on the national interest.

In 1995, for example, the House Ways and Means Committee sought to craft a plan to secure the financial foundation of the Medicare and Medicaid programs into the twenty-first century. But instead of effective negotiating sessions, the open markup meetings of the committee became a forum for political posturing and one-upsmanship. Shouting matches ensued, and the minority walked out in protest. The cameras recorded everything. And Americans had yet another good reason for disgust with their government.

Secrecy is always suspect in a democracy. But it is worth remembering that our Constitution was written in secret and that many of our most important decisions are made beyond public view. The Supreme Court deliberates and decides in secret. The Federal Reserve Board does as well. American diplomats are constantly engaged in secret negotiations with their foreign counterparts. Policy choices are often made in the White House in secret and in most of the executive agencies and departments as well. In each case, however, accountability comes when a decision is announced, a position is taken, or a bargain is arranged. The layers of checks and balances in our politics, the enormity of the contemporary press corps, and the intensity of special interest concern all assure that nothing will be overlooked, that second-guessing will proceed on many fronts.

Secrecy, in proper doses and subject to proper review, facilitates democratic decisionmaking. The postwar notion that all secrecy is bad and antidemocratic was rooted in a peculiar definition of democracy that elevated process above outcome, that unwisely placed individual accountability above collective accountability. In responding to that notion over the past quarter century, we have opened up many of the processes of democracy at great cost to our collective purposes. Nowhere is that cost more evident than in the work of congressional committees.

Committees should hold hearings in public as they do now. They should record the final vote of each member on the bills they send to the floor. But their deliberations on the shape and substance of legislation should be afforded protection from the intense pressures and publicity that now so impede the crystallization of collective purpose in congressional committee rooms.

5. The elected party leaders in Congress should have larger authority to assign committee members and appoint committee chairs.

In 1995 Americans had occasion to observe two contrasting approaches to congressional leadership. For the first time in forty years, Republicans controlled both houses of Congress. In the House, the new Speaker, Newt Gingrich, seized the opportunity to impose potent leadership on his party by acts of the political equivalent of sheer hustle. Before the new Congress convened, he worked with other Republican leaders to reshape committee jurisdictions and to handpick all the committee chairs. House Republicans were new to majority status, so no one was losing power he or she had once had in this shuffle. Gingrich saw his opportunities, and he took them. It was a vision—perhaps only fleeting—of how a strong legislative leader operates.

Later in 1995 the contrast emerged in the Senate. Senator Bob Packwood was forced to resign after years of criticism for his interactions with women. Packwood chaired the Senate Finance Committee, and the resignation occurred in the middle of that committee's deliberation on such critical issues as welfare reform, Medicare and Medicaid, and tax cuts. The vacancy in the chair created by Packwood's resignation led to the ascendancy through the routine reliance on seniority of Senator William Roth of Delaware, a seventy-four-year-old, twenty-five-year Senate veteran. Roth commanded little respect among his colleagues for his legislative creativity or his leadership skills. There was no perceptible enthusiasm for his assumption of the committee chair. But operating as most congressional leaders have in the postwar period, Senate Majority Leader Bob Dole made no attempt to interfere with the seniority tradition in filling the vacancy.

Weakened party leadership has been one of the principal characteristics of the postwar Congress. Over the decades House and Senate leaders have seen a steady deterioration in their ability to influence the votes of other members and to control the flow and shape of legislation. I noted in Chapter 4 that the members of Congress are brighter than ever before and very hard working. I also noted the enormous gains that have been made in recent decades in building the institutional infrastructure of Congress with more staff support and other resources. The absence of strong leadership mechanisms, however, has kept Congress from functioning very effectively in spite of these other advances. Like an all-star team without a captain or coach, the individual skills of the members greatly exceed their collective competence. Someone has to run the show, and in Congress, for most of the period since 1970, no one has.

It is no simple matter to create potent leadership in a Congress whose members are accustomed to independence and autonomy. It is especially hard to create strong congressional leaders in a political system where leaders in Congress have no influence over the nomination of candidates for Congress from their own party. We have had some historical experience with strong congressional leaders, however, and there are lessons to be learned from that. Primary among them is that rank-and-file members of Congress are likely to be responsive to party leaders who control committee assignments and the appointment of committee chairs.

Party leaders—the Speaker of the House, the majority leader of the Senate, and the minority leaders in each chamber—should have sole responsibility for assigning individual members to committees and for appointing the chairs of all the committees. Their exercise of that authority could be overturned in specific cases by majority vote of the relevant party caucus, but the vote would not be automatic. The caucus could vote to alter the leader's assignments and appointments only in individual cases and only on presentation of a petition by a dissatisfied member signed by at least one-third of the members of the caucus.

This approach would make individual members significantly more attentive to their party leaders because desired committee assignments and appointments to committee chairs could be used as rewards for responsiveness to the leadership and for good work performed on legislative matters and coalition-building efforts. Leaders would have much more latitude to shape committee memberships in anticipation of important legislative initiatives, to minimize obstructionism and grandstanding. We would be less frequently exposed to the spectacle of congressional committees forced to work around chairs who are so old or infirm or out of touch that they have no capacity to provide real leadership. The forces of decentralization and atomization would remain strong, but party leaders, the principal centralizing forces in Congress, would have much greater capacity to confront and conquer the tendencies that pull Congress apart instead of together.

The Electoral Process

We cannot begin to correct the breakdowns in our policymaking process until we repair the electoral process. The contemporary electoral process, especially the presidential selection process, is a widely acknowledged failure. It takes too long. It tests the wrong candidate characteristics. It gives too much influence to some states and too little to others. It costs too much and relies too heavily on special interest funding. The formidable obstacle course it presents deters too many of our best potential leaders from entering the race. But the most significant indictment of the presidential selection process is that it fails to produce presidents with broad support or to generate enduring coalitions to govern. The distance between politics and government has never been greater.

6. The presidential nominating process should be altered to enlarge the role of party leaders and public officials in selecting candidates.

To reconnect politics and government, we should begin by reestablishing some of the control that party leaders once had over the nominating process. This does not require a return to smoke-filled rooms and backroom deals, nor does it necessitate the elimination of popular participation in nominations. There is a broad middle ground between boss rule and anarchy. The nominating process needs to move into that middle ground.

Perhaps a way to do that is to have the nominating conventions meet at the beginning of the process, instead of at the end. Let them nominate four or five candidates, who would then compete in a national primary held all on one day. If no candidate receives 50 percent of the vote in the first round, a runoff would follow two weeks later among the top two vote-getters.

The conventions would take place in midsummer and would allow party leaders, party regulars, and elected officials to serve as a clearinghouse for designating candidates with appropriate experience, policy vision, existing and successful political relationships, and the political and rhetorical skills necessary to be an effective president. The state delegations at the conventions would be composed of members of Congress, statewide elected officials, state legislators, and members of the state party leadership from the relevant party. These could be shorter and smaller conventions than those that now exist. They would provide opportunities for all those who wished to be on the nominee list to come and present themselves to the delegates, to make the case for themselves, before the convention voted. The conventions would be a lot less like show business and a lot more like working sessions of real political parties doing the important work of national politics.

The four or five candidates on the nominee list would then have a period of about a month to campaign nationally. Candidates for the nomination would use federal funds distributed and allocated by their party in equal amounts to each of them. They would not be permitted to raise or spend other funds, including their own. Party control of the funds would permit the party to attach strings such as a requirement that the nominees appear in joint debates or campaign in certain places together. The national primary would occur for both parties on the same day, perhaps shortly after Labor Day. A runoff, if necessary, would occur two weeks later. The general election between the candidates of the two parties would follow a month or so after that.

This approach would correct many of the flaws in the current nominating process. It would eliminate the advantage that some states gain by positioning themselves early in the sequence of primaries and caucuses. It would broaden the range of real candidate choice for most Americans. It would concentrate the candidates' attention on national, rather than state, interests in the primary. It would test nationwide communication skills and broad policy understanding of the sort most relevant to presidential leadership. By enlarging the role of party and political leaders, this approach would help reconnect electoral politics to the task of governing. The process would be shorter and less repetitive, thus maintaining the interest and enthusiasm of more voters. It would cost less and greatly reduce the impact of fund-raising. Since the ultimate goal has to be to win a majority, not a plurality, it would provide incentives for coalition building in the center of the political spectrum. Most important, it would provide much greater likelihood of producing presidents with the popular support and skills necessary to lead a complex country.

7. Organized special interests should not be permitted to contribute to candidates for public office.

Our current system for financing national elections is an open sore. It infects every aspect of our politics and deeply undermines public trust in government. Any change in current practice has to begin with the realistic assumption that modern elections cost money. The American population grows steadily. Candidates for president and Congress have more voters to reach than ever before, and those voters are more dispersed, more mobile, better educated, and less well organized politically than in the past. They can be reached only through the broadcast media and through travel to the many places where they reside. Campaigns are inevitably expensive.

So the key question is, Who pays? The money to run campaigns has to come from somewhere: from special interests, from candidates' personal resources, from government, or from individual citizens. The worst of all of these options is the one currently at the center of our campaign finance system: support from special interests through their PACs. PACs rarely provide a majority of the funding for campaigns for national office. But their impact, especially in congressional elections, is so large and the implicit assumption of a quid pro quo so widespread that PAC funding is a dominating and often revolting presence in contemporary elections. Elections should not be auctions in which candidates are sold to the highest bidder. But elections have come to seem that way to voters and to feel that way to candidates.

We should ban political action committees and prohibit special interest contributions to political campaigns. No business corporation, no labor union, and no organized interest group of any kind should be permitted to contribute to a candidate for national public office. The taint of special interest financing has given our politics a very bad odor.

What should be done instead? Government financing has worked rather successfully in presidential elections, although that, too, has suffered growing infection from independent or so-called soft money expenditures by special interests. There seems to be no compelling reason to end the recent practice of public financing of presidential elections if some effort is made to control the impact of independent expenditures (the elimination of PACs would contribute substantially to that) and to ensure sound funding through the income tax checkoff for future presidential campaigns.

The extension of government financing to congressional campaigns is more problematic. It would be expensive, and it would be difficult to construct a funding formula that fairly assimilated the political cultures of 50 different states and 435 different congressional districts without creating unintended advantages for some kinds of candidates or political parties. The better alternative is to rest the financing of congressional campaigns on individual contributions. The limits on these—$1,000 per candidate per election—have not increased in twenty years and are unrealistically low. They should be raised now to the equivalent value in current dollars and then indexed to rise with future inflation. The ability to raise funds from individual sources in relatively small amounts is a useful test for potential congressional candidates. The failure to raise funds successfully is a demonstration of narrow appeal and an entirely proper deterrent to quixotic campaigns.

The problem then is to contain the costs of elections in order to save candidates from the need to spend all of their time on fund-raising. Most analysts of the costs of contemporary campaigns agree that they are spending driven, especially by the cost of televised advertising. This suggests that there might be a role for government in purchasing time for candidate presentations or in making the provision of such airtime at small or no cost a condition of a broadcast outlet receiving a broadcast license. The provision of such free time should be tied to certain requirements on those who use it: that they participate in debates or respond to reporters' questions, for example. Determining the right approach here is difficult, however, in the current transitional state of broadcast communications. It is not at all clear how candidates will present themselves to voters when most homes are wired to receive hundreds of television channels, when laser discs, video on demand, and other emerging technologies take us further and further away from the narrow channel choices that were the norm in the first age of television. Perhaps the problem of the high cost of televised campaign advertising will simply disappear as it becomes impossible to reach any significant group of voters through television at all.

CONCLUSION: REALITY CHECK

I have presented here a list of seven suggestions for fixing the problems identified in the earlier chapters of this book. In the contemporary context of tepid and isolated reforms, these will probably be regarded as radical and often as heretical suggestions. Perhaps they are.

I bear no illusion that any of these changes will soon occur. The contemporary political dynamic is stacked against them. Those best positioned to make changes of this character or magnitude are also those most likely to lose influence as a result. For years, for example, we have watched the ugly spectacle of Congress knotted in fruitless debate over relatively limited proposals to alter the system by which congressional campaigns are financed. We can only imagine its disinclination to undertake some of the other forms of suicide suggested here. But it is precisely the inability to right itself, to connect behavior to goals, and to develop a federal government that serves national purposes that is the most damning indictment of the political system that we Americans created for ourselves in the period after World War II.

I have focused on that process throughout this book. I have argued that this has been one of the great periods of change in our history. But I have also noted that this was a unique kind of change because it has occurred in different ways at different times, for different reasons, at different places on the political landscape. The postwar changes have been isolated, disconnected, and coincidental. They possess none of the coherence of the American Revolution, of Jacksonian democracy, of the Progressive movement, of the New Deal. They were inspired by no single idea or ideology, driven by no coherent mass movement, responsive to no shared sense of what the problem was. No one sought this change, not the sum of it, and no one much likes it.

And so on the eve of the millennium, after nearly four centuries on this continent and more than two centuries of constitutional practice, the

American people find themselves wondering what went wrong with their experiment in self-government. How did we get into this mess?

The answer is that we did it to ourselves, but not intentionally. We did it through hundreds of small and isolated actions in which self-interested Americans sought to shape government for their own purposes and self-righteous Americans sought to "protect" government from the taint of politics. God knows, we did not mean to make such a mess of things. But we have. And if we are to find our way together through the even more perplexing century that lies ahead, we will have to undertake a radical renewal of politics and government that forces us to break a lot of old habits and accept more sacrifice than we ever have before.

NOTES

Chapter 1

1. Joseph G. Goulden, *The Best Years: 1945–1950* (New York: Atheneum, 1976), p. 5.

Chapter 2

1. Unless otherwise indicated, the data reported in this chapter are from the *Statistical Abstracts* and the *Historical Statistics* series published by the U.S. Bureau of the Census.

2. Geoffrey Perrett, *Days of Sadness, Years of Triumph: The American People, 1939–1945* (New York: Coward, McCann and Geohegan, 1973), pp. 10–11.

3. James A. Michener, "After the War: The Victories at Home," *Newsweek*, January 11, 1993, p. 27.

4. Quoted in Perrett, *Days of Sadness*, p. 356.

5. Quoted in Congressional Quarterly, *Congress and the Nation, 1945–1964* (Washington, D.C.: Congressional Quarterly, 1965), vol. 1, p. 349.

6. Kenneth T. Jackson, *The Crabgrass Frontier* (New York: Oxford University Press, 1985), pp. 234–235.

7. Joseph C. Goulden, *The Best Years: 1945–1950* (New York: Atheneum, 1976), p. 139.

8. Michael Barone, *Our Country* (New York: Free Press, 1990), p. 199.

9. "Nearly Half in the U.S. Are Living in Suburbs," *New York Times*, May 27, 1992.

10. Bryant Robey, *The American People: A Timely Exploration of a Changing America and the Important New Demographic Trends Around Us* (New York: Dutton, 1985), p. 2.

11. William Issel, *Social Change in the United States, 1945–1983* (New York: Schocken Books, 1985), p. 71.

12. Quoted in Felicity Barringer, "18% of Households in U.S. Moved in '89," *New York Times*, December 20, 1991.

13. Ibid.

14. Barone, *Our Country*, p. 199.

15. Barringer, "18% Households."

16. Paul C. Light, *Baby Boomers* (New York: Norton, 1988), p. 145.

17. Martin P. Wattenberg, *The Decline of American Political Parties, 1952–1984* (Cambridge, Mass.: Harvard University Press, 1986), pp. 114–115.

18. Robey, *The American People*, p. 168.

19. Barone, *Our Country*, p. 178.

20. Juliet B. Schor, "Americans Work Too Hard," *New York Times*, July 25, 1991.

21. Barone, *Our Country*, pp. 289–290.

22. The history of the development of the electronic computer is described in Joel Shurkin, *Enigmas of the Mind: A History of the Computer* (New York: Norton, 1984).

23. Robey, *The American People*, p. 55.

24. Angus Campbell, Philip E. Converse, Warren Miller, and Donald E. Stokes, *The American Voter* (New York: Wiley, 1964), pp. 86–87.

25. Stephen Earl Bennett, *Apathy in America, 1960–1984: Causes and Consequences of Citizen Political Indifference* (Dobbs Ferry, N.Y.: Transnational Publishers, 1986), pp. 78ff.

Chapter 3

1. Charles Taylor and David Jodice, *World Handbook of Political and Social Indicators* (New Haven: Yale University Press, 1983), pp. 76–77.

2. Theodore Caplow, Howard Bahr, John Modell, and Bruce Chadwick, *Recent Social Trends in the United States, 1960–1990* (Montreal: McGill University Press, 1991), p. 237.

3. CBS/New York Times Poll reported in Robin Toner, "Turned Off by Campaigns or Just Too Busy to Vote," *New York Times*, November 7, 1990.

4. In 1848 Zachary Taylor, a Whig, confronted Democratic majorities in both houses. In 1876 Rutherford B. Hayes, a Republican, was elected with a Republican-controlled Senate and a Democratic House. In 1884 Grover Cleveland's Democratic Party controlled the House, but the Republicans controlled the Senate.

5. In fact, split-ticket voting had been a growing trend for most of the twentieth century. But the emergence of this voting pattern as a norm for a large percentage of American voters did not come until after World War II. See Martin P. Wattenberg, *The Decline of American Political Parties, 1952–1984* (Cambridge, Mass.: Harvard University Press, 1986), pp. 18ff.

6. Angus Campbell, Philip E. Converse, Warren E. Miller, and Donald E. Stokes, *The American Voter* (New York: Wiley, 1960), p. 67.

7. Wattenberg, *The Decline*, p. xiii.

8. Walter Dean Burnham, *Critical Elections and the Mainsprings of American Politics* (New York: Norton, 1970), p. 133.

9. Michael Barone, *Our Country* (New York: Free Press, 1990), p. 386.

10. Because presidential primaries are operated under laws established by the state governments, the implementation of the McGovern-Fraser recommendations, and those of subsequent Democratic Party reform commissions, often required the enactment of new state laws. Since in most cases those laws applied to the Republicans as well as the Democrats, the reforms of the Democratic Party were widely echoed in the Republican Party.

11. Howard Reiter, *Selecting the President* (Philadelphia: University of Pennsylvania Press, 1985), p. 64.

12. Jeane Kirkpatrick, *The New Presidential Elite: Men and Women in National Politics* (New York: Russell Sage, 1976).

13. An exception to this pattern has been the growing participation of public school teachers at Democratic conventions. Their interest in politics, however, is much more typical of the new- than the old-style delegate since their jobs are rarely dependent on the outcome of elections and most teacher-delegates have demonstrated a significant interest in policy issues.

14. Nelson Polsby wrote brilliantly about these characteristics of the contemporary nominating process in *Consequences of Party Reform* (New York: Oxford University Press, 1983).

15. The one notable candidate who sought to use the nominating process to that effect, Edmund Muskie in 1972, was out of the race a few weeks after the first primary (which, ironically, he won).

16. Alexis de Tocqueville, *Democracy in America* (New York: Knopf, 1948), vol. 2, p. 106.

17. Ibid., vol. 1, pp. 191–192.

18. These data are drawn from research done by Mark Petracca and reported in "The Rediscovery of Interest Group Politics," in Mark P. Petracca, ed., *The Politics of Interests: Interest Groups Transformed* (Boulder: Westview Press, 1992), pp. 3–31.

19. *Encyclopedia of Associations* (Detroit: Gale Research, various years).

20. Petracca, "The Rediscovery," p. 13.

21. See the description of Japanese efforts to influence American policy in Pat Choate, *Agents of Influence* (New York: Knopf, 1990).

22. Ronald G. Shaiko, "More Bang for the Buck: The New Era of Full-Service Public Interest Organizations," in Allan J. Cigler and Burdett A. Loomis, eds., *Interest Group Politics, 3d ed.* (Washington, D.C.: CQ Press, 1991), p. 109.

23. Ibid., p. 112.

24. Jeffrey M. Berry, *The Interest Group Society* (New York: HarperCollins, 1989), pp. 20–21.

25. "Prepared Text of Carter's Farewell Address on Major Issues Facing the Nation," *New York Times*, January 15, 1981.

26. Jack L. Walker Jr., *Mobilizing Interest Groups in America: Patrons, Professions, and Social Movements* (Ann Arbor: University of Michigan Press, 1991), p. 40.

27. Ronald J. Hrebnar and Ruth K. Scott, *Interest Group Politics in America*, 2d ed. (Englewood Cliffs, N.J.: Prentice-Hall, 1990), p. 166.

28. Alexander Hamilton, James Madison, and John Jay, *The Federalist: A Commentary on the Constitution of the United States* (New York: Tudor Publishing, 1937), p. 62.

29. Some of the arguments and assessments in the previous paragraphs draw on Benjamin Ginsberg and Martin Shefter, *Politics by Other Means: The Declining Importance of Elections in America* (New York: Basic Books, 1990). I gratefully acknowledge my intellectual debt to them.

30. E. J. Dionne, *Why Americans Hate Politics* (New York: Simon and Schuster, 1991).

31. Kevin Phillips, *Post-Conservative America: People, Politics, and Ideology in a Time of Crisis* (New York: Random House, 1982), p. 75.

Chapter 4

1. Hubert H. Humphrey, *Beyond Civil Rights: A New Day of Equality* (New York: Random House, 1968), p. 67.

2. Robert A. Caro, *The Years of Lyndon Johnson: Means of Ascent* (New York: Knopf, 1990), p. 129.

3. Calculated by the author from Congressional Quarterly, *Congress and the Nation*, vol. 1, *1945–1964* (Washington, D.C.: Congressional Quarterly, 1965).

4. Alexis de Tocqueville, *Democracy in America*, (New York: Knopf, 1948), vol. 1, p. 204.

5. Joe Martin, *My First Fifty Years in Politics* (New York: McGraw-Hill, 1960), p. 49.

6. See Congressional Research Service, *Reelection Rates of House Incumbents, 1790–1988* (Washington, D.C.: Library of Congress, March 16, 1989); and Congressional Research Service, *Reelection Rates of Senate Incumbents, 1790–1988* (Washington, D.C.: Library of Congress, May 15, 1989).

7. Hugh Davis Graham, *The Civil Rights Era* (New York: Oxford University Press, 1990), p. 452.

8. The pattern of self-nomination is explained at length and incisively in Alan Ehrenhalt, *The United States of Ambition* (New York: Random House, 1991). The discussion of that pattern in this chapter benefits greatly from Ehrenhalt's work.

9. Burdett A. Loomis, *The New American Politician: Ambition, Entrepreneurship, and the Changing Face of Political Life* (New York: Basic Books, 1988), pp. 28–29.

10. Richard Bolling, *House Out of Order* (New York: Dutton, 1964), p. 12.

11. Congressional Quarterly, *Congress and the Nation*, vol. 3, *1969–1972* (Washington, D.C.: Congressional Quarterly, 1973), p. 377.

12. Quotes in previous three paragraphs are from John E. Young, "How the Watergate Class of '74 Played Kings of the Hill," *Washington Post National Weekly Edition*, June 22–28, 1992, p. 12.

13. Another school of thought, best articulated by David Rohde, argues that, in fact, the congressional reforms of this period strengthened the leadership of the Democratic Party and were centralizing in their effects. See David W. Rohde, *Parties and Leaders in the Postreform House* (Chicago: University of Chicago Press, 1991). Although it is clear that the instruments of party leadership, especially the Democratic caucus in the House and the powers of the Speaker, were strengthened, they were done so by the rank-and-file members to serve the purposes of individual members, not the leadership. Stronger central mechanisms were used to overcome the stranglehold that the committee chairs had once had in the House. But those instruments of party leadership were placed under tight scrutiny and held to a standard of real accountability by the rank and file. The recent reforms produced a House that bears little resemblance to the institution that existed at the turn of the last century, where party leaders truly dominated.

14. Televising of Senate sessions followed in 1986.

15. In 1983 in *Immigration and Naturalization Service* v. *Chadha*, the Supreme Court struck down most versions of the legislative veto. Congress has subsequently imposed similar constraints on executive branch discretion through less formal devices.

16. Benjamin Ginsberg and Martin Shefter, *Politics by Other Means: The Declining Importance of Elections in America* (New York: Basic Books, 1990), p. 131.

17. These percentages indicate the portion of all House and Senate votes on which a majority of Democrats were on one side and a majority of Republicans on the other.

18. References in this paragraph to the "1970s" include the years 1971–1980; references to the "1980s" include the years 1981–1990. All data calculated by the author from Congressional Quarterly sources.

19. Timothy E. Cook, *Making Laws and Making News: Media Strategies in the U.S. House of Representatives* (Washington, D.C.: Brookings Institution, 1989), p. 73.

20. Loomis, *The New American Politician*, p. 84. It should be noted that this inflates the number of journalists actually working on Capitol Hill at any given time. Many reporters use their membership in the congressional press corps only to cover a congressional angle on a story that is part of their regular beat.

21. Cook, *Making Laws*, p. vii.

22. David R. Mayhew, *Congress: The Electoral Connection* (New Haven: Yale University Press, 1974), p. 62.

23. Michael J. Robinson, "A Twentieth-Century Medium in a Nineteenth-Century Legislature: The Effects of Television on the American Congress," in Norman J. Ornstein, ed., *Congress in Change: Evolution and Reform* (New York: Praeger, 1975), p. 241.

24. Quoted in David Broder, *Changing of the Guard* (New York: Simon and Schuster, 1980), pp. 36–37.

25. See Ginsberg and Shefter, *Politics*, p. 173, for a broader discussion of this point.

26. Aaron Wildavsky, *The New Politics of the Budgetary Process* (Glenview, Ill.: Scott Foresman/Little, Brown, 1988), pp. 280–281.

27. See Kenneth A. Shepsle, "The Changing Textbook Congress," in John E. Chubb and Paul E. Peterson, eds., *Can the Government Govern?* (Washington, D.C.: Brookings Institution, 1989), pp. 238–266, for discussion of this point.

28. Morris P. Fiorina, "The Decline of Collective Responsibility in American Politics," *Daedalus*, 109 (Summer 1980):44.

29. See Jeffrey H. Birnbaum and Alan S. Murray, *Showdown at Gucci Gulch: Lawmakers, Lobbyists, and the Unlikely Triumph of Tax Reform* (New York: Random House, 1987).

30. Ehrenhalt, *The United States*, p. 246.

Chapter 5

1. Woodrow Wilson, *Constitutional Government in the United States* (New York: Columbia University Press, 1908), p. 40.

2. Herman Hagedorn, *The Roosevelt Family of Sagamore Hill* (New York: Macmillan, 1954), p. 173.

3. Richard Rose, *The Postmodern President: George Bush Meets the World,* 2d ed. (Chatham, N.J.: Chatham House, 1991), p. 21.

4. Herbert Hoover, *The Memoirs of Herbert Hoover, 1920–1933* (New York: Macmillan, 1952), p. 217.

5. Quoted in Arthur M. Schlesinger Jr., *The Crisis of the Old Order, 1919–1933* (Boston: Houghton Mifflin, 1957), p. 246.

6. Quoted in Frank Freidel, *Franklin D. Roosevelt: A Rendezvous with Destiny* (Boston: Little, Brown, 1990), p. 498.

7. Address at Oglethorpe University, Atlanta, Georgia, May 22, 1932.

8. Herbert Croly, *The Promise of American Life* (New York: Macmillan, 1909), p. 69.

9. James Bryce, *The American Commonwealth* (New York: Macmillan, 1891), vol. 1, p. 206.

10. Quoted in Clinton Rossiter, *The American Presidency,* 2d ed. (New York: New American Library, 1960), p. 106.

11. Richard Neustadt, "Presidency and Legislation: The Growth of Central Clearance," *American Political Science Review* (September 1954):641–668.

12. Quoted in James T. Barron, "Advising the President," *Princeton Alumni Weekly* (November 24, 1975):10.

13. The best of the books on this development is Samuel Kernell, *Going Public: New Strategies of Presidential Leadership* (Washington, D.C.: CQ Press, 1993).

14. Quoted in Richard Neustadt, *Presidential Power* (New York: Wiley, 1960), p. 103.

15. Arvind Raichur and Richard W. Waterman, "The Presidency, the Public, and the Expectations Gap," in Richard W. Waterman, ed., *The Presidency Reconsidered* (Itasca, Ill.: F.E.A. Peacock, 1993), p. 3.

16. Quoted in Michael Nelson, ed., *Guide to the Presidency* (Washington, D.C.: Congressional Quarterly, 1989), p. 464.

17. Roderick P. Hart, *Verbal Style and the Presidency* (Orlando, Fla.: Academic Press, 1984), p. 2.

18. Lou Cannon, "Speaker Calls President Insensitive," *Washington Post,* January 29, 1986.

19. John Orman, "Covering the American Presidency: Valenced Reporting in the Periodical Press," *Presidential Studies Quarterly* 14 (1984):381–382.

20. Larry J. Sabato, *Feeding Frenzy: How Attack Journalism Has Transformed American Politics* (New York: Free Press, 1991), p. 49.

21. Robert E. DiClerico, "The Role of Media in Heightened Expectations and Diminished Leadership Capacity," in Richard W. Waterman, ed., *The Presidency Reconsidered* (Itasca, Ill.: F.E.A. Peacock, 1993), p. 118.

22. Television Information Office, "America's Watching 30th Anniversary, 1959–1989" (New York: Television Information Office, 1989), pp. 27–28.

23. Gary King and Lyn Ragsdale, *The Elusive Executive: Discovering Statistical Patterns in the Presidency* (Washington, D.C.: CQ Press, 1988), p. 262.

24. Sidney Blumenthal, "Marketing the President," *New York Times Magazine*, September 13, 1981, p. 118.

25. Arthur M. Schlesinger Jr., *The Imperial Presidency* (New York: Popular Library, 1973), p. 389.

26. Peri E. Arnold, "The Institutionalized Presidency and the American Regime," in Richard W. Waterman, ed., *The Presidency Reconsidered* (Itasca, Ill.: F.E.A. Peacock, 1993), p. 222.

27. Nelson Polsby, "Some Landmarks in Modern Presidential-Congressional Relations," in Anthony King, ed., *Both Ends of the Avenue* (Washington, D.C.: American Enterprise Institute, 1983), p. 20.

28. See Robert S. Gilmour and Alexis A. Halley, eds., *Who Makes Public Policy? Co-Management by Congress and the Executive* (Chatham, N.J.: Chatham House, 1993).

29. Charles L. Schultze, *The Public Use of the Private Interest* (Washington, D.C.: Brookings Institution, 1977), p. 7.

30. On the impact of new types of issues on the postwar presidency, also see Paul C. Light, *The President's Agenda: Domestic Policy Choice from Kennedy to Carter (with notes on Ronald Reagan)* (Baltimore: Johns Hopkins University Press, 1982).

31. Neilsen Media Research, cited in "Tale of the Tube," *Newsweek*, August 2, 1993, p. 6.

32. Data from a CNN–USA Today poll cited in Michael Wines, "It's August; How Much Policy Can a Nation Take?" *New York Times*, August 15, 1993.

33. Milton J. Rosenberg, Sidney Verba, and Philip E. Converse, *Vietnam and the Silent Majority* (New York: Harper and Row, 1970), pp. 25–26.

Chapter 6

1. Harold W. Stanley and Richard G. Niemi, *Vital Statistics on American Politics,* 3d ed. (Washington, D.C.: CQ Press, 1992), p. 306.

2. Alexis de Tocqueville, *Democracy in America* (New York: Knopf, 1948), vol. 1, p. 280.

3. "An Abundance of Lawyers," *New York Times*, August 14, 1991.

4. U.S. Department of Commerce, Bureau of the Census, *Statistical Abstract of the United States, 1993* (Washington, D.C.: GPO, 1993), p. 204.

5. For a fuller discussion of changes affecting the supply of attorneys, see the interesting analysis of Richard L. Abel, *American Lawyers* (New York: Oxford University Press, 1989), p. 139.

6. Ibid., p. 138.

7. Ibid., p. 137.

8. U.S. Department of Labor, *Occupational Outlook Handbook* (Washington, D.C.: GPO, 1992), p. 103.

9. Robert B. McKay, "Law, Lawyers, and the Public Interest," 55 *University of Cincinnati Law Review* (1986):351.

10. State Justice Institute, *State Court Caseload Statistics: Annual Report 1990* (Alexandria, Va.: State Justice Institute, 1992), p. 6.

11. Richard A. Posner, *The Federal Courts: Crisis and Reform* (Cambridge, Mass.: Harvard University Press, 1985), p. 81.

12. Jethro K. Lieberman, *The Litigious Society* (New York: Basic Books, 1981), p. 152.

13. Posner, *The Federal Courts*, p. vii.

14. Ibid., pp. 102–103.

15. Ibid., p. 104.

16. Alvin B. Rubin, "Views from the Lower Court," 23 *U.C.L.A. Law Review* (1976):448, 456.

17. See Sheldon Goldman, "The Bush Imprint on the Judiciary: Carrying on a Tradition," *Judicature* 74 (April-May 1991):298–299.

18. "George's Choice," *New Yorker*, January 18, 1993, p. 32; and Deborah Pines, "Jacobs to Ascend Second Circuit Bench with Democrats' Aid," *New York Law Journal* (November 10, 1992):1.

19. This section draws heavily on data gathered and analyzed by Professor Garrison Nelson of the University of Vermont.

20. Cited in Robert A. Katzmann, "The Underlying Concerns," in Robert A. Katzmann, ed., *Judges and Legislators: Toward Institutional Comity* (Washington, D.C.: Brookings Institution, 1988), p. 11.

21. Lieberman, *The Litigious Society*, p. 25.

22. Ibid., p. 306.

23. Gary L. McDowell, *Curbing the Courts: The Constitution and the Limits of Judicial Power* (Baton Rouge: Louisiana State University Press, 1988), pp. 52–53.

24. "N.Y.C. Salaries Down; Others Hold the Line," *National Law Journal* (March 18, 1991):2; "Sampler of Partner Income at Large Firms," *National Law Journal* (April 27, 1992):S4.

25. Neil D. McFeeley, *Appointment of Judges: The Johnson Presidency* (Austin: University of Texas Press, 1987), p. 73.

26. Deborah Barrow and Gary Zuk, "An Institutional Analysis of Turnover in the Lower Federal Courts, 1900–1987," *Journal of Politics* 52 (May 1990):460.

27. Posner, *The Federal Courts*, p. 237.

28. Rosenberg, *The Hollow Hope*, p. 50.

29. Ibid., p. 179.

30. Ibid., p. 338.

Chapter 7

1. See, for example, Charles Murray, *Losing Ground: American Social Policy, 1950–1980* (New York: Basic Books, 1984); George Gilder, *Wealth and Poverty* (New York: Basic Books, 1980).

2. See, for example, Sidney Blumenthal, *Our Long National Daydream* (New York: Harper and Row, 1988); Thomas Byrne Edsall, *The New Politics of Inequality* (New York: Norton, 1984).

3. Jack L. Walker Jr., *Mobilizing Interest Groups in America: Patrons, Professions, and Social Movements* (Ann Arbor: University of Michigan Press, 1991), p. 39.

4. Walter Dean Burnham, *The Current Crisis in American Politics* (New York: Oxford University Press, 1982), p. 260.

5. Nelson W. Polsby, *Consequences of Party Reform* (New York: Oxford University Press, 1983), p. 136.

6. Quoted in Jethro K. Lieberman, *The Litigious Society* (New York: Basic Books, 1981), p. 106.

7. E. E. Schattschneider, *The Semisovereign People* (New York: Holt, Rinehart and Winston, 1960), p. 2.

8. E. J. Dionne, *Why Americans Hate Politics* (New York: Simon and Schuster, 1991), p. 332.

9. Benjamin Ginsberg and Martin Shefter, *Politics by Other Means: The Declining Importance of Elections in America* (New York: Basic Books, 1990), p. 173.

10. John E. Chubb and Paul E. Peterson, "American Political Institutions and the Problem of Governance," in John E. Chubb and Paul E. Peterson, eds., *Can the Government Govern?* (Washington, D.C.: Brookings Institution, 1989), p. 5.

11. Robert Shogan, *None of the Above: Why Presidents Fail—and What Can Be Done About It* (New York: New American Library, 1982), p. 5.

12. Harold W. Stanley and Richard G. Niemi, *Vital Statistics on American Politics*, 4th ed. (Washington, D.C.: CQ Press, 1993), p. 212.

13. Cited in *Debate on the Constitution* (New York: Library of America, 1993), part 2, p. 318.

14. Jeffrey H. Birnbaum and Alan S. Murray, *Showdown at Gucci Gulch* (New York: Random House, 1987), p. 178.

READINGS CONSULTED

Abel, Richard L. *American Lawyers*. New York: Oxford University Press, 1989.

Arnold, Peri E. "The Institutionalized Presidency and the American Regime." In Richard W. Waterman, ed., *The Presidency Reconsidered*. Itasca, Ill.: F.E.A. Peacock, 1993.

_____. *Making the Managerial Presidency: Comprehensive Reorganization Planning, 1905–1980*. Princeton: Princeton University Press, 1986.

Barone, Michael. *Our Country*. New York: Free Press, 1990.

Bennett, Stephen Earl. *Apathy in America, 1960–1984: Causes and Consequences of Citizen Political Indifference*. Dobbs Ferry, N.Y.: Transnational Publishers, 1986.

Berry, Jeffrey M. *The Interest Group Society*. New York: HarperCollins, 1989.

_____. *Lobbying for the People*. Princeton: Princeton University Press, 1977.

Bickel, Alexander, and Harry Wellington. "Legislative Purpose and the Judicial Process: The Lincoln Mills Case." *Harvard Law Review* 71 (November 1957).

Burnham, Walter Dean. *The Current Crisis in American Politics*. New York: Oxford University Press, 1982.

Campbell, Colin. *Managing the Presidency: Carter, Reagan, and the Search for Executive Harmony*. Pittsburgh: University of Pittsburgh Press, 1946.

Ceasar, James W. "Improving the Nominating Process." In A. James Reichley, ed., *Elections American Style*. Washington, D.C.: Brookings Institution, 1987.

Chayes, Abram. "Public Law Litigation in the Burger Court." *Harvard Law Review* 96 (1982).

_____. "The Role of the Judge in Public Law Litigation." *Harvard Law Review* 89 (1976).

Choate, Pat. *Agents of Influence*. New York: Knopf, 1990.

Chubb, John E. "Federalism and the Bias for Centralization." In John E. Chubb and Paul E. Peterson, eds., *The New Direction in American Politics*. Washington, D.C.: Brookings Institution, 1985.

Chubb, John E., and Paul E. Peterson "American Political Institutions and the Problem of Governance." In John E. Chubb and Paul E. Peterson, eds., *Can the Government Govern?* Washington, D.C.: Brookings Institution, 1989.

_____, eds. *The New Direction in American Politics*. Washington, D.C.: Brookings Institution, 1985.

Cook, Timothy E. *Making Laws and Making News: Media Strategies in the U.S. House of Representatives*. Washington, D.C.: Brookings Institution, 1989.

Crawford, Kenneth G. *The Pressure Boys: The Inside Story of Lobbying in America*. New York: Julian Messner, 1939.

Crovitz, L. Gordon, and Jeremy Rabkin, eds. *The Fettered Presidency.* Washington, D.C.: American Enterprise Institute, 1989.

Delli Carpini, Michael X. *Stability and Change in American Politics: The Coming of Age of the Generation of the 1960s.* New York: New York University Press, 1986.

Destler, I. M., Leslie Gelb, and Anthony Lake. *Our Own Worst Enemy.* New York: Simon and Schuster, 1984.

DiClerico, Robert E. "The Role of Media in Heightened Expectations and Diminished Leadership Capacity." In Richard W. Waterman, ed., *The Presidency Reconsidered.* Itasca, Ill.: F.E.A. Peacock, 1993.

Dionne, E.J. *Why Americans Hate Politics.* New York: Simon and Schuster, 1991.

Easterlin, Richard A. *Birth and Fortune: The Impact of Numbers on Personal Welfare.* Chicago: University of Chicago Press, 1987.

Ehrenhalt, Alan. *The United States of Ambition.* New York: Random House, 1991.

Ferejohn, John A., and Morris P. Fiorina. "Incumbency and Realignment in Congressional Elections." In John E. Chubb and Paul E. Peterson, eds., *The New Direction in American Politics.* Washington, D.C.: Brookings Institution, 1985.

Fiorina, Morris. *Congress: Keystone of the Washington Establishment.* New Haven: Yale University Press, 1977.

_____ "The Decline of Collective Responsibility in American Politics." *Daedalus* 109 (Summer 1980).

Gais, Thomas L., Mark A. Peterson, and Jack L. Walker Jr. "Interest Groups, Iron Triangles, and Representative Institutions." In Jack L. Walker Jr., ed., *Mobilizing Interest Groups in America: Patrons, Professions, and Social Movements.* Ann Arbor: University of Michigan Press, 1991.

Gais, Thomas L., and Jack L. Walker Jr. "Pathways to Influence in American Politics." In Jack L. Walker Jr., *Mobilizing Interest Groups in America: Patrons, Professions, and Social Movements.* Ann Arbor: University of Michigan Press, 1991.

Ginsberg, Benjamin, and John C. Green. "The Best Congress Money Can Buy: Campaign Contributions and Congressional Behavior." In Benjamin Ginsberg and Alan Stone, eds., *Do Elections Matter?* Armonk, N.Y.: M. E. Sharpe, 1986.

Ginsberg, Benjamin, and Martin Shefter. *Politics by Other Means: The Declining Importance of Elections in America.* New York: Basic Books, 1990.

Ginsberg, Benjamin, and Alan Stone, eds. *Do Elections Matter?* Armonk, N.Y.: M. E. Sharpe, 1986.

Gormley, William T. *Taming the Bureaucracy: Muscles, Prayers, and Other Strategies.* Princeton: Princeton University Press, 1989.

Goulden, Joseph G. *The Best Years: 1945–1950.* New York: Atheneum, 1976.

Hamilton, Alexander, James Madison, and John Jay. *The Federalist: A Commentary on the Constitution of the United States.* New York: Tudor Publishing, 1937.

Hart, John. *The Presidential Branch.* New York: Pergamon Press, 1987.

Heclo, Hugh. *A Government of Strangers.* Washington, D.C.: Brookings Institution, 1977.

Horowitz, Donald L. *The Courts and Social Policy.* Washington, D.C.: Brookings Institution, 1977.

Hrebnar, Ronald J., and Ruth K. Scott. *Interest Group Politics in America*. 2d ed. Englewood Cliffs, N.J.: Prentice-Hall, 1990.

Huntington, Samuel P. *American Politics: The Promise of Disharmony*. Cambridge, Mass.: Harvard University Press, 1981.

Issel, William. *Social Change in the United States, 1945–1983*. New York: Schocken Books, 1985.

Jamieson, Kathleen Hall. *Eloquence in an Electronic Age*. New York: Oxford University Press, 1988.

Johnson, Paul Edward. "Organized Labor in an Era of Blue-Collar Decline." In Allan J. Cigler and Burdett A. Loomis, eds., *Interest Group Politics*. 3d ed. Washington, D.C.: CQ Press, 1991.

Katzmann, Robert A. *Judges and Legislators: Toward Institutional Comity*. Washington, D.C.: Brookings Institution, 1988.

Kernell, Samuel. "Campaigning, Governing, and the Contemporary Presidency." In John E. Chubb and Paul E. Peterson, eds., *The New Direction in American Politics*. Washington, D.C.: Brookings Institution, 1985.

_____. "The Evolution of the White House Staff." In John E. Chubb and Paul E. Peterson, eds., *Can the Government Govern?* Washington, D.C.: Brookings Institution, 1989.

_____. *Going Public: New Strategies of Presidential Leadership*. Washington, D.C.: CQ Press, 1993.

King, David C., and Jack L. Walker Jr. "The Origins and Maintenance of Groups." In Jack L. Walker Jr., *Mobilizing Interest Groups in America: Patrons, Professions, and Social Movements*. Ann Arbor: University of Michigan Press, 1991.

King, Gary, and Lyn Ragsdale. *The Elusive Executive: Discovering Statistical Patterns in the Presidency*. Washington, D.C.: CQ Press, 1988.

Kirkpatrick, Jeane. *The New Presidential Elite: Men and Women in National Politics*. New York: Russell Sage, 1976.

Ladd, Everett Carl. "Party Reform and the Public Interest." In A. James Reichley, ed., *Elections American Style*. Washington, D.C.: Brookings Institution, 1987.

Lieberman, Jethro K. *The Litigious Society*. New York: Basic Books, 1981.

Light, Paul C. *Baby Boomers*. New York: Norton, 1988.

_____. *The President's Agenda: Domestic Policy Choice from Kennedy to Carter (with notes on Ronald Reagan)*. Baltimore: Johns Hopkins University Press, 1982.

Loomis, Burdett A. *The New American Politician: Ambition, Entrepreneurship, and the Changing Face of Political Life*. New York: Basic Books, 1988.

Loomis, Burdett A., and Allan J. Cigler. "Introduction: The Changing Nature Of Interest Group Politics." In Allan J. Cigler and Burdett A. Loomis, eds., *Interest Group Politics*. 3d ed. Washington, D.C.: CQ Press, 1991.

Lowi, Theodore W. *The End of Liberalism*. 2d ed. New York: Norton, 1979.

Lunch, William M. *The Nationalization of American Politics*. Berkeley and Los Angeles: University of California Press, 1987.

Mann, Thomas E. "Is the House of Representatives Unresponsive to Political Change?" In A. James Reichley, ed., *Elections American Style*. Washington, D.C.: Brookings Institution, 1987.

McDowell, Gary L. *Curbing the Courts: The Constitution and The Limits of Judicial Power.* Baton Rouge: Louisiana State University Press, 1988.

McFeeley, Neil D. *Appointment of Judges: The Johnson Presidency.* Austin: University of Texas Press, 1987.

Perrett, Geoffrey. *Days of Sadness, Years of Triumph: The American People 1939–1945.* New York: Coward, McCann and Geohegan, 1973.

Petracca, Mark P. "The Rediscovery of Interest Group Politics." In Mark P. Petracca, ed., *The Politics of Interests: Interest Groups Transformed.* Boulder: Westview Press, 1992.

Pika, Joseph A. "Reaching Out to Organized Interests: Public Liaison in the Modern White House." In Richard W. Waterman, ed., *The Presidency Reconsidered.* Itasca, Ill.: F.E.A. Peacock, 1993.

Polsby, Nelson. *Consequences of Party Reform.* New York: Oxford University Press, 1983.

Posner, Richard A. *The Federal Courts: Crisis and Reform.* Cambridge, Mass.: Harvard University Press, 1985.

Rabkin, Jeremy. *Judicial Compulsions.* New York: Basic Books, 1989.

Raichur, Arvind, and Richard W. Waterman. "The Presidency, the Public, and the Expectations Gap." In Richard W. Waterman, ed., *The Presidency Reconsidered.* Itasca, Ill.: F.E.A. Peacock, 1993.

Reichley, A. James. "The Electoral System." In A. James Reichley, ed., *Elections American Style.* Washington, D.C.: Brookings Institution, 1987.

_____. "The Rise of National Parties." In John E. Chubb and Paul E. Peterson, eds., *The New Direction in American Politics.* Washington, D.C.: Brookings Institution, 1985.

_____, ed. *Elections American Style.* Washington, D.C.: Brookings Institution, 1987.

Robey, Bryant. *The American People: A Timely Exploration of a Changing America and the Important New Demographic Trends Around Us.* New York: Dutton, 1985.

Rohde, David W. *Parties and Leaders in the Postreform House.* Chicago: University of Chicago Press, 1991.

Rose, Richard. *The Postmodern President: George Bush Meets the World.* 2d ed. Chatham, N.J.: Chatham House, 1991.

Rosenberg, Gerald N. *The Hollow Hope: Can Courts Bring About Social Change?* Chicago: University of Chicago Press, 1991.

Sabato, Larry J. *Feeding Frenzy: How Attack Journalism Has Transformed American Politics.* New York: Free Press, 1991.

_____. "Real and Imagined Corruption in Campaign Financing." In A. James Reichley, ed., *Elections American Style.* Washington, D.C.: Brookings Institution, 1987.

Schwartz, Herman. *Packing the Courts: The Conservative Campaign to Rewrite the Constitution.* New York: Charles Scribner's Sons, 1988.

Shaiko, Ronald G. "More Bang for the Buck: The New Era Of Full-Service Public Interest Organizations." In Allan J. Cigler and Burdett A. Loomis, eds., *Interest Group Politics.* 3d ed. Washington, D.C.: CQ Press, 1991.

Shepsle, Kenneth A., "The Changing Textbook Congress." In John E. Chubb and Paul E. Peterson, eds., *Can the Government Govern?* Washington, D.C.: Brookings Institution, 1989.

_____. "Representation and Governance: The Great Legislative Trade-Off." *Political Science Quarterly* 103, 3 (1988).

Shogan, Robert. *None of the Above: Why Presidents Fail—and What Can Be Done About It.* New York: New American Library, 1982.

Skowronek, Stephen. *Building a New American State: The Expansion of National Administrative Capacities, 1877–1920.* Cambridge: Cambridge University Press, 1982.

Smith, Steven S. "New Patterns in Decisionmaking in Congress." In John E. Chubb and Paul E. Peterson, eds., *The New Direction in American Politics.* Washington, D.C.: Brookings Institution, 1985.

Sorauf, Frank J. "PACs and Parties in American Politics." In Allan J. Cigler and Burdett A. Loomis, eds., *Interest Group Politics.* 3d ed. Washington, D.C.: CQ Press, 1991.

Spitzer, Robert J. "Is the Separation of Powers Obsolete? The Congressional-Presidential Balance of Power." In Richard W. Waterman, ed., *The Presidency Reconsidered.* Itasca, Ill.: F.E.A. Peacock, 1993.

Stanley, Harold W., and Richard G. Niemi. *Vital Statistics on American Politics.* 3d ed. Washington, D.C.: CQ Press, 1992.

Sundquist, James L. *Constitutional Reform and Effective Government.* Washington, D.C.: Brookings Institution, 1986.

_____. "Strengthening the National Parties." In A. James Reichley, ed., *Elections American Style.* Washington, D.C.: Brookings Institution, 1987.

Tocqueville, Alexis de. *Democracy in America.* New York: Knopf, 1948.

U.S. Department of Commerce, Bureau of the Census. *Historical Statistics of the United States: Colonial Times to 1970.* Washington, D.C.: GPO, 1975.

_____. *Statistical Abstract of the United States, 1993.* Washington, D.C.: GPO, 1993.

Walker, Jack L. Jr. *Mobilizing Interest Groups in America: Patrons, Professions, and Social Movements.* Ann Arbor: University of Michigan Press, 1991.

Waterman, Richard W. "Closing the Expectations Gap: The Presidential Search for New Political Resources." In Richard W. Waterman, ed., *The Presidency Reconsidered.* Itasca, Ill.: F.E.A. Peacock, 1993.

Wattenberg, Martin P. *The Decline of American Political Parties, 1952–1984.* Cambridge, Mass.: Harvard University Press, 1986.

Weaver, R. Kent. *Automatic Government: The Politics of Indexation.* Washington, D.C.: Brookings Institution, 1988.

_____. "Controlling Entitlements." In John E. Chubb and Paul E. Peterson, eds., *The New Direction in American Politics.* Washington, D.C.: Brookings Institution, 1985.

ABOUT THE BOOK
AND AUTHOR

Americans are disenchanted with politics, their government, and their leaders. For evidence, we do not have to look very far: The elections of 1994 turned over control of Congress to the Republicans for the first time in forty years, and the new House Republicans' Contract with America was the biggest single antigovernment initiative since the Boston Tea Party, with term limits, campaign finance reform, and a balanced budget amendment high on its list of priorities.

But before Americans climb again on a new bandwagon of government restructuring, they would do well to listen to Cal Mackenzie's admonitions in *The Irony of Reform*. The trouble with contemporary government, he explains, is not a lack of change or "restructuring" over the years but rather the disjointed, inadvertent, and unpredictable pattern of reform we have followed since World War II.

Mackenzie traces the roots of our current distress, noting that more tinkering will lead only to more—though perhaps different—problems. Something much bolder is needed—a new approach that enables leadership, facilitates coalition building, and enhances accountability. Mackenzie proposes a cure for the political ills diagnosed here—a hard and painful cure for a very crippled body politic.

G. Calvin Mackenzie holds the endowed chair of Distinguished Presidential Professor of American Government at Colby College.

INDEX